The Churches
and the Soviet Union

By the same Author

SAINTS OF RUSSIA

His Holiness Patriarch Alexei of Moscow and all the Russias

The Churches
and the Soviet Union

Constantin de Grunwald

TRANSLATED BY
G. J. ROBINSON-PASKEVSKY

THE MACMILLAN COMPANY
NEW YORK
1962

Originally published by Plon, Paris, as
La Vie Religieuse en U.R.S.S.

Published in Great Britain under the title
God and the Soviets

Contents

Illustrations

Preface

Destiny has seen fit to have me live at the extremes of the two worlds which are in open hostility to one another today. I was born and raised in St Petersburg, and made my university studies in that city. It was there, too, that I began my career in the service of the Imperial Government. I have never ceased to be a loyal citizen of my native country, but since 1921 I have made my home in Paris and been highly influenced by Western thought and the Western way of life.

A specialist in my country's history, I was bold enough to consider myself qualified to undertake an extremely delicate project: to give readers in the West a full picture of the religious situation in my native land and of the bitter struggle now going on there between believers and unbelievers.

To make my documentation as complete as possible, I spent a large part of the summer of 1960 in the Soviet Union, visiting not only the large urban areas such as Moscow, Leningrad and Kiev, but also the most far-removed provincial regions. The long journey was made entirely at my own expense and at no time was I extended any extraordinary privilege not given to all tourists under the usual agreement made available by Intourist.

I had heart-to-heart talks with people on all levels of Soviet society: heads of various religious groups and simple village priests, directors of the anti-religion campaign and university agnostics, workers, students, humble peasants and taxi-drivers. With an extraordinarily moving candour, they all expressed their most heartfelt convictions to me, whom they recognized as a fellow-countryman.

I am neither a theologian nor a philosopher, nor can I claim a penetrating familiarity with Marxist theory. Aware of the limitations of my own knowledge, I have tried to formulate as precise an idea as possible of the predominant tendencies in Russia's spiritual life today, and to put forth my observations as objectively and sincerely as possible.

I should like to contradict in advance those who would like to see in me an involuntary victim of some sort of insidious propaganda. If any such attempts to deceive me had been made, I was forearmed, not only by my understanding of the workings of the Russian mind, but by occasional but long journalistic experience. My forecasts of the future may be unduly optimistic, but my statements as to fact are based on unimpeachable evidence. To claim the contrary would be to suppose that the accredited representatives of all existing religious communities in Russia were in league with my numerous personal friends, known to me since childhood, to present me with a distorted picture of the reality. The absurdity of such an allegation does not need to be enlarged upon. As remarked by so eminent a writer as George Kennan in his recent work *Russia and the West under Lenin and Stalin:* 'There is . . . nothing in nature more egocentric than the embattled democracy. Its enemy becomes the embodiment of all evil. Its own side, on the other hand, is the centre of all virtue.' It seems to me that the moment has come to adopt a more balanced viewpoint in our attitude to the Soviet Union. Let us shake off our prejudices. Good and Evil are not determined by the nature of the social regime: they fight for mastery within the soul of each one of us.

I must express my heartfelt thanks to everyone who was kind and helpful enough to make my task easier by sharing his personal attitudes with me on the problem I was investigating. Above all, I owe a special debt of gratitude and acknowledgment to the eminent clergyman who was more than generous by reading through my manuscript and making some invaluable suggestions.

From the Pavillon Dauphine to the *Laura*
of St Alexander

W E WERE at a delightful luncheon at the Pavillon
Dauphine given in honour of Nikita Khrushchev by
the Paris Diplomatic Press Association. It was a lovely
spring day and through the great windows we could see the
blossom-laden trees in the Bois de Boulogne.

The group's president had been gracious enough to invite me
to the luncheon so that I might make fresh contact with leading
Moscow circles.

My neighbours at table were two men of impressive stature,
broad-shouldered and with heroic heads and muscular arms. I felt
that an American seeing them would almost probably conclude
that they were the bodyguards of the Soviet Prime Minister. He
would be mistaken, however; both men belonged to the intelligentsia of their country, perhaps even to the Kremlin's 'brains
trust'. One was the director of a large political journal and the
other held a post high in the Ministry of Culture. Naturally,
therefore, our conversation covered the broad field of ideas in
general.

'You are acquainted with the magnificent achievements of the
Soviet Union,' one of them said to me. 'Not content with our
technical progress alone, we have succeeded in developing a new
society, a classless society conceived entirely on the basis of
dialectical materialism. All the old prejudices and dogmatic
doctrines have been thrown out, along with a heritage of medieval superstition. Historically, religion is a product of ignorance.'

The other elaborated on this theme: 'Why do we need anything like God when we live in an age when automation trans-
mits thought mechanically from one machine to another? We
have got beyond that sort of thing entirely. You must come and
travel about the country. See for yourself what we mean.'

I had often thought about this problem and there and then
decided that I should once more travel along the high roads
from Moscow, the new Mecca of the world of irreligion.

Several weeks later I was comfortably installed in a bright
new ship flying the red flag with its hammer and sickle. We
crossed the surprisingly calm North and Baltic Seas on our way
to Leningrad, my native city.

The journey was a real cruise, with stops at all the northern
capitals—Copenhagen, Stockholm, Helsinki. I had all the time
in the world to marshal my thoughts and prepare for what was
to be rather a complicated undertaking.

Most of the passengers belonged to a nationality of whose
existence I had until then been ignorant: they called themselves
'Ukrainian-Canadians'. Their manner was somewhat brusque
and it seemed to me that the language they were talking was as
far from Shakespeare's English as it was from Pushkin's Russian.
From all that I could see, they had nothing to offer me.

But chance arranges things and one sunny afternoon I was in
my deck-chair and discovered that my neighbour was a Soviet
Russian, though he looked for all the world like a Western
intellectual. We introduced ourselves and I learned that I was
talking with Mr Victor Mikheev, member of the Russian section
of UNESCO and author of a doctoral thesis entitled *La Critique
des tendances phénoménologiques dans la philosophie bourgeoise con-
temporaine*. Obviously, I could not have found a better man with
whom to discuss the problem I was on my way to investigate.

I had no trouble at all getting him to express his ideas as we
both sat and watched the lovely panorama of the Swedish
archipelago go by, with its rocky islands covered with firs, and
attractive villas and chalets.

He began by quoting Karl Marx: 'The traditions of dead generations are as heavy as a nightmare on the minds of the living.' 'We have gone through all of that,' he said. 'In my youth our churches were crowded with people. Like my contemporaries, I venerated the philosophy of Spinoza, who fought against the reactionary ideas of his time; we even excused him when he almost imperceptibly arrived at that same "good God" whose existence he should logically have denied. But we've got beyond that stage now. We know now where human evolution is leading. Every metaphysical system sinks its roots deep into the realm of fantasy; it cannot have the slightest relevance to reality and our times no longer need it.

'All religious notions are products of one social structure or another; thus, for instance, monotheism is a direct derivative of the idea of monarchy. The only valid understanding of the world is based on "reason" and reason diligently examines and investigates matter, of which it is nothing more than one manifestation.

'I am in a good position to observe modern trends of thought and I am convinced that religion is dying everywhere. In this area, however, as in so many others, we Soviet Russians are in the van. We are well away towards creating a new society in which religious concepts will be done away with, once and for all.'

·   ·   ·   ·   ·

Our cruise had ended. The day after this encounter we were getting near Kronstadt, the old strongly fortified city built by Peter the Great at the mouth of the Neva. I could see the great domes of a cathedral shining on the horizon—this was one of the first things I saw in atheist Russia. We passed into the harbour, which had recently been enlarged and was lined with huge factories and mammoth cranes, and disembarked on the dock at Leningrad.

Immediately after his arrival in the former imperial capital every tourist makes a point of visiting the Hermitage. Since the Revolution, Catherine the Great's 'folly' has been enriched by many collections, once the property of Russian nobles, and now extends through almost all of the Winter Palace, of which it used to be merely an annex.

Masterpieces of art are displayed there in a brilliant setting. Beautifully decorated rooms, elegant furnishings and large porphyry urns combine to create a magnificent background for creations of every age, from examples of the famous Greco-Scythian silversmiths' craft down to Picassos and the work of other modern painters.

I have known the Hermitage Museum since I was a youth. During the time I spent as a prisoner of the Gestapo I often tried to ease the loneliness of my cell by going through all the rooms in the Hermitage in my mind, recalling as many details of the various collections as possible.

This time I had decided that I must not let pass the opportunity of seeing the unequalled Rembrandts which make up one of the museum's most marvellous collections. To that end, I had asked one of the curators, a friend who had been my guide two years before, to show me through the rooms.

Once again, however, chance stepped in and things took a different course than I had planned. My friend never found the opportunity or time to be my guide; once I had shaken his hand and explained why I was in Russia—to study the religious problem—he led me to the hanging gardens of the Semiramis of the north, had me comfortably seated and then began to give me his ideas on the subject.

As I was leaving Paris, the thought came that perhaps I would run up against a blank wall if I tried to get Soviet Russians involved in a discussion of religion. In the West we avoid conversation of this type, either because we are indifferent or because we are loath to run the risk of offending the sensibilities of others; we prefer to talk about the theatre, sports or politics.

Things are different in the Soviet Union, however, as I found out on my first day there. In the old days people used to make fun of the young Russian revolutionaries and say that they never finished one of their long and drawn-out discussions before bringing up the question of God's existence—usually at about two o'clock in the morning! The social structure has changed, since, but the Russian mind has the same bent.

'You should not be surprised that we are still most pre-occupied with the religious problem,' my learned friend began. 'We scholars and intellectuals of the new Russia are faced with a gigantic task—we must create a new structure. Survivors of the old days are dying out; the last war decimated our ranks. People in the West have been given a poor idea of how much the people of Leningrad lost during World War II. The heroism of the fighters at Stalingrad has overshadowed the glory our defenders earned during an eighteen-month-long siege.

'In 1939 the museum had about a thousand people [on its staff]; now we have only about forty. All the others have simply disappeared; the young men were killed during the war and the older ones were the victims of cold and hunger.

'All our energies are devoted to creating new elements. We are working very hard to give them a technical education, but that is not enough. Some type of moral education is absolutely necessary as well. Can the Church give it? Like so many of our intellectuals, I doubt it. Our clergy have always been corrupt, and they are worse today than they ever were. I know personally a priest who thought he had found his vocation during the last war in a storm on the Arctic Ocean. With death staring him in the face, he made a vow to become a priest and is now a curate in a parish in the north. The first thing he did was to decorate the church with tin boxes, to look like a ship's cabin. He plays the accordion to summon his flock and, like the sailor that he still is, he appreciates a good bottle and pretty girls. He admits his shortcomings and agrees that he would probably do better to go off and try his luck as a factory hand. But he is used to an easy life by this time and the idea of regular employment puts him off completely.

'Surely this type of man is not the teacher that our country people need.

'While the Church is losing prestige, a new school, a new teaching, constructive socialism, is coming to the fore. We were just talking about a sailor and that brings to mind those five sturdy men who attracted attention by keeping themselves alive for forty days in complete isolation on an ice-floe. Would the owner of a yacht, brought up on your Western doctrine of individualism, be capable of such an heroic act? And is not their exaggerated individualism a direct derivative of so-called spiritual doctrines?

'Our young people are given a different sort of training; every one of them knows that the individual is worthless outside collectivity and that, like the ants, they cannot hope to survive apart from the anthill. They dedicate and sacrifice themselves to this collectivity. Our society rejects spiritual values because they give no answer at all, except an irrational one, to basic problems. On the other hand, that same society fully realizes that reason alone is the basis of the solutions proffered by materialism.'

At this point, my friend began to warm to his subject.

'The logical development of individualism leads to a society's turning out traitors and cowards, while materialism creates heroes. It does not deny human dignity, far from it; it stimulates it and goes as far as promising that the man who has worked to deserve it will be remembered for ever by the other members of his community. Whether we belong to the Party or not, this is the frame of mind in which we are raising our new generation, completely without recourse to the Church.

'But go on with your investigation. You will see that the vast majority of the Soviet people share my ideas.'

Later that evening what he said was confirmed during an entirely unexpected encounter.

Despite the length of our talk I was able to see my beloved

Rembrandts before the museum closed. As dusk was falling, I took a long and aimless walk through the sleepy city. I met a group of French tourists and joined them, showing them the house where my grandparents had lived, and the Imperial Yacht Club, beyond whose windows formerly sat young, idling, elegant grand dukes and heavily decorated old generals. I took them to the square of the Winter Palace, in front of the famous semicircular government building known in the diplomatic world as the Pont de Chantres, where I had my office as a young attaché. I described to them the times when the Tsar reviewed his troops there. My tourist friends must have thought that I, too, was some sort of ghost, come back to scenes of former glory and splendour.

Suddenly, when I was just a few steps from my hotel, a stranger called me by name. The first thought that came to me was that, finally, an operative of the 'secret police' had got on to me. Actually, the prospect of a new and exciting adventure made me almost hope I had guessed right.

The man who had recognized and called out to me in the dark would have found it easy to secure employment as a physiognomist at the casino in Monte Carlo; only a few hours earlier he had seen my photo on the mantelpiece of some mutual friends who told him that I was expected to arrive shortly.

His powers of recognition were not the only thing surprising about him, however. Fifteen minutes later we were seated alongside one another in Senate Square, a few yards away from the spot where the Decembrist Revolt broke out in 1825. The shades of these aristocratic and romantic revolutionaries drifted above us; like them, we too, already, were busy discussing the basic problems of philosophy and religion. Midnight struck; the Russians really are indefatigable talkers.

My new friend was a professor and the first thing I asked him was to what extent young students were acquainted with religion and religious problems. Had I not heard that the new Soviet generation did not even know the name of the Lord?

And that a student had burst into loud guffaws on learning that Christ, born in Palestine, was just a 'Jew'?

'That is nonsense,' he answered. 'We are not that stupid. Don't believe anyone who tells you that modern Russians have never heard of the Bible. As a matter of fact, one of my colleagues is in the midst of a series of lectures on scripture at the Popular University of Science and Culture, which has about a hundred branches throughout the city where anyone who wants may enrol in an evening course.

'I can even tell you what material he covers in his lectures. One of them discusses the Bible as an historical source, and the other considers it as a classic of literature. My friend takes a scientific point of view and admits that paleography and archaeology bear out the truth of the larger part of the Bible narratives; he admits that the greatest writers of the past were greatly inspired by these narratives.

'There will be a third series of lectures soon. It will concentrate on the masterpieces of painting and sculpture whose subjects have been taken from the Old and New Testaments, such as Leonardo's "Last Supper", Michelangelo's "Moses" and Raphael's Madonnas.

'You see, what we want to do is strip historically undeniable facts of the halo of mysticism which has been put round them. We no longer need religion as such; we no longer believe.'

Thus, as in all my previous conversations, I had come to the point when I heard the same ideas rehearsed once again.

But my professor friend was not content to stop there. He himself had read the Bible and had concluded that many of the mysterious and miraculous events narrated in Holy Scripture might be reconciled with scientific data. The only thing needed was a bit of imagination, and he had that.

He offered to prove it to me and we arranged that I should visit him the next day.

I need hardly say that I was on time for our meeting. The professor had a modest but very comfortable flat; no young Parisian intellectual could have asked for anything more. A handsome library, outmoded but comfortably upholstered armchairs and no glaring lights.

My host did not have a manuscript before him, but simply referred to some notes he had made, rather like Oriental story-tellers, to tell a story reminiscent of the style of Dostoievsky's 'Grand Inquisitor' sequence. He promised that he would later send me a written transcription of what he said, but, of course, that promise was never kept.

I shall try to reproduce as accurately as I can what he said:

'Recent archaeological excavations in northern Africa turned up some fragments which had led to the conjecture that, about two thousand years before the beginning of our era, the earth was visited by astronauts who had come from far off in the cosmos. They had some ideas of their own about our planet and had decided to come to look for living beings on the white areas they had been able to make out near the Equator.

'They landed in Egypt, and were awestruck when they saw the pyramids. Some of the peasants of the area approached the three travellers very warily and accepted them as having come peacefully.

'That was the first manifestation of the Holy Trinity.

'The three astronauts stayed on earth for several years and made themselves familiar with life and conditions here. Then they left.

'With them, however, they took a human, as a specimen. He was the man the Bible calls Enoch. Before going, though, they promised their hosts that they would return one day. A light in the sky, like a star, would announce their coming.

'Succeeding generations never forgot this promise. The people who had been witnesses to the actual promise constantly talked about it and reminisced about the heavenly visitors.

'But they had to flee from Egypt, because they were being persecuted on account of their "mystical" beliefs. They settled in Palestine, where they were called *Ibrim*, "the men who come from afar".

'At the time when King Herod was on the throne of Judea, the sign they had been waiting so many generations for finally appeared and the *Ibrim* saw a mysterious light in the heavens. At once, they delegated messengers to go and welcome the space travellers.

'These latter had landed in the desert, and there were seven of them [the number of angels mentioned in the Apocalypse]. One of them left with the messengers to go off towards the Jordan; he was the man tradition calls John the Baptist.

'The Baptist was later followed by another man, for whose arrival he made preparations; this was Christ. Christ's knowledge of the physical world far outstripped what any human knew, and he easily cured the sick. The situation was rather similar to what we have seen in our time when Soviet doctors perform "miracles" among the native populations of Central Asia.

'This Messiah profoundly impressed everyone who heard him when he described the unimaginably more developed and merciful social structure which existed on his planet. When he was arrested, he said that his kingdom was "not of this world".

'When he was about to be taken to his torture and death on Golgotha, he used "wireless" to contact his companions, who had stayed in Egypt, and let them know what was happening.

'His friends could not get to him quickly enough, but they took his body, which disappeared for ever.

'His admirers concluded that he had risen from the dead and gone up into the heavens.

'Thus was Christianity born. People began to construct places of worship that looked like interplanetary rockets.

'They even thought that the day would come when he would reappear. Believers are still waiting. . . .'

The professor had finished his tale. Disturbed and moved, I left, thanking him for his hospitality.

This, then, was one of the modern Marxist intellectuals. Convinced and zealous atheists, torn by metaphysical anguish, striving to construct a new moral structure, inspired by a communal spirit, some of them have become biblical scholars whose research ends up in science fiction!

Nietzsche said that 'a Russian atheist remains a believer'. My initial contacts with members of the upper levels of Soviet life and culture had certainly given me that impression—but I wondered what the situation was among the ordinary people.

The following Sunday was the Feast of the Trinity, and I decided to attend the liturgy at the Monastery of St Alexander Nevski.

This was the imperial monastery of Tsarist Russia. Peter the Great had brought there the relics of the famous medieval prince, who had victoriously defended Orthodoxy, and repulsed the incursions of the Swedes and Teutonic Knights. They rested in a huge reliquary of engraved and chased silver which once was above his tomb but is now in one of the rooms in the Hermitage. His memory is still as venerated as it ever was, however.

Bishop Alexei of Luga, who is the Metropolitan-Vicar, officiated before a great crush of almost 6,000 people; and there had been as many people at an earlier liturgy.

Most of the congregation were middle-aged women, obviously in modest circumstances and all wearing the conventional neat white headscarves. There were not many younger people in the cathedral, but I could see quite a few men who seemed to me to be workers and ordinary wage-earners.

I was struck by the fervour and attentiveness of all of them; two of the most moving moments, perhaps, were when they joined with the choir in singing the Creed and the Lord's Prayer in an exquisite mixture of rich Russian basses and full sopranos.

Nothing else could compare to the atmosphere in the cathedral that day, with its truly gorgeous decorations and the hundreds of lighted candles mixing their light and odour with the smoke and scent of the incense—it was like being back in old Holy Russia once again.

Outside the cathedral I struck up a conversation with a man I had noticed during the service.

'Don't be taken in,' he said. 'Our people have lost their faith; they don't believe in anything any more. I'm a taxi-driver, so I see a lot of people and get a good look at them; no more than ten per cent of them still believe in religion. Even my own children won't go to church. I read the Bible regularly and I'm waiting for the catastrophe predicted in Paul's second Epistle to the Thessalonians. We'll end up the way Lot's daughters did.

'I've said the same thing to my mates, but they just laugh in my face; and when I start to read some religious book, St Dmitri of Rostov maybe, they just yawn and walk away.

'That's the way it is with us. I'd be ready and willing to be a martyr for Christianity—but nobody's asked me to yet, and maybe that's the root of our trouble.'

I don't think the whole question of religion and irreligion in the Soviet Union could be better summarized than the way this unassuming taxi-driver did. There is a great deal to ponder there.

2

The Russian Church in History

THE Church has played an enormous part in the thousand-year-long history of Russia. Nothing else, in any other Christian country, matches this close link.

Our civilization rests on a threefold basis: Greek beauty, Roman strength and the wisdom of Jerusalem. Russia had no direct contact with Rome, but the entire framework of her spiritual life is built on the Greco-Judaean and Christian heritage she received from Byzantium.

Though it had been in preparation for a very long time, the final and actual evangelization of Russia was late. It was not until 958 that St Vladimir, the Great Prince of Kiev, decreed that all his people should be baptized. Once this step had been taken, however, the Russians were completely penetrated by the teachings of Christianity, which they adapted to their own thought and mentality.

While Christians in the West submitted to the supra-national papal authority, the Russian Orthodox soon threw off Byzantine domination and gradually made of their Church a strictly national institution.

Their clergy went further than merely teaching them the essentials of morality, such as the idea of family responsibility and respect for women, and it did more than arouse their innate Russian feeling for charity and justice. What it did do was to make a concrete contribution towards unifying national territory and establishing centralized government. It identified itself with the people and their country, with the nation, and bolstered up their courage during the most trying times in their history.

Christianity in Russia spread with astonishing speed, as it did in other European countries. Scarcely a hundred years had gone by since Vladimir's baptism, and Kiev already shone with the thirteen golden domes of its Cathedral of St Sophia, which adapted the traditional Russian architecture in wood to a beautiful stone building. Russian artists soon became expert in fresco-painting and mosaics and, beginning with the eleventh and twelth centuries, ikon-painters left Kiev to bring the benefits of their art and skill to the entire country.

At that time Russia and her rulers were established as members in full standing of the community of European nations.

Later, when the country ran with the blood spilt by feudal quarrelling, based on nothing but brute strength, the Church pointed out that the only way to salvation and safety lies in Christian brotherhood. And when the Mongolian hordes stifled the rich surge of Kievan culture, and submitted the entire Russian nation to foreign domination for two centuries, it was once more the Church who used faith and the churches as the treasure-houses of nationalism, keeping it intact until this, the worst period in Russian history, finally came to an end.

When the idea arose of creating a new centre of political life in Moscow the clergy were its enthusiastic promoters. The first metropolitans of the city encouraged the faithful to support to their utmost a series of aspiring and far-seeing rulers. Men who were saints in the fullest sense of the word, such as St Sergei Radonezh-ski, all had a part in reviving the moral strength of the country, which had almost been brought to its knees. Their work was to influence deeply the lives of succeeding generations, who transformed the memory of them into an enduring national heritage.

Backed by the clergy, the Moscovite sovereigns who gathered the different feudal dukedoms of Russia into a strong unity had succeeded by the sixteenth century in transforming an immense region buried deep in forests into a powerful state.

After marrying Sophia Palaeologus, the niece of the last Byzantine emperor, Ivan III proclaimed himself autocrat of all the Russias. Taking advantage of his right of succession, which was actually not indisputable, his grandson, Ivan IV, called 'the Terrible', declared that he was the heir of the Emperor of the East and assumed the title 'Tsar' (from Caesar) at his coronation. Some good and holy clerics busied themselves at concocting a new doctrine aimed at glorifying the position of their rulers as successors to the work of Constantine and defenders of the true faith.

Russian messianism was first formulated in a message to the Kremlin from the wise monk Philotheus: 'The holy and apostolic Church, the Church of the Third Rome, the Church of Thy kingdom, shines with a brilliance purer than the sun's. . . . Thou alone, beneath all the heavens, art the sole, truly Christian ruler. Two Romes have fallen but the third Rome stands—nor will there be another.'

Constantinople, now under Moslem rule, was lost in Moscow's shadow. A few years after the death of Ivan the Terrible, while Boris Godunov was regent, the election of the first Patriarch of All the Russias was held at the Kremlin on 23 January 1589.

Though they had established their influence on the level of religious affairs, the Moscovite clergy did not stop there; they were as diligent in fulfilling the responsibilities their position imposed on them in social and political affairs. During the reign of Ivan the Terrible the only one to raise his voice against the Tsar's tyranny and despotism, which were irreconcilable with Christianity and Christian morality, was Metropolitan Philip, who ended by being put to death by one of Ivan's specially chosen and trusted henchmen.

The old Rurik dynasty had ended. At the beginning of the seventeenth century serious troubles developed because the throne was vacant. Indeed, Russia's very existence was threatened by concerted interference in her affairs by Poland and Sweden. Once more the Church showed that she was part of the strong foundation of the national idea. The patriotic activity of Patriarch Hermogenes, who was killed by Poles, and the ultimately victorious resistance given to the enemy through long months of a siege by the Monastery of the Trinity and St Sergei, are shining passages in the history of the national revival of patriotism.

When the new Romanoff dynasty ascended the throne in 1613 it seemed that the collaborative union of Church and State was permanently established. The very young Tsar's father was Patriarch Philaret, who actually held the reins of government.

It was during this period that the words 'Holy Russia' achieved their full meaning. The Orthodox Church had succeeded in imposing upon the people a disciplined fidelity in fulfilling their religious duties which it would be difficult to find elsewhere, even during the Middle Ages. The bells never ceased ringing.

The Sabbath rest and Lenten fasts were observed with utmost scrupulousness and the least offence against these regulations was severely punished. 'Moscovite monks and nuns,' wrote a Western observer, the diplomat, J. Korb, 'are obviously more poor and lead lives of greater austerity than our religious do. No other people in the world can pride themselves on so widespread a manifestation of upright piety.'

Too often, however, devotion to these external customs was bereft of any internal meaning of significance. It seemed that the formative work done by St Theodosius and the other Kievan monks of the Petchersky Monastery to bring the light of religion to the pagan population had gone by the board. If we take the word of foreign visitors, respect for priests was concentrated almost entirely on their hats: 'If anyone wants to pick a fight with a pope[1],' stated another contemporary visitor, 'he must first take off the priest's hat and, after having respectfully put it to one side,

---

[1] 'Pope' is the old Russian title given to priests; it now has disrespectful overtones and should never be used by a foreigner unaware of those connotations.

may belabour the priest with as many blows as he likes, with no fear of punishment.'

Christianity's essential principles had been overlooked and misplaced.

When J. Perry, an English visitor to Russia in those days, tried to discuss God and morality with Russian clerics, they swerved off the main subject to concentrate on fasting and the intervention of the saints.

In the eighteenth century the Dane Juel was to declare that 'our thirteen-year-olds with any education at all know more about the subject than most Russian adults'. And he went on, adding this sharply evaluative comment: 'After what I have seen, I should say that barely one man out of five can recite the Lord's Prayer. . . .'

But how could the situation be otherwise, when almost all the 150,000 members of the 'white' and 'black'[1] clergy were recruited from the lowest levels of society? The few monks who were members of noble families were in monasteries because they had been sent there by the Tsar, who, for one reason or another, considered them in disgrace.

At first a priest was chosen to serve in a particular parish by the people of that parish, though later the bishops usually appointed the sons of former parish priests to their fathers' posts, without expecting them to give any evidence of learning or even preaching skills. This system promoted the establishment of genuine clerical dynasties, some of them lasting for several generations, within most parishes.

Or, again, how can we suppose that circumstances would have been different when we realize that there had been no theological faculty in Russia for several centuries, nor even a seminary to train men for the priesthood, since the first Ecclesiastical Academy (where the profane sciences were also taught) in Kiev was not

---

[1] The 'white' clergy are married priests; the 'black' clergy are monks, who are celibate and bishops, who are usually chosen from among the monks since, except in some small schismatic sects, Orthodox bishops must be celibate. *Trans.*

established until 1613? Besides, the situation was further complicated when scholars attached to this academy instituted a reform
of liturgical books, to bring them back to their original texts and
meaning, and thereby brought on a schism which rocked the
Orthodox Church to its foundations and robbed it of some of its
most ardent and fervent members.

'Medieval Russia,' wrote W. Weidle, 'had no St Bernard nor
St Thomas Aquinas; she had no *Divina Commedia* and no Gothic
cathedrals; there were no eminent theologians or influential
monastic order. . . . Her Christianity had by now been
absorbed by popular piety, which was at once sentimental and
ritualistic.'

Despite these things on the debit side, however, the Church
of Russia still enjoyed enormous influence in Russia's cultural
life. She played a very large part in the creation of a national
artistic style which found expression in magnificent liturgical
music, exquisite churches and ikons of a deeply mystical
beauty.

In old Moscovite Russia only the clergy were capable of giving
young people of the ruling classes even the scantiest introduction
to learning. To them also the Church owed that vast and varied,
though entirely religious, body of literature in which the 'lives' of
saints are pre-eminent.

But more than anything else the clergy are to be credited with
preserving the glorious traditions of the Churches of the East,
traditions heavy with spiritual wealth and which are concentrated
on contemplation, Christian humility, the teaching of the Holy
Spirit and the transfiguration of all the universe.

These advances and contributions notwithstanding, the fact
remains that various historical upheavals and difficulties retarded
the Russian Orthodox Church's pace of development. Isolated as
she was in a haughty retirement from what was going on about
her, and progressively more and more disdainful, blindly clinging
to the forms of worship though without any sort of properly
organized system of instruction, and consequently incapable of

correcting the profound ignorance of her flock and training them to a genuine social discipline, she had, by the end of the seventeenth century, become an institution which hobbled the free strides of the people's energy by her stubborn obscurantism.

In his sweeping modernization of Russia, Peter the Great was to bring about a radical change even in the life of the Church. As soon as he began enforcing his initial reformative legislation he was met by the head-on opposition of the clergy. At first, when the Patriarch expressed his indignation that Peter had insisted that a new form of dress should be adopted, the Tsar contented himself with replying: 'Leave the tailor to take care of fashion; the Church alone is your affair.'

But the clergy were so stubbornly against Peter's educational reforms that he was forced to take drastic measures. After hesitating a few weeks, he finally decided, on 16 December 1700, to abolish the Patriarchate. The reform thus initiated was brought to full term twenty-two years later with the creation of the Holy Synod. This institution was collegiate in structure and was composed of several archbishops selected by the sovereign; they were to direct all Church business and had a jurisdiction at least as broad as the former Patriarchs, which included: the maintenance of true Orthodox doctrine; selection of bishops; administration of Church property; jurisdiction over the clergy; supreme authority in marriage cases and judgment of trials involving blasphemy, heresy and witchcraft; supervision of parochial schools and direction of seminaries; publication of devotional books and censorship of other books; charitable aid to the poor, the sick, orphans, etc.

In the Ecclesiastical Regulations, promulgated by Peter at that time, the idea behind the reforms was thus explained:

'The Orthodox Tsar, guardian of the true Faith and of the welfare of Holy Church, aware of her spiritual needs and eager to have her administration directed in as perfect a way as possible, has authorized the creation of the Holy Synod, whose task it will be to work diligently and untiringly for the Church's welfare, so that all things may be in order and that there may be no disorder, according to the mind of the Apostle and the will of God himself. . . .

Our ordinary subjects cannot distinguish between the authority of the Church and temporal authority. Impressed by the renown and honour paid to the Supreme Pastor, they came to look on him as another sovereign who was equal to the Autocrat, or even more powerful. . . . The perfect union of the two powers will, before anything else, be to the advantage of the Church herself.'

Peter the Great was obviously repelled by the idea that he might have a sort of Russian Pope within his own empire. But it is the most extraordinary kind of exaggeration to accuse him of giving Russia some sort of Caesaro-papism, which would make the Church completely subject to temporal power. Neither Peter nor any of his successors ever considered extending his authority to include the doctrines of religion; their jurisdiction covered only the administration of the Church, which was taken care of by a Procurator General. Peter was not working to leave the clergy without a single leader and superior; he wanted nothing more than to get them back into step, revive some sort of order in their ranks and be able to depend upon them to keep all the levels of society disciplined and organized.

According to a formula coined later during Nicholas I's reign, it was the destiny of 'Orthodoxy' to become side by side with 'Autocracy and Populism', the creed upon which the entire Russian politic was established.

On the whole the clergy did not have too much to complain about, no great reason to pity themselves; they were not especially inconvenienced by the Tsar's authority nor even by certain imperial commands ordering them to participate in specified political activities.

Their anxieties and preoccupations were of a more mundane

sort. There was no conflict of principles or interests; but they found that they were expected to perform many wearisome tasks, such as keeping civil registers and assisting the civil authorities in the prosecution of schismatics. Most priests in rural areas had very small means compared with the wealth of some monasteries and the privileged position enjoyed by certain bishops (the Metropolitan of Kiev, for example, received a salary of 4,000 rubles, but got about 50,000 more from the Petchersky Monastery). The restraints put on theological development and on attempts to penetrate social, economic and political reform movements with genuine Christian teaching all provided far more serious grounds for complaint.

Actually, the genuinely dramatic period through which the Church in Russia was to live for the next two centuries was not so much generated by the creation of the Holy Synod as by the spirit which was, on the whole at least, behind Peter's reforms. On his own admission, the Tsar had hoped that 'the people would not be so involved merely in observing their fasts, in genuflexions, and lighting candles and burning incense, but that they would have genuine confidence in God and realize what faith, hope and charity really are'.

In effect, however, what he succeeded in doing was secularizing the Church and creating a deep abyss between the two classes in the country, the one which was becoming more and more rapidly Europeanized and the other which was stubbornly devoted to traditional customs but no less steeped in poverty and ignorance, just as they had been before

Henceforth, religion for the upper levels of Russian society was to be nothing more than attendance at various solemnities. Spiritual perfection meant nothing at all to people who were swept up in the 'Enlightenment' and, later, the 'Age of Reason'. Russian Freemasons, basically faithful Christians who wanted to take their place 'midway between Voltairianism and Christianity', were only influential for a very short time. And Alexander I, the 'Protector of Orthodoxy', did not even know that there was a very great and holy man, Seraphim of Sarov, among his countless subjects. Even if he had known, however, the Mystic Tsar, devoted disciple of Boehme and Baader as he was, could hardly have found common ground with the humble hermit who lived hidden away in the forests.

Surprising as it may seem (but how typical, really), we have no history of the Russian Church in modern times. The few major works on the subject do not go past the eighteenth century.[1] In these circumstances, consequently, it is difficult to give a complete outline of its activities during the final period of the old regime.

The Church of Russia did everything it could to raise the cultural and social levels of the people by struggling bravely against crime, alcoholism and illiteracy. It was responsible for opening 21,000 parochial schools during the years between 1859 and 1865, but this initial burst of enthusiasm for education was doomed to a short life, because neither the Government nor public opinion had enough confidence in the clergy to leave public education in their hands. The initiative was taken up again, however, at the end of the last century, under the Procurator General of the Holy Synod, Constantine Pobiedonostsev. This was a man of towering scholarship, member-correspondent of the *Institut de France*, translator of the *Imitation of Christ*, but also a fiercely intransigent reactionary. Uneasy and frightened to think of the day when his country, 'this immense desert shrouded in ice and snow', would 'thaw', he thought that in the parochial school system he had found a means of fighting the revolutionary spirit in the country. By the end of the century there were 42,000 such schools—and it was at one of them that Nikita Khrushchev was later given the elementary education which still enables him to quote frequently from the Gospels.

The Russian higher clergy had long since put aside their

[1] A prohibition issued by Pobiedonostsev, procurator of the Holy Synod, prevented Father Golubinski from completing his *History*, which was acclaimed as a classic. An untimely death interrupted the remarkable work begun by Professor A. Kartashov, two volumes of his *Histoire de l'Eglise Russe* were published in Paris in 1959.

medieval prejudices and fanatic intolerance, so that by this time they were able to point to eminent theologians and moving preachers in their ranks (one of the most famous was Metropolitan Philaret of Moscow). Missionary groups were organized and worked in eastern Siberia and the Kamchatka peninsula, bringing Christianity to the tribes living there and eventually extending their evangelizing work as far as Japan and China.

But progress had also been made among the ordinary parish priests and by this time most of them were better educated than the majority of their flocks.

Notwithstanding these advances, the influence brought to bear by both levels of the clergy was still as weak and impotent as it had been in the past. The hierarchy was as much an efficient tool in the hands of the autocrat as it had ever been and parish priests were no less dependent on their parishioners for their material subsistence. Churchgoers were left unmoved and uninstructed by the sermons they heard preached in a mixture of Church Slavonic and the vernacular, and the duties and responsibilities of the clergy more often than not levelled themselves off at nothing more or less than strict and painstaking celebration of various services—so that no development from the old attitudes was obvious here, either.

So far as ritualistic observances were concerned, however, they had completely won the day. There was a law—more often disregarded than observed—which made it obligatory for all imperial officers and civil servants to receive Holy Communion at least once every three years, and the liturgy was celebrated in military camps for the slightest reason. Each evening the men would line up to sing the liturgical responses, and I recall very clearly the many times when it was my duty in the field to give the command: 'Prayer call. Caps off!' to my small unit.

Country people without fail celebrated the feasts of the patron saints of their churches, but these holy days were really nothing more than occasions for long drinking-bouts.

G.A.T.S.—C

And even among the Russian upper classes there was not a woman who would not attend Matins on Easter Eve wearing a white dress and a necklace of jewels fashioned to imitate Easter eggs.

It would be wrong, of course, to say that the Russian people's religious life consisted in nothing more than these external manifestations of affected piety. Tsarist Russia had not experienced the religious renewal that had spread through Catholicism and Protestantism during the romantic period after the Napoleonic wars. Orthodox spirituality's vibrant underground current survived among the people, however, and was alive and fervent amidst the lowly and oppressed people who were concentrated at the very instant when nineteenth-century rationalism was winning its greatest victories among the intelligentsia. Christianity helped the popular classes to hang fast to traditional ideas of morality and charity. It was the dynamic force behind the unselfish activities (too often stymied by the stupidity of administrative offices) of those marvellous priests Lesskov so vividly describes in his stories. Striking evidence of its activity was given by the work of a group of monks who were imbued with wisdom and Christian holiness and known as the Startsi of the Monastery of Optina.

It was in the cell of one of these mystic-hermits that Ivan Kireyevsky, founder of the Slavophile School, discovered the source of his inspiration. It was the first time since the reform made by Peter the Great that parallel activity could be seen in the notions championed by secular Russia and the teachings of the Church presented in their loftiest character. Slavophile thought was shot through with a thread of religion, and one of the leaders of the movement, Khomiakov, can be rightly considered as the greatest of Russia's lay theologians. The movement's doctrine was that Russia's mission in the world was different from any Western country's; Russia was a living unit, an organism, which had deep within itself its own law of morality, and its own modes of spiritual and intellectual activity. Religion was an essential element in Russia's evolution and had to purge Orthodoxy of the vestiges of ruinous historical influences; it had to penetrate deeply into the souls of the Russian people once they had been able to blot out the stains left on them by the State's absolutism and rationalism. Rural Russian communes were the archetype of the *sobornost* (communal life and inspiration) which should be the mode of living of all true Christians.

The 'Elders [*startsi*] of Optina' had more far-reaching influence than this, however; the leading representatives of Russian religious thought—Dostoievsky, Tolstoy, Soloviev—would all come to the monastery to be aided and directed in their search for eternal truth.

Russia's future was not laid out by this movement of religious thought, however. The so-called 'Western' school outstripped the slavophiles and it was due to them that Russian youth soon became steeped in the rationalist, socialist and atheist ideas dignified by French and German thinkers. 'Humanism', which made each man his own god, soon became the cry. The new school of thought took over as its own that myth of the modern world, 'progress', and expected science to furnish it with weapons against religion and to give it fresh means to interpret human destiny. It would quickly turn to studying Karl Marx and strive to make practical application of dialectical materialism by interpolating philosophical data into an economic and social system.

Russia was moving into her pre-revolutionary period. As it did in France, it was to last a good fifty years.

It was at this time that a new type of student, idealistic, enthusiastic and fanatic, appeared on the scene. They soon came to be known though far from accurately, as 'Nihilists'. The name was a misnomer because these romantic revolutionaries were actually motivated by a faith which was compelling. Like the Slavophiles, they were convinced of the reality of the *Messianic* mission of the Russian people; on the other hand, they also believed that republicanism and integral socialism would, in the long run, triumph.

They were disciples of writers of mediocre talents but ardent devotion to the new ideas, and who are now idolized as the precursors of the Revolution—Chernichevsky, Dobrolubov, Pissarev.

As far as religion was concerned, their whole approach was negative; the young atheists reproached the clergy for their submission to the government, their servility towards property owners, and their inability to raise the intellectual level of the people and shake them out of their almost idolatrous devotion to various saints. They were Russia's first socialists, but, in the beginning at least, they were a very small minority and the people hardly paid any attention to them.

In 1905 the already riddled foundations of Tsarism were shaken by their first shock. Under pressure from an overwhelming popular movement Tsar Nicholas II was forced to grant the rudiments of a constitution, convoke a national assembly (the Duma) and authorize religious freedom.

Even in Church life there was a repercussion from the intellectual and social tremors making themselves felt in Russia at that time. Count Sergei Witte, one of Russia's great statesmen, originally brought up the question of Church-State relations and urged sweeping reforms. Pobiedonostsev, the formidable Procurator General of the Holy Synod, opposed to any reform whatever, had to resign. A 'Religious and Philosophical Society' was formed in St Petersburg and included high-ranking prelates and other leading figures (such as the author Merezhkovski and the theologian Bulgakov) among its members. Once again Russian intellectuals and a newly revivified Church set out to co-operate with one another, as they had done at Optina. But Russian society had its mind on other things, and was not affected by the work done by the group, any more than the lower classes were.

A movement began within the clergy themselves, however, and was soon to have results which were important, but in another area.

In 1906 sixty-three bishops collaborated in issuing a four-volume report in which they outlined an important reform-programme and, among other things, demanded the calling of a Church Council whose task it would be to re-establish the independence of Orthodoxy. With the approval of the Holy Synod and the authorization of the Tsar, a special commission was set up immediately, to get ready for the assembly of this council and prepare its agenda. The commission had not finished its work by 1917.

Meanwhile, the Duma was no more immune to political agitation than the rest of Russia was. Political parties, formerly forbidden, began to form and the clergy saw in them the opportunity to become involved in politics. Unfortunately, the right-wing groups benefited more than any others because they were able to enrol some reactionary bishops as members. Most rural parish priests did not, of course, share the opinions of these ranking prelates, but the latter went to great lengths to have their viewpoint prevail; besides, things were not at all helped by the presence of some inflammatory left-wing priests in the Duma, who certainly did nothing to advance the Church's prestige.

A fatal blow was struck this prestige by the tragic Rasputin affair.

Externally at least, the Church of the final years of Tsarist Russia was still an impressive power. There were almost 100 million faithful, 67 bishops–ordinary and 82 auxiliary bishops, 50,105 priests, 15,210 deacons, 21,330 monks and 73,299 nuns. Despite her apparently flourishing condition, however, she too, like all the other national institutions, was affected by the widespread degeneration of the country's social structure. While Russia was heading for shipwreck, violent quarrels began in monasteries and the members of the Holy Synod took advantage of the fact that they were no longer answerable to a disciplinary authority and became embroiled in some shocking conniving.

An ordinary man, the child of illiterate peasants, almost illiterate himself, and utterly unscrupulous, profited by this disordered situation. Despite what is widely believed, Rasputin was neither a priest nor a monk; he never even claimed that he was a cleric. He did, however, call himself a 'man of God' and had connections in high ecclesiastical circles; some bishops helped him achieve his eventually influential position. Despite the fact that she had no close or intimate connections with him, the Church would one day find herself compromised by the wicked hold that Rasputin had over the imperial couple while he lived and his malevolent influence on Russia's fate.

The times could not have been more ill chosen—so far as the Church was concerned—for Tsarism to come to an end and a new governmental system to begin. At first glance, however, it seemed that the abdication of Nicholas II and the establishment of the provisional Government held out promise of a new and brighter future for the Church. Determined to grant complete religious freedom, the new Government abolished the office and duties of the Procurator General of the Holy Synod and, from deep down in the files, took out the dusty and yellowed records of the commission which, twelve years earlier, had been set up to prepare for a council.

On 15 August 1917 the Supreme Council of the entire Russian Church met for the first time since 1696. Among its 564 delegates were 278 laymen, representatives of sixty-seven dioceses. The first business taken care of was the composition of a new set of statutes for the Church, which provided for the restoration of the Patriarchate, the election of bishops by the interested dioceses, and the inclusion of laymen as members of parochial and diocesan councils, and within the supreme administrative organization of the Patriarchate.

These reforms had long been considered necessary and so were immediately set into operation—but they came too late. War with Germany was going on and throwing the country into confusion. Political strife broke out all over Russia and shook its social structure right down to bedrock. The Communist Party lifted its banner and marched on to victory.

On 5 November 1917 the Council elected Metropolitan Tikhon of Moscow Patriarch. Two days later, the Communists had overthrown the provisional Government and Lenin was in power.

3

The Church and the Revolution

THE time has not yet come to give an objective and impartial picture of religious life in Russia during the first twenty years of the Soviet regime. We are still too close to everything that happened; memories of the fierce struggle between Church and State are still too sensitive; survivors of those tragic times are still too numerous and the documentary evidence we have on which to reconstruct what actually happened is scanty and incomplete.

However, official and semi-official documents which are available give us enough information to define, at least, the attitudes adopted by the government and the leaders among the clergy from 1917 to our own day.

As everyone knows, the extraordinary personality who was to become the leader of the Bolshevik (later changed to Communist) Party was a convinced atheist and, on principle, the enemy of all Churches. He had got the essence of his doctrine from Karl Marx:

'Conscience does not determine life, life determines conscience; mind is nothing more than the evolutionary expansion of matter. . . . Religion is the lament of the oppressed, the soul of a world that has no soul, the hope of a humanity which has lost all hope; it is the opium of the people.'

Engels taught him that 'Christianity more and more became the birthright of the influential classes, which they used as a bridle to check the lower classes'.

Knowing what life in rural Russia was like, Lenin was over-come by a profound contempt for the ordinary priests, whom he considered poorly trained, avaricious and implacably determined to keep the people in superstitious ignorance. As far as the hier-archy were concerned, his hatred for them, the 'enemies of the people', grew out of what he saw of the behaviour of the bishops and their cronies in the Duma.

Determined as he was to smash the chains of oppression and set total revolution under way, Vladimir Lenin was still too principled an individual to adopt any programme which would sanction the violation of consciences. Product of ignorance as it is, religion would disappear by itself, he thought, once it no longer had the support of the exploiting privileged classes. All that need be done was to separate the Church from the State as completely as possible and leave the people, who had not yet completely evolved socially, the possibility of venerating their idols and remaining faithful to whatever belief they wanted.

This (not entirely uncontradictory) attitude was put forth by Lenin many, many times in what he said and what he wrote. In an article dated 1909, he took up Engels' argument, which was a categorical denunciation of 'any interdict against religion in a socialist society' and which blamed Bismarck's errors on his completely inefficient struggle with clericalism. The only struggle which seems worth while to him is the one which takes place 'in relation to the concrete practice of the movement of the classes'. Socialism's essential task is to fight against religions 'as deeply rooted in capitalistic domination'. If the workers are to be enlisted in this struggle, the first and principal thing to be careful of is that their religious feelings are not offended.

He returned to this subject in November 1918, when he was already head of the Government:

'Religious prejudices must be fought against with the utmost prudence, so as not to offend the sensibilities of believers; one must carry on the battle with propaganda and education. To go into the struggle headlong and without restraint would be to risk the hatred of the masses and their alienation on religious grounds, whereas all our strength lies in our being united. Poverty and ignorance are the real sources of religious prejudice and they are the evils against which we must do battle with every means at our disposal.'

Despite these reservations, Lenin never lost sight of his ultimate objective. 'We must fire and let our bullets pierce the skin of Holy Russia,' the hero of the famous poet Alexander Blok (*The Twelve*) had cried in a work which appeared during the early months of the Revolution. Lenin did not use the language of a mutinous soldier, of course, but he, no less than anyone else, wanted to have done, once and for all, with the old pseudo-theocratic regime and snap the traditional links binding 'the altar and the throne' to one another and thus trammelling the free development of national dynamism in Russia. Two months after he assumed power, he had the Council of People's Commissars approve the famous 'Decree on the Separation of Church and State'. It was published on 23 January 1918 and still remains the fundamental basis for relations between the secular and religious powers in the Soviet Union.

The legislation stipulated that, thenceforth, the Church in Russia would be separated from the State and forbade any activity likely to hamper freedom of conscience. Every citizen was free to profess the religion of his choice, or to profess none at all. Any restriction of civil rights stemming from practice or non-practice of religion was abolished. Official documents would no longer note a citizen's membership, or non-membership, in a religious community. Official activities of the State and all other activities of a juridic nature would be henceforth carried on without any religious rite or ceremony whatever.

Freedom of worship was permitted insofar as it would not affect public order and did not interfere with the rights of the citizens of the Soviet Republic. If there should be any such interference, local authorities were authorized to take whatever steps considered necessary to guarantee order and the public interest.

No citizen could appeal to his religious beliefs as exemption from the performance of his civic duties. If a case arose in which one such civic duty was to be replaced by another, individual exemptions would be granted in particular cases by the people's tribunal.

Religious oaths were forbidden. In cases where oaths were necessary, a solemn promise would be sufficient. Civic acts of the State (marriages, births, deaths, etc.) were within the competence of the proper secular offices which would also keep relevant records and registers.

Education was taken out of the Church's hands. Religious education was forbidden in state-operated or private schools, except special schools of theology. Citizens were free to teach and study religion privately.

Considered from an entirely juridic point of view, this decree is not so very different from various other modern codes of legislation which regulate Church-State relations in most contemporary secular states. What is striking, however, is the prohibition of religious education in all schools without exception and the deprivation of all religious associations of their right to own property. But the essential difference lies elsewhere: it can be found in the very particular political climate prevailing in Russia during the revolutionary period when the decree was published.

Afterwards, when tempers and excitement had cooled, one of the most qualified representatives of the Church, Metropolitan (late Patriarch) Sergei, was in a position to insist on the positive side of the decree. In March 1942 he wrote:

'The separation of Church and State destroyed any barriers which had kept within the Church any people who were Christians in name alone. Under the Tsarist government, the Church was an organ of the State. . . . The decree freed the

Church from supervision from without. She benefited immensely by ceasing to be autocratic power's tool in fettering the religious consciences of people of other beliefs. . . . By the decree of January, 1918, every religious society, including our own Orthodox Church, was guaranteed the right and the possibility of existing and administering its own affairs in accord with the demands of its own belief.'

In 1918, however, immediately after the Tsarist regime had collapsed and on the eve of the outbreak of the Civil War the clergy were not yet able to judge the situation in such a detached way. Trained according to entirely different principles, fervently loyal to the reigning dynasty and bound in hundreds of ways to land-owners and merchants they could not help be horrified to see a crowd of revolutionaries, avowed deniers of everything and every idea they held sacred, come into power. Their hostility towards the usurpers was shared by a great number of their fellow-citizens who, like themselves, were unable to evaluate the historic im-portance of what they saw going on before their bewildered eyes.

The ruling authorities of the Russian Orthodox Church were equally thrown off balance. In November 1917 and March 1918 representatives of the council (which still had its headquarters at Moscow) made completely ineffectual overtures to the govern-ment, which was determined to work alone, proposing to chart a programme of Church-State relations acceptable to both parties. Even Patriarch Tikhon, very shortly after his installation, thought it appropriate to excommunicate the 'avowed or secret enemies of Christ' by a decree issued from his residence in Moscow on 19 January 1918:

'By the authority invested in me by God, We forbid you to approach the Mysteries of Christ [the liturgy and sacra-ments]; We declare you anathema, if you bear the name of Christians and were born members of the Orthodox Church. . . . I call upon you others, you loyal sons of the

Church, to defend our Holy Mother, who has been outraged and oppressed. . . . And if it should be necessary to suffer for Christ's cause, We exhort you to follow Us along the path of suffering. . . . And you, my brother bishops and priests, . . . organize religious associations immediately, and call on them to fight amongst those spiritual enemies who would use physical strength to overcome the power of the Spirit. We are firmly convinced and believe that the enemies of Christ's Church will be crushed and scattered by the power of His cross.'

Though they were not mentioned by name, it was easy enough for the Communists to recognize the references to themselves in this document which was medieval in inspiration, and which left them entirely indifferent and, rather, gave them material for arguments for their counter-attack. The same thing can be said of the exhortation to mercy sent directly to Lenin in October 1918 by Patriarch Tikhon. The Civil War had already broken out and it was no longer within Lenin's or anybody else's power to 'stop this bloodshed' as he was asked.

Naturally, this attitude of the clergy and their many sympathizers was bound to irritate to the extreme all the people on the other side of the fence. When violence finally broke out, the 'popes', along with the nobility and police, became the target of the popular frenzy.[1]

Actually, Church leaders never went as far as supporting outright the counter-revolutionary movement in Russia at the time. In another appeal to his flock in September 1919, the Patriarch asked them to 'abstain from any activity which might provoke the suspicion of Soviet authorities and fulfil all civil obligations, to the extent that they are not contrary to faith and religious observance'. Several bishops gave similar instructions to their own

[1] Two excellent books will give the interested reader more details about this period: Paul B. Anderson, *People, Church and State in Modern Russia*, New York: 1944; Jean Meyendorff, *l'Eglise orthodoxe hier et aujourd'hui*, Paris: 1960.

flocks. Thus, for example, Metropolitan Benjamin of Petrograd, who had been given certain information that the relics of St Alexander Nevski were going to be profaned, sent a delegation to Zinoviev, the President of the Petrograd Soviet, asking him to withhold the action and solemnly promising in return that any cleric who aided the 'Whites' would be immediately suspended.

Unfortunately, prudential measures like these were not enough to prevent the outbreak of an open war against the Church. Conflict became inevitable and was given the pretext it needed when the Church took steps to help the victims of the awful famine in 1921–2. The Government by no means intended to allow the Church the satisfaction of fulfilling a responsibility which it considered came within its own competence; on 27 February 1922 a new decree appeared which ordered the confiscation of the treasures (precious metals or stones) still retained by Churches but which had already become the property of the State by virtue of a decree of January 1918.

As a reply, the Patriarch issued a circular letter which permitted the clergy to surrender to civil authorities any of these treasures which were not consecrated (candelabra, ikons, *ex votos*, various ornaments) but forbidding them to hand over any properly liturgical objects (chalices, patens, vestments, etc.). As a substitute, he called on the faithful to organize collections and give the Government the cash value of the sacred vessels.

Without meaning to, Patriarch Tikhon had just given the signal for the beginning of open war against the Church. The Government fell on his letter as a way of propagandizing what they presented as the avarice of a hierarchy too grasping to make available the means necessary for relieving millions of people's suffering.

There were violent clashes between the laity and clergy in several cities. Crowds burned churches and sacked monasteries. Two years before, at the insistence of the 'working masses', fifty-eight tombs of holy people had already been broken into in several provinces and their relics profaned. Clerics were now brought to public trial; forty-four people, priests and laymen, were tried at Moscow and eleven of them were condemned to death.

In Petrograd, Metropolitan Benjamin himself was condemned to death and shot with some of his followers—despite his repeated protestations of loyalty and his sincere good will in wanting to reach a satisfactory arrangement concerning the Church treasures. In Ukrainia, which was the cradle of Christianity in Russia, reprisals included the closing and sacking of the famous Petchersky Monastery, and were especially violent. No one will ever know exactly how many Orthodox priests were killed; some émigré publications have given statistics (more than 2,000 priests and about fifty bishops, killed or deported) but there is no way of checking their figures and they should not be taken on face value.[1]

The day was to come, however, when tribute would be paid to some of these clerics who sacrificed their lives to show their devotion to their faith. In Paris I once met Metropolitan Benjamin's defence counsel, Mr Gurevitch, a rationalist of Jewish origin; giving me his impressions of the Metropolitan and his trial, he said: 'I felt that I had a genuine saint sitting behind me on the accused's bench.' And we can be certain that Metropolitan Benjamin was not the only victim of whom this could be said.

It was inevitable that the Government's enmity towards the stubborn Orthodox clergy should eventually extend to affect other religious groups, the Armenians, the Moslems, etc. Roman Catholics, especially, found themselves in a particularly delicate situation following Vatican intervention. After 1919 Pope Benedict XV had sent Lenin a message protesting against the persecution of the Orthodox clergy; its only result was that Archbishop von der Ropp, Metropolitan of Mohilev, was arrested and banished. In 1922 Pope Pius XI, in turn, sent the diplomatic

---

[1] According to Anderson, op. cit., there were, in addition to the more important trials (231 cases tried by 55 tribunals with 44 death penalties out of a total of 738 accused), countless other less important trials which centred on the interpretation of the law or appeals referring to Church property.

conference at Genoa a memorandum asking them to insist that the confiscation of liturgical vessels and vestments stop.

Even authors of recent books which are clearly hostile to the existing Soviet Government have recognized that the attitude of the Holy Father was bound to encourage the Roman Catholic clergy in the Soviet Union to condemn Communism in their sermons.[1] No one had to wait long for the consequences of the Vatican's move. Moscow's newspapers opened up a full-scale onslaught against the Pope and accused him of trying to organize a world-wide campaign against Soviet Russia. Archbishop Cieplak, who had succeeded Archbishop von der Ropp and was now Vicar-General of Mohilev, was accused with fourteen other priests of opposing Government decrees. He was condemned to death but the penalty was reduced to ten years' imprisonment; after a time he was pardoned and banished. The priests tried with him were either condemned to imprisonment or exile; one of them was executed.

More and more churches were closed. Vacant episcopal sees were not filled. Bishop Michel d'Herbigny, s.j., entered the Soviet secretly to consecrate new bishops, but they were discovered and exiled.

The point to remember in recalling these tragic times is that the Soviet Government always held on to its basic principles. They always claimed that their judicial and administrative actions were based on strictly political motivation. The clergy were accused and tried for disobedience to civil authority or counter-revolutionary activity and, unfortunately, that was precisely the case in most instances, no matter how pure individual motives may have been. No one was ever persecuted because of his religious beliefs; because of circumstances, freedom of religion was to be more and more restricted and gradually less apparent.

Even when the reprisals began, it was an easy matter to realize that they would only achieve part of their aim. At the same time

[1] Nadezhada Teodorovich 'The Roman Catholics' in the collection *Religion in the U.S.S.R.*, Munich, 1960, p. 84.

The Patriarch Alexei (centre, in a mitre surmounted by a cross) surrounded by leaders
of the oriental Churches

An open-air service at the Monastery of the Trinity and St Sergei

At the Monastery of the Trinity and St Sergei. Constantin de Grunwald, with a group of visitors, leaving the beautiful chapel of St Sergei

Young Christians meet at the monastery during the sixth World Festival of Youth

as they broke down the opposition of the clergy once and for all, they excited the religious fervour of the people by creating new martyrs for them.

But perhaps an even greater danger to the Church lay in internal movement which was already gaining momentum and was counting on the support of the civil authorities. An authentic schism, the 'Living Church', was about to come into full existence.

'The Living Church [also known as the Church of the Renovation, the Synodal Church, the Church of Ecclesiastical Revival] must be considered in the light of the revolutionary times in which it was born,' declared a qualified expert on the subject.[1] Among the people who were behind it and, certainly, among its leaders and faithful, there were many men who sincerely desired the welfare of all of Christianity in Russia. They wanted to correct the mistakes made by the old regime, make the Church 'democratic' and popular and help it throw off the monastic caste's domination.

Orthodox canon law reserves the episcopacy for the black clergy; ordinary priests, who must be married men (though they may not remarry if widowed), cannot be consecrated bishops. The innovators in the Living Church wanted to destroy the monks' privileged position, give priests the possibility of governing dioceses and allow them to remarry. They proposed a liturgical reform which would simplify the complicated traditional services and replace Church Slavonic with modern Russian. Above all, they considered it indispensable to accept the existing state of affairs and adapt themselves to an authority which, to their mind, 'was the only one in the world which had used governmental processes to establish the ideal of the kingdom of God'.

A Council (*Sobor*) convened by this group on 6 August 1922 declared in no uncertain terms that 'every earnest Christian should take his place in the ranks of those fighting for humanitarian truth

---

[1] Archbishop Andrei of Saratov to an American journalist, quoted by Anderson, op. cit.

and use every means at his disposal to concretize the great ideals of the October Revolution'.

The few priests at the head of the movement, Archpriest Vvedensky and his cohort, were men consumed with ambition and completely without scruples. They did not hesitate at using the most shameful methods to get what they wanted. On 9 May 1922, when Patriarch Tikhon had been arrested after using his authority to try to protect the guilty parties in the 'Trial of the 44', Archpriest Vvedensky and his group immediately took advantage of this unexpected development and installed themselves in the offices of the Patriarchate, where they announced that they were the 'Provisional Government of the Russian Church'.

Confident of Government support, they very soon had brought a number of provincial churches under their jurisdiction. Many bishops of the legitimate Church joined them, as also did the Metropolitans of the autonomous Churches of White Russia and Ukrainia.

By 1925, the Living Church had 12,593 parishes, 16,540 priests and deacons and 192 bishops (as opposed to the 105 bishops there were in Tsarist Russia). It had even succeeded in getting official recognition from the ancient Patriarchal sees of Antioch, Constantinople and Jerusalem.

Though it had come to the fore and achieved power with such a burst of energy, the whole Living Church undertaking was destined to be cut off by a single blow. The one thing it needed to succeed, precisely the thing it had not got, was the support of the people. Faithful Orthodox refused to have anything to do with these clergymen who seemed to them more like renegades than anything else (a situation rather similar to what happened in France during the Revolution with the *prêtres assermentés*); they no longer felt at home or comfortable in the group's churches, where the priest no longer officiated at the altar but in the midst of the congregation, and read from liturgical texts of which not only had certain passages, considered useless, been suppressed, but everything else had been translated into the vernacular instead of retaining the old phraseology, difficult to understand but hallowed by tradition. The innovators had underestimated the almost superstitious attachment of the Russian people to each and every word used in their services. Quarrels soon broke out among the leaders of the Living Church. Extremists of varying convictions broke away and new, but entirely unimportant, splinter groups were formed.

While all this was going on, a new and effective movement sprang up among the clergy who had remained loyal to the Patriarch. Many clerics were living in exile or had been deported, but they maintained contact with their families and friends, and kept up an exchange of ideas with other priests. Now that they were no longer allowed to perform their church duties, they found time for reflection. Though they reaffirmed the primacy of spiritual values, which Communism, of course, denied, they nevertheless arrived at the conclusion that 'the Church should not interfere in any way in the activities of the civil government, which has assumed the responsibility of ensuring the material welfare of the people'. This is the gist of a document attributed to some bishops who had been deported to the Solovetzk Monastery on an island in the White Sea.

Thus it was that the basis for a reconciliation of Church and State, a move which had the support of the entire country, was laid.

During this time, the Russian Orthodox Church was without a leader. After he had been kept in detention for a year, Patriarch Tikhon was released by the civil authorities after they had got his signature on an official document in which he admitted his mistakes: the condemnation of the peace treaty of Brest-Litovsk, the anathema laid on the Government and his circular letter written on the subject of the Church's treasures. He died two years later, after having solemnly condemned the activities of the Living Church (several of whose members immediately submitted to his authority and did penance) and after he had brought it to the attention of 'monarchists at home and abroad' that he was not to be considered hostile to the Soviet Government.

After his death, the patriarchal see remained vacant. Each of the three men whom he had designated as *locum tenentes* of the Patriarchal Throne, in the eventuality that elections should be impossible, was successively prevented from assuming the duties of the office. Indeed, the first two he had named were in prison and the third, Metropolitan Piotr of Krutitsa, was officially installed but was to be exiled to Siberia at the end of the following year.

Finally, according to the provision laid down by Patriarch Tikhon in his will, the patriarchal succession devolved upon Metropolitan Sergei of Nizhni-Novgorod, who was given the strange title of 'Substitute to the *locum tenens* of the Patriarchal Throne', which he would continue to use until 1944.

The attitude of all these prelates towards the Soviet Government remained the same, however. 'We desire to be Orthodox,' Metropolitan Sergei declared on 30 March 1927, 'but, at the same time, we want to acknowledge the Soviet Union as our civically constituted country, whose trials, no less than her joys and achievements, are ours.'

No one outside Russia has ever really understood this attitude, and many people have persistently awaited the imminent downfall of Soviet authority. In the country itself, people were in a better position to make a judgment, however. They were all conscious of their personal responsibility for the tragic events of the Revolution. The errors made by the upper classes had eventually led to an upheaval in the working and peasant classes, and later the extremes to which the masses had gone led more conservative elements to take up arms and join in a civil war.

Now that the counter-revolutionary elements had been crushed, was it up to the Church to bear the burden of stubborn opposition singlehanded? If the only way that religion could be safeguarded was by adapting to existing circumstances and equitable compromise, which was what the hierarchy envisaged, should she not take that way?

There are in every Russian, no matter how strong his mystical impulses, vast resources of native realism, and while Orthodox emigré groups set up their own autonomous Churches which were not supposed to be subject to 'the forces of darkness', the Moscovite Orthodox went on venerating the dead Patriarch Tikhon as the man who had said, shortly after his release: 'We declare that there is no earthly power strong enough to inhibit Our conscience as head of the Church or restrict the Liberty of Our patriarchal utterance.' Pilgrimages are still made to the tomb of this holy man, in anticipation of his future canonization.

But the Soviet authorities were no less realistic. They realized, not without some surprise, that religious feeling was still very active among the people, even after the disappearance of the so-called exploiting classes—the Tsar, wealthy landowners, capitalists and even the comfortable large-scale farmers (*khulaks*). It was obvious that the analysis of the religious phenomenon formulated by the German founders of Marxism did not entirely apply to conditions in Russia. Would it not be possible to retain the fundamental programme of the Party intact, but employ other methods than closing churches and prosecuting priests?

But not even the anti-religion propaganda campaign, undertaken with too little preparation, was as successful as it had been hoped it would be. In the beginning, the activity of the League of the Godless, which was headed by the old revolutionary Yaroslavski, a determined atheist, had succeeded in arousing great curiosity. The league had several million members; tens of thousands of students were given an atheistic education in its schools; there were hundreds of study groups; and even twenty-six anti-religious universities were especially established for workers.

And still all the churches which had not yet been closed were crowded!

The Soviet Government had its strength in the unified support of the people; it could not forget that fact. Besides, there was a gradual softening of its policy.

In May 1924 the thirteenth Congress of the Communist Party declared itself firmly in favour of 'the abolition of all administrative efforts against religion, such as the closing of churches'. At the insistence of Stalin himself, the new constitution restored the civil rights of the clergy.

After 1927 Metropolitan Sergei had permission to set up a 'Patriarchal Holy Synod' to handle the affairs of the Orthodox Church.

Thus it was that the way towards a genuine reconciliation was opened up a long time before 1941, when German aggression would provide the occasion for its final realization.

On the very day of the invasion (22 June 1941) Metropolitan Sergei sent to all the parishes of Russia a message of lofty patriotism which resounded throughout the entire world:

'Fascist gangs have attacked our homeland, violating treaties and promises; they have burst in upon us without warning and the blood of peaceful citizens is already staining our native land. The times of the Tartars, of the Teutonic Knights, of Charles of Sweden and of Napoleon have returned. The wretched successor of these enemies of Orthodox Christianity once more would have us bend our knee before falsehood. . . . Let us recall the holy leaders of the Russian people, such as Alexander Nevski and Dmitri Donskoy, who vowed their lives to their people and their country. . . .

Our Orthodox Church has always shared the lot of the people. She has suffered with them, and rejoiced in their victories. Today, she will no more abandon them than she has ever done. She calls down Heaven's blessing on the sacrifices now being offered by the entire country. . . .

The Church of Christ gives her blessing to all those

Orthodox who are defending the sacred frontiers of their homeland. God grant you victory!'

And, in a prayer recommended to be used in all Orthodox Churches, the following passage was especially striking:

'Grant victory to our combatants in Your Name; and should they appear before You for judgment, having lost their lives in battle, forgive them their sins and put aside the wrath of Your justice. Grant them the crown which tarnishes not.'

In a sermon which he delivered on 22 August of that year, Metropolitan Sergei explained the meaning of this blessing in these moving terms:

'The Church calls on us to pray for all the men who are killed in general, whether they are bound to us or not, whether they were our friends or relatives or not, even though they may be complete strangers to us—we pray for them not because they were relatives or friends, but because they sacrificed their lives in fighting for our country, for each one of us, therefore. . . .

Someone may say: "But people today are indifferent to religious belief; they have even repudiated it. How can prayers said for someone who does not want them have any sense?"

First of all, everyone has not repudiated religious belief. Secondly, regardless of what the words in the prayer are and regardless of what an individual's attitude towards prayer may be, we must all fulfil the obligation laid upon us by gratitude and love. Especially must we remember the difference between a man's attitude in normal circumstances and his attitude at the point of death.

At that supreme moment, when the soul is leaving the

body, men are often capable of an extraordinary effort and their final moments can often have infinitely more bearing on their final destiny than all the rest of their life on earth.'

Once more, then, the Orthodox Church had reiterated, in the most solemn manner, her indestructible attachment to the fate of the people. The words 'Stay with us, O Lord. Hear us and we shall be victorious' were echoed again in one of the later messages of the Metropolitan.

The Orthodox Church gave her moral support to the Soviet armies. Men on their way into battle were reassured that if they died they would be sacrificing their lives for a holy cause.

But support went farther than that. Clergy and laity all made great sacrifices to provide their defenders with material aid. Collections were organized in all parishes and contributions to the national defence fund would soon add up to millions—almost all donated by ordinary simple people. Steps were taken to take care of everything from aid for the wounded and orphans, and warm clothing for the armies, to the construction of aeroplanes and, even, the organization of an entire column of tanks, dedicated to Dmitri Donskoy, Russia's liberator from the Tartars.

The Soviet Government could hardly fail to appreciate all this patriotic activity for what it was really worth; it was not done merely to encourage the nation's soldiers and draw the people at home into a solid body of defence and support, but also to bolster up Soviet prestige abroad.

The turning point came on 4 September 1943, at a meeting at the Kremlin between Stalin and Metropolitan Sergei, who was accompanied by the two men most intimately involved in his work, Metropolitans Alexei and Nikolai. We do not know the details of what went on during the meeting, but we do know that the head of the Soviet Government gave his approval for an immediate convocation of a council of bishops to elect a patriarch and select the members of a Holy Synod.

Four days later, on 8 September 1943, ten archbishops and

bishops met in Moscow and unanimously chose Metropolitan Sergei as head of the Russian Orthodox Church.

It was impossible, from every point of view, to make a better choice. A member of a provincial clerical family which, since the thirteenth century, had already given bishops to the Orthodox Church, Patriarch Sergei had long enjoyed the reputation of being a leading theologian. He had been Rector of the Theological Academy of St Petersburg and attracted attention by his active participation in the debates of that Religious and Philosophical Society which, from the beginning of this century, had united so many eminent scholars, both lay and clerical. Archbishop of Finland, of Vladimir and then of Nizhni-Novgorod, he later gave evidence of his wisdom and unparalleled courage while holding the office of *locum tenens* of the Patriarchate for the seventeen years before his election.[1]

The task he had just been given was overwhelming. Since the Revolution, the ranks of the clergy had been, almost literally, decimated: of the 46,457 churches there were, in 1917, only 4,225 left; the 1,026 monasteries had dwindled to thirty-eight; the rolls of the clergy had fallen from 50,000 in Tsarist Russia to 5,600. Though the Living Church had, as it were, died out, various autonomous and collaborationist religious movements had started in occupied territory (eastern Ukrainia, the Balkan states, Rostov).

It was up to him, and the Holy Synod which was constituted at the same time as his election, to restore order to a Church which was disorganized from top to bottom. He had to appoint bishops to vacant diocesan sees, supervise the training of a new generation of priests and resume interrupted contacts with other Churches.

Finally, he had to nourish an atmosphere of mutual confidence and establish permanent relations with the Council for Orthodox Church Affairs, a branch of the Council of Ministers which had been recently formed along with another council in charge of the affairs of other religious groups in Russia.

Patriarch Sergei died on 15 May 1944, shortly after his

[1] Cf. *Patriarch Sergei and his Spiritual Heritage* (in Russian), Moscow: 1947.

election, and therefore left some work unfinished. Nevertheless, the first impetus had been given; relations between the Church and the Government had taken on a completely new character. After the Patriarch's death, the Council of People's Commissars hastened to express their condolences, which they had published in the official Press. During the meeting of the council which was convened on 21 November 1944 to elect a new patriarch, G. V. Karpov, President of the Council for Orthodox Church Affairs, told fifty archbishops and bishops that:

'The present phenomena manifested in the relations between the State and the Church are not at all surprising nor temporary, as our detractors sometimes say they are. They are a natural outgrowth of tendencies which were evident before the war and became very clear during the war. The steps taken by the Soviet Government are in complete accord with the constitution and have the character of an approval of the Church's position with regard to the State.'

After Metropolitan Alexei had been raised to the patriarchal dignity, Mr Karpov made the following statement at the Patriarch's enthronement on 4 February 1945: 'Our government and our people are in deepest sympathy with activities of the Russian Orthodox Church.'

Two months later, on 10 April 1945, Patriarch Alexei and two of his staff were received at the Kremlin by Stalin and Molotov. It was decided to enlarge the school system for the clergy and the first Theological Institute was opened at Moscow in June of that year.

Shortly afterwards, Patriarch Alexei went on a pilgrimage to Jerusalem; he visited Damascus, Beirut, Cairo and Alexandria and established fraternal contacts with the heads of the other Eastern Churches. Metropolitan Nikolai, who accompanied him, went on to England, where he was cordially received by King George VI and the Archbishops of Canterbury and York. On their return to Moscow, the Patriarch and the Metropolitan immediately set to work at giving religious life in Russia a new impetus.

During the next ten years real wonders were to take place. Russia's patron saints watched over her destiny; armed with patience, an essentially Christian virtue, the Orthodox faithful found within themselves the strength necessary to come out of the struggle with unshaken faith. To the confusion of unbelievers, the Church quickly rose again out of her ashes: neglected churches were reopened and renovated in cities and rural areas; old priests resumed their ministry, and candidates for the priesthood flocked to be admitted to the re-established seminaries. The dynamism was soon to spread to other confessions, whether they were Catholics, Protestant, Moslems, Jews or members of other, smaller, sects.

Without insisting further on the truly extraordinary events of this period, I should like to be allowed one personal reminiscence.

During my first visit to the Soviet Union, in 1958, the fortieth anniversary of the Patriarchate's re-establishment was celebrated by a solemn liturgy attended by representatives of all the Eastern Churches. Moscow's newspapers had made no mention of the ceremony and, according to their usual practice, were withholding their report until the following day. Nevertheless, the bells of the patriarchal Cathedral of the Epiphany were enough to arouse the excited curiosity of people living in all the neighbouring quarters. Though I had been invited to the service, it was only with the greatest difficulty, and the help of policemen on foot and on horses, that I was able to push my way through the great crowds filling the neighbouring streets and squares.

Finally, once we had got to the cathedral, my wife and I lived through one of the most unforgettable hours of our existence. All the liturgical splendour of Holy Russia came alive again for us in the lighted candles, the incense, the magnificent singing and the huge crowd, breathless in their fervour. Surrounded by the Patriarchs of Antioch and of Alexandria, and many other prelates of various other Eastern Churches, all wearing superb vestments,

Patriarch Alexei officiated at the liturgy. His melodious voice, gentle but at the same time firm, filled even the farthest corners of the cathedral. At the close of the service, I was among those who went up to the Patriarch to receive his benediction.

As we left the cathedral, our eyes were so clouded with tears we could barely see. Outside, there was a crowd larger than the congregation in the cathedral, and all of them were as moved and fervent as the people who had been able to get in to the service.

Had Soviet Russia become a Christian country again?

4

Nero or Renan?

WHEN I returned to Moscow in 1960 I had ample time to
see that, once more, there was a change in the relations
between the Church and the State; all I had to do
was read through one of the official newspapers to gauge the
change.

Today the Soviet Union is a country in the throes of rapid
transformation. My personal judgment is that the time of
revolutionary upheavals is over and done with; under the present
Government—in the unanimous opinion of everyone I talked
with during my zigzagging tour across the whole country—the
rule of the law grows stronger every day.

The country's constructive efforts have been carried out on a
mammoth scale. Wounds left by the war have finally healed over
and are now only scars; the large cities, most of them badly burned
and devastated, are regaining their normal appearance, but have
been enlarged and improved; new cities are springing up all over
with as many as 200,000 to 500,000 inhabitants; industrialization
and the collectivization of agriculture are making astonishing
strides forward; the general level of culture is rising rapidly and
secondary education is becoming obligatory and free for everyone.

The twentieth Congress of the Communist Party, which met
in 1956, was content to acknowledge the huge scope of the results
already attained, elaborate new economic development projects
and condemn tendencies towards exaggerated ideological
dogmatism.

After its twenty-first congress in January 1959, however, the Party developed new dynamism. In the speeches and resolutions which accompanied its approval of an ambitious seven-year plan, a new feature was evident: the time had come—it was emphasized —to give serious consideration to the shift from socialism, by this time sufficiently consolidated in the Soviet Union, to integral Communism, under which the labours of the individual would be rewarded not only according to his merits but also according to his needs. There was no question, of course, of accomplishing this undertaking without first stepping up the rates of production and consumption tremendously; this acceleration had, in fact, to be raised to a rate which the world had never previously experienced.

A new type of man was needed for this gigantic effort; a man who had thrown off not only the grasp of capitalism, which ceased to exist, but also any vestiges of outmoded ideologies. Thus, once again, the problem of struggling against religious ideas came up in its fullest scope.

As a result, the Party decisively reverted to its initial programme: the astonishing success enjoyed by the Church during the previous fifteen years could not be left unanswered. Obviously, no one could seriously consider resuming the impotent methods used at the time when the Party was still, in the words of Lenin, 'beset by the childhood diseases of Communism'. If anyone had dared risk setting fire to a church or assaulting a priest, the police would be on the spot to stop him.

There could be no repetition of the errors made during the old anti-religious campaign. Soviet Russia had outgrown the days when lecturers would travel through rural areas explaining to the *muzhik* that 'man has descended from the ape', only to be asked, 'And who created the ape?' It was indispensable that other, more efficient arguments be developed and used among the educated and 'evolved' masses.

Besides, the main lines of an anti-religion campaign had already been laid out in a decision of the Central Committee of the Party on 10 November 1954. In formal but explicit terms, the decree stated that:

'Instead of having recourse to a systematic and persistent operation by which knowledge of the natural sciences would be propagated, and instead of an ideological battle against religion, the press and lecturers allow themselves to indulge in insulting attacks against the clergy and convinced church-goers, who are sometimes described as though they were people who had no right to political confidence.

In several areas, local organizations and some individuals have permitted themselves to interfere in the administrative activities of religious associations and have affected a dis-courteous attitude towards the clergy.'

The text proceeds to a harsh condemnation of these illegitimate practices and adds:

'No one should lose sight of the fact that there are some citizens who, though they are active participants in the life of the country and earnestly fulfil all the civil obligations laid upon them by the country, are still influenced by different religious confessions. The Party's attitude towards these adherents to religion has always been, and will continue to be, one of attention and understanding.

It would be nonsensical and inadmissible to call into question the loyalty of Soviet citizens because of their religious convictions. Penetrating and patient propaganda will help them to throw off religious errors of their own accord, while insulting attacks will merely serve to confirm them in their error.'

Naturally, nothing in this categorical condemnation of past abuses was changed by the situation set up by the twenty-first Party Congress. In conformity to instructions given the secretaries of all regional organizations by the Central Committee, the battle against religion after 1958 was fought with renewed strength on the ideological level, and its new and more subtle form was to make it an even greater menace to the future of religious faith.

.   .   .   .   .

Who are the men entrusted with the Soviet Union's anti-religious campaign? How do they think? What motivates them? Which are their favourite methods?

These were the questions running through my mind as I arrived at Moscow. After making a courtesy call at the patriarchal residence, I was eager to establish personal contact with the leaders of the atheistic movement.

There is in the Soviet capital a special committee attached to the Council of Ministers which handles cultural relations with foreigners; anyone who comes to Russia from abroad to study cultural life in the Soviet and goes to the offices of the committee for advice and help, is always assured of a friendly welcome. I had long been acquainted with the President of the Committee, G. A. Zhukov, who was now minister but had formerly been *Izvestia's* correspondent in Paris; I was not mistaken when I hoped that he would prove the best of guides. He put me in the hands of Mr Grigolenko, one of his aides and himself an expert in religious problems.

Mr Grigolenko did more than give me a few helpful addresses; he gave me a detailed summary of his own point of view which, I suppose, is very close to the attitude of the Government and the Party:

'I am sure you are aware of Lenin's basic position towards the religious problem, but I should nevertheless like to draw your attention to a passage in his *Materialism and Empirio-criticism*, which highlights our teacher's train of thought and his ultimate goal.

'"As we follow the line laid out by Marxist theory," Lenin wrote:

The inspector of the Leningrad Theological Academy with two students and the author

Students at the Seminary of the Trinity and St Sergei celebrating the birthday of their Rector

The Great Cathedral of the Dormition in the Monastery of the Trinity and
St Sergei

' "We get closer and closer to objective truth, though we shall never be capable of grasping it entirely. If we follow any other line, we end up in the confusion of falsehood (error). . . . If there is no objective truth, then truth (and I include scientific truth) is only an organized form of human experience and, in admitting its existence, we recognize the fundamental premises of the priests, we open the door to religion and make way for the 'organized forms' of religious experience."

'In another place (*Socialism and Religion*), Lenin wrote:

' "Religion teaches the man who labours and leads a life of suffering and hardship that he must have patience and humility during his earthly life; it consoles him with the notion of a heavenly reward. The man who lives by the work of others is urged to philanthropy, which is a cheap justification for his exploitation and gives him a ticket to celestial beatitude at a reduced rate."

'This is why Lenin's disciples have come to look upon religious groups as instruments of bourgeois reaction, helping to defend exploitation and keeping the working classes in a lethargic state. The Churches had their strength in the unconditional support of the governments, whose tractable instruments they were.

'This is why, long before it seized power, the Party included the complete separation of Church and State in its programme. Religion had to remain a personal matter.

'Paradoxically, what we were doing was actually following a lead given by the bourgeoisie themselves at an important moment in history, 1789, when they enlisted the help of the common people in their struggle to throw over the feudal aristocracy. The bourgeoisie, however, did not keep their promises.

'What sense is there in talking about separation of Church and State in the United States where the sessions of Congress are opened with a prayer, where the late Mr Dulles read the lessons during a church service and where some states forbid public office to atheists?

'Throughout the entire capitalist world, bourgeois governments persist in using the Church to fight political movements: Communism and even socialism.

'Things are different here. The principle of separation between Church and State is enforced in its entirety. After getting rid of capitalism and the bourgeoisie, we did not wish—nor was it feasible—to get rid of the Church. She continues today as a relic of the past. Religion has become an entirely personal matter. Every religious confession is allowed; the police do not prosecute anyone for adhering to any of them; the police arrest only criminals and protect believers. Because, you see, though we are officially opposed to religious prejudice, we are equally opposed to any violation of the religious convictions of our citizens and to any sort of religious discrimination; anyone who dared dismiss an employee because of his religious belief would be severely punished.

'There is nothing about religious affiliation in the questionnaires given to Party members. As a matter of fact, Stalin himself was furious on one occasion when he learned that one of his generals had broken with his son because the young man had become a monk.

'Our attitude is tolerant—but it is not therefore passive. We sometimes find ourselves obliged to attack the Vatican, which has now become the centre of warlike activity against Communism. It is impossible for us to give responsible positions to men whose philosophical convictions are diametrically opposed to ours and could not, therefore, sincerely co-operate with us in pushing our programme forward. We have an immense task facing us. Those of our colleagues who thought that old ways could disappear in a few years were sadly mistaken; it takes a very long, sustained effort to re-educate the masses.

'The strength of religious prejudice comes from a lack of genuine education. We have depended upon scientific propaganda to fight wrong ideas. In doing this, we had to keep in mind some objective conditions which were in the Church's favour: we, too, like other countries, have our share of unhappy, afflicted and suffering people who turned to religious belief as the best source of consolation. But we were always sure that, in the final accounting, our ideas would win through.

'Despite what people say, the religious spirit is not innate in men. It did not exist at the beginning of history; religious prejudice only developed after a long evolution of social structure. At one time, I agree, 99 per cent of mankind believed in God. But civilization's evolution has brought it past that stage.

'Religious prejudice is already seriously weakened and will completely disappear when Communism triumphs. We are not fanatics nor adepts of a new religion. Do not put too much stock in what some dreamers in Leningrad may have told you along these lines. We no longer have to resolve religious problems. Scientific ideas about economic and social evolution give us hope that a new society will develop in which the notion of *homo homini lupus* will be a thing of the past. With everyone enjoying material satisfaction, the only way some people will be able to consider others will be with feelings of fraternal affection and, thus, without having recourse to religion but proceeding in our own way, we shall concretize the traditional ideal of Christianity.'

A few days later I was to hear the changes rung on the same theme at the huge offices of Alexei Kuznetsov, Vice-Minister of Culture, who very cordially received me in the absence of his chief, Mme Nina Furtseva. The mention of religion was enough to loosen every tongue.

To get on to the subject, I jokingly asked Mr Kuznetsov if he intended to have me shot because I still believed in God. He burst out laughing and answered: 'You can put your mind at ease about that; your life is not in jeopardy! . . . The difference between us is purely philosophical. We still have a great many people who have held on to idealistic notions—but that is their own business.

'We who have responsible positions, however, are convinced

that the Church's influence will get gradually weaker as the cultural level of the country rises. People will not have to go to priests for consolation any more; Western influences will be less strong than they were in the past.

'Besides, I am personally convinced that we need not exclude the possibility of a synthesis between the two systems of thought which are so at loggerheads today.

'We try to be tactful in our propagandizing. We are well aware of the fact that more people got comfort during the last war from their parish priest than from their local trade union. We are not going to offend their sensibilities; we are determined not to tolerate the excesses sometimes indulged in by our Communist young people's groups. But we do intend to strengthen our propaganda to enlighten the masses and we are ready to burn all our bridges behind us to achieve that end.

'My office directs and supervises the work of our publishing houses, theatres and film industry. We use them to spread the ideas we think appropriate. In the first place, we want to counteract propaganda put out by various religious sects whose tendencies run counter to the properly understood commonwealth of any society at all. I am thinking especially of the Jehovah's Witnesses and groups like them.

'I should not say that everything we do is eminently successful. For example, we had quite an amusing time with a certain play.[1] The plot revolved around a priest and a scholar who was a member of the Academy and a notorious atheist. The role of the priest was played by a very accomplished actor, and he got all the applause! . . .

'But we are more interested in our publishing houses than in the theatre. In accordance with the wishes of the twenty-first Congress of the Party, we have given priority to publications aimed at destroying religious superstition. With that end in view,

[1] He was probably referring to Alyoshin's play, *The Torch*, which was produced at Tbilisi, the capital of Georgia. The author's purpose was to show that a highminded nonbeliever will not be afraid to die once he has fulfilled the responsibility towards the community set him by his destiny.

we are organizing very complex programmes; we give advice and counsel to our authors and submit their manuscripts to a critical scrutiny. On the whole, we are satisfied with the results.

'I should especially suggest that you pay a visit to Mr Kolonitski, who is a leading expert in the matter and edits a new magazine, *Science and Religion* [*Nauka i Religia*]. He could give you a little more information about the things I have just touched upon.'

I could hardly fail to take his advice. Peter Kolonitski is in his forties, a lively and enthusiastic man. While studying for a degree in philosophy in 1958, he published a pamphlet which gave a masterful exposition of the connections between Marxism and religion. He said that the entire social structure of the Soviet Union promotes a scientific conception of the world, a conception which is entirely free of religious belief. 'This,' he writes, 'explains the incontrovertible fact that millions of Soviet citizens, who previously believed in God, have now thrown over their religious convictions, and that the younger Soviet generations who have been raised according to scientific principles are, generally speaking, completely devoid of any religious errors.'

Like his vice-minister, Kolonitski further admits that religious prejudice still exists in a great part of Soviet society. He goes even further: he admits that there are many cases of an 'increase of religious prejudice'.

He claims that this increase cannot be explained merely by referring to the hardships endured by the people during World War II; 'The capitalist world never lets pass an opportunity,' he says, 'for directly influencing Soviet citizens, through various channels, by using the vestiges of capitalism (among which are included religious prejudices) as a basis for bourgeois propaganda.'

Finally, he concedes that the support believers have given the Soviet regime has created a favourable atmosphere for the work of the clergy and that the Church has taken advantage of this atmosphere. No one can deny that the clergy are making an active contribution to the propaganda for peace which is now going on. Nor can anyone deny that most people who still believe in God have become 'loyal and earnest workers of the socialist society'. These facts force the Marxist–Leninists to take into account the deep-rooted feelings of these men who, despite their particular interests, have so much in common with the whole country. It would be absurd to close their churches, curtail their services and shut their theological academies.

But there is a better way than reprisal to fight against religious ideas. The Communist Party 'considers any reconciliation with religion, or even a passive attitude towards it, impossible', and has its most effective weapon in science, exact science which, without recourse to the Bible, explains man's ultimate origins and describes a bright future for him, which was foreshadowed by the construction of the sputnik.

It was obvious to me that Mr Kolonitski is a man absolutely convinced of the ultimate victory of his doctrine. His ideas are spreading: the magazine already has a circulation of more than 100,000. Originally intended to reach propagandists especially, it is read by a wide public.

And the day is getting nearer when there will no longer be any room for religious prejudice:

'Our ideological enemies declare that we cannot form a concept of the inconceivable. But I answer that whatever is "inconceivable" does not exist. Marxist philosophy is perfectly ready to grant that there are many phenomena of the world which are not yet understood or even classified. But why should they remain like that?

'Science is making great strides forward, and if she encounters new problems at every stage, there is also a single, fundamental conclusion which will be valid from now on: God has no place in the world we are living in.

'This world of ours emerged from matter, and was not created from nothing; it has always existed and will continue in existence for ever. Its present form is the result of an evolutionary process which has taken millions of years. Religion's explanation of the world has to have recourse to intuition and inevitably winds up in fantasy and the "sighs of the oppressed" which, in the long run, is what it really is.

'I am willing to admit that, over and above certain superstitious prejudices, the Church is founded on some gnoseological concepts which will always be with us, in one form or another, but will never be enough for formulating a religion in the real sense of the word. On the contrary, the social phenomena which allowed the constitution of the various Churches are far from eternal; they are fated to disappear with socialism's triumph and, to an even more drastic degree, with the final victory of Communism.

'You may argue against me and say that although the Soviet Union has adopted socialism as its form of government from now on religious belief still exists in the country. Yes, of course, it still exists, and it is like a small mole on the body of our social system. And so long as religion continues, the clergy will continue. The clergy will disappear when belief has been stifled.

'For the time being, we have no means of ridding our society of the clergy, who do their utmost to stand in our way. But we have to respect the religious beliefs of our workers and the Constitution forces us to respect their rights, whether we like it or not. We know that prayer saps the energy of our workers by leading them to hope for something which is impossible. We also know that there is much common ground which Communism and Christianity share, with the difference however that we are reaching our goals and ideals on the earth we live on and not in some unknown beyond, and that our morality is based on the interests of the human community and not on some divine words or other.

'How long will it take us to reach the goal we have fixed for ourselves? That question is only of secondary importance. Science, of course, is still a long way from having solved all problems; perhaps it never will. But religion could disappear very soon, say within twenty or thirty years.

'Social conditions in the West are such that there are many people who believe in God there. We in the Soviet Union have already reached the stage where a cultured man no longer believes.'

It would be difficult to produce more categorical explanations and predictions. Still, there was some room for doubt. For whom did Mr Kolonitski and people like him, all of them secure in their beliefs, speak? Was I to consider them survivors and heirs of the great revolutionary tradition—or were they the spokesmen of a new generation; heralds of a world to come?

To get a clear picture of the situation, I could not have done better than contact a very young scholar whose address had been given me by mutual friends. He was a foreigner by birth but had been raised in Soviet Russia and was married to a Russian woman. For several years, he had been studying at the University of Moscow and was preparing for his degree. A Party member, like his parents and his wife, he was a fervent supporter of Party doctrine.

Without actually being actively involved in propaganda work (he was conserving his energies for more important activities in the future), he was well placed to give me the kind of information I wanted because of his many and strong contacts in university circles.

I therefore invited him and his wife to dine with me on the terrace of the famous Praha restaurant. For once the exasperatingly slow service which is traditional in Soviet restaurants did not get on my nerves; it was a clear, warm evening and the gilded domes of some of the churches of Moscow shone above us in a cloudless night. We had all the time we needed for our discussion as we waited to be served our 'cutlets à la Kiev', the *pièce de résistance* of Russian cuisine.

My dinner companion's explanations were clear and precisely put:

'There are no believers left in the university. But that does not mean that we are unaware of the religious problem. There are frequent heated discussions of the subject in "students' seminars", which are devoted to studying Marxist philosophy, but, even after long and complicated exchanges of opinion, everyone always arrives at the same atheistic conclusion. You claim that the number of educated young people who continue as Party members after they have reached their majority and finished their studies is relatively small. That is right, but what it really proves is that these young people know what their responsibilities are and that they realize they are not yet mature enough and still unable to give back to the Party everything they got from it while they were students.

'The officials you have spoken to were perfectly right. Religion is fated to disappear, and not only because scientific ideas are getting an increasingly broad hearing in our society, but because there is also a dynamism and energy accumulating in our social structure which is making men able to achieve magnificent results without having to run to beg the intercession of some occult power. In this way, we shall eventually reach the point where no one will any longer need "revealed truth".

'But if you conclude from all this that we are also going through a time when interest in metaphysical problems is disappearing, you would be mistaken. The truth is that this interest expands as problems in the material order are taken care of. Dialectical materialism is an excellent means towards understanding things as they really are and devising appropriate formulas to explain them. Why should we not admit that, at rock bottom, materialism's basic notions coincide somehow with the fundamental principles of all spiritual philosophies, and that the difference between the two systems is essentially terminological?

'We are already busy studying Hegel, that great philosopher who tried to reconcile the two streams of thought. And did not Lenin write in his philosophical journal that: "An intelligent idealism is closer to an intelligent materialism than an unthinking materialism is"?'

.   .   .   .   .   .

'I love Russian atheists,' Dostoievsky cried in his *Adolescent*. 'I love them because they do not believe in God but comfort Christ by their good works.'

How far could this insight, truly Christian in its forgiveness, be applied to the four qualified representatives of Soviet atheism who had been good enough to share their innermost thoughts with me? It is not up to me to say; but this much is certain, those 'Godless' individuals had nothing in common with some of the 'priest-eaters' the world has seen. They struck me as intelligent, dignified, courteous and, in a word, very likable people. All four of them talked to me with complete candour and did not withdraw when I made any objections. Nothing in the world could make me doubt their good faith and sincerity. Enemies of the Church as they admit they are, they remind me more of Renan than of Nero.

The next step was to make a detailed and critical survey for myself of the results of this anti-religious propaganda in which they put so much stock.

5

Is There a God?

As I write this chapter in my library in Paris, I can look up and see a great pile of books, magazines, journals, etc., all of them anti-religious propaganda materials, lying on the desk before me. Some of them were given me by Government offices; others I bought in bookshops or chose at random from bookstalls in the streets of Moscow. Some of them are thick, cloth-bound volumes, others are slender pamphlets, leaflets, etc. Leading authors wrote some of them, and hacks turned out some of the others. Some of them were meant to be read by educated people, the others were addressed to the masses. In a word, something for every taste.

In 1958 the *Bible for Believers and Unbelievers* was re-issued. Filed with blasphemous interpolations, it was first published by Emilian Yaroslavski in 1922 and was a 'best seller'. It ridicules everything: Moses marries a priest's daughter and gibes: 'Hand over the money'; the manna in the desert becomes 'your heavenly partridges'; the Kings of Israel fall into drunken stupors and commit heinous crimes.

This kind of foolishness has always entertained a certain type of reader, and some great authors did their best to cater to this taste (Voltaire, for instance, with his *Pucelle* and Tolstoy and his caricature of the liturgy in the *Resurrection*).

But the Church has never seriously suffered because of them, and modern Soviet writers know it. Their attacks on the Bible have been more serious-minded. A recent book[1] attempts to

[1] I. Kryvelev, *The Book of the Bible* (in Russian), Moscow: 1959.

uncover the origins of Scripture by using scientific methods and beginning with theological research done by Protestant theologians and Anglo-Saxon archaeologists. It lists the historical errors and inaccuracies which swarm through the entire Old Testament. Its rather facile conclusion is that the morality of the Bible developed by enslaving exploiters 'is useless to a worker who is sensible of the interests of his class and human dignity'. Perhaps his arguments would have been a little more convincing if the author had given a little more time to discussing the doctrine of Christian love, which he merely treats in passing.

Vatican activities are another favourite topic of Moscow propagandists. A very learned author has discussed them in a book published under a pseudonym.[1] He was kind enough to give me a copy—very cordially inscribed—and I read through it with uninterrupted attention.

His documentation is extraordinary; it includes all the annals of the papacy and all the recent literature on the subject, whether Italian, German, Polish or American, and he even cites the *Informations catholiques internationales*.

But one's attention is first of all drawn to the economic activity of the Roman Curia: simony during feudal times, colonial exploitation during the sixteenth century, close co-operation with the capitalist bourgeoisie during the nineteenth century and with the world of high finance in our time.

Only in his last chapter does the author make a point of noting that Catholicism is now in the throes of a crisis brought on by a desire for purity and revival.

We must grant that this book can be a very useful instrument of political propaganda at the moment, when the Vatican shows no hesitation in declaring itself the open enemy of the Soviet.

In the framework of anti-religious propaganda, however, it does not seem that an historical account like this could have much effect on someone who believes in God.

[1] Lavretski, *The Vatican; Religion, Finances and Politics* (in Russian), Moscow: 1957.

Everyone in the West has known about the crimes of the Borgias for centuries, and secular newspapers teem with stories about the financial dealings of Cardinal Spellman and his contacts with New York banks. But where is the Catholic whom that sort of thing is going to keep from going to Mass?

As far as the Russian Orthodox are concerned, anyone of them reading this book might be grateful to the author for giving him a look at what goes on behind the scenes, but he would also tell himself at the same time that it does not concern him directly, since he belongs to a Church which is not subject to the authority of the Holy See.

Any Soviet citizen who is still hesitating between atheism and religious belief would certainly get whatever documentation he might be looking for in *The French Freethinkers of the Eighteenth Century*, which was published in Moscow in 1960 and is a very large and complete book. Opening it, he would find what Montesquieu, Voltaire, Lamettrie, Diderot, Helvetius and other *dii minores* wrote against the abuses of the clergy and the wealth of monasteries, and against intolerance and fanaticism. It gives a detailed explanation of the materialist doctrines of Baron von Holbach.

The only thing that is missing is a statement to the effect that generations of Frenchmen, Germans and Englishmen have read these passages—and still the Church lives on. But why this silence? For a Marxist, the reply goes without saying: religion has every possibility of existing in so far as capitalism provides it with a suitable atmosphere by oppressing workers and keeping them in ignorance.

The Atheist's Guide (*Sputnik Ateista*, Moscow: 1959) is a book of more or less the same type but it brings us more up to date. Edited by a collaborative group of specialists in the field, this illustrated, 500-page manual is intended to give detailed information about the various religions of mankind. Important mention is given to the Orthodox Church, which is no longer trying to oppose progress but is endeavouring to reconcile the 'two faces of the coin of Truth', science and religion. This, we are warned, is a tactical approach we should be most cautious of, because the goal of Communism 'is not only to liberate man from material fetters, but to free him from spiritual shackles as well'.

The book covers in detail the teaching of theologians who manifest progressive tendencies; these tendencies are as much to be repudiated as any others. Also attacked is the World Council of Churches, which demonstrated its hostility towards democracy 'by approving imperialist aggression in Korea and refusing to endorse the appeal of the Stockholm Peace Conference for atomic disarmament'.[1]

A little work[2] devoted to the struggle now going on between material and spiritual forces struck me as impressive in quite a different way. Using as his authorities Protestant theologians, the author emphasizes the fact that science has destroyed traditional dogmatic notions based on the Bible, thanks to recent progress in astro-physics and biology. Put in the position where they cannot argue against this progress, religious ideologists are now depending on facile manoeuvres which, they pretend, are aimed at finding a common ground for science and religion.

Science, they claim, has demonstrated the impossibility of reducing all life's phenomena to physical and chemical data or to an 'abstract and mechanical concept' (Antonio Aliotta). Like religion, they go on, science is based on non-rational and metaphysical principles which are reconciled in an absolute (O. Klohr).

Actually, however, neither the quantum, nor relativity theories, nor atomic disintegration jeopardizes Lenin's dialectico-materialist doctrine; on the contrary, what they do do is confirm it. It is impossible, on this earth, to have a 'double account-ability', such as E. Frank and Al Farrer propose. 'Peaceful

[1] An article published by L. P. Kharahorkin in the review *Problems of Philosophy* (I, 1960) put forth and defended almost the same point of view. Though obviously eager to be as objective as possible, the author insists that Orthodox doctrine, even in our day, is reactionary and anti-scientific.

[2] I. Kryvelev, *Modern Theology and Science* (in Russian), Moscow: 1960.

co-existence' involving religion and science is completely inadmissible; science does not need any 'support' from religion and its mystical terminology.

No one claims that science can provide moral principles, but as it reveals the essence of all natural and social phenomena, it leads us to the 'single truth' and affords us the possibility of making whatever deductions are necessary, even in the field of ethics. Today's man need not hesitate to put aside those so-called 'mysteries of transcendence' that some thinkers cling to (J. Hessen, T. MacPherson). He can also have done with that faith which is beyond human experience and is awakened by divine 'grace' which some Protestant theologians (Karl Barth) persist in considering the source of all Christian teaching.

If there are still scholars who have not yet given up religious faith, that only goes to prove that, experts in mathematics and physics though they may be, they have not been able to rise above old-fashioned ideologies and still allow their reason to be ruled by their emotions.

If a man like Max Planck can declare that man is, at best, capable of 'apprehending' the essence of the order in the world, but not of 'comprehending' it; if he maintains that, exactly like religion, science depends upon symbols in this area, he cannot help arriving at some sort of pantheist conception, which is bound to shock theologians because it does not imply the presence of a God. What he is really doing, therefore, is simply giving a debased demonstration of the idealist point of view and proving to us that his reputation and authority as a scientist do not extend to other areas of human thought.

The same thing could be said about various lucubrations of Albert Einstein, when he allowed his tendencies to emotional thinking get the better of his reason. Opposition between genuine science and genuine religion remains insurmountable

This entire line of argument is obviously serious enough to deserve a detailed refutation; we shall have to return to it.

An equally dignified position could not be given some of the other widely circulated little pamphlets I have, though, which are clearly the products of a simplist—if not downright naive—frame of mind. Thus, for example, in *Why we are Battling against Religion* (Moscow: 1960), F. Dolguikh and A. Kurantov refer to the close relations between American monopolists and clergy, the discussion between the Lutheran Bishop Dibelius and Bonn's Minister of War regarding religious services in the *Bundeswehr's* camps, and even the approval voiced by an Anglican bishop of the departure of English and American troops for Lebanon and Jordan.

Or, in another such pamphlet, Professor I. Pantshava, doctor of philosophical sciences, traces atheistic activity from ancient India and the Peloponnesian wars down to Lenin including, of course, references to the Renaissance humanists, to Spinoza and Hobbes, and mentioning Rabelais and the Encyclopedists.

L. Serdobolskaya's effort is aimed at uncovering *The Reactionary Essence of Baptism* (Moscow: 1960), while Mr Eryshev attacks *Religious Sectarianism* in general and accuses some fanatical associations of being nothing less than dens of anti-social elements.

Another series (with a circulation of 200,000 to 300,000) is devoted to ridiculing the sacraments. I. Skvortsov-Stepanov devotes about thirty illustrated pages to *The Sacrament of the Eucharist* (Moscow: 1959), which he claims is simply a survival of old pagan rites already observed in different ways in Peru, Cyprus, Persia and elsewhere. In his pamphlet *I Marry the Servant of God* (Moscow: 1959) G. A. Suglobov gives us a catalogue of unhappy women who have been married with the Church's blessing to rich old men, sometimes as the result of an advertisement in a 'Personal Column'.

It is hard to assess the effect this sort of material has on ordinary farmers or workers. In the early days of the Revolution, of course, they would have had an impact on those levels of society which were still immersed in ignorance. Now that every young Soviet citizen will soon be receiving free secondary education, it seems to me that caricatures of lecherous monks or of aged civil officials standing at the altar to be married to unhappy girls who have been sacrificed for wealth and position have outlived their usefulness.

I have even seen a little book entitled *Is There a God?* by P. Pavelkine. A hundred thousand copies of it were printed and it is sold on Moscow streets for the low price of eighty kopecks. When I offered my copy to a young schoolmistress, she smartly replied: 'Thanks very much, but I've got another little pamphlet that only costs twenty kopecks and tells how to get rid of tooth-ache. I hope you won't be offended, but I haven't got time to read that other nonsense.'[1]

. . . . . .

Under the Soviet Government the Russian Press has always given a prominent position to anti-religious propaganda, but since the twenty-first Party Congress, a new and obviously more energetic approach has been taken. A foreign journalist, well armed with statistics, told me that, during 1959 and 1960, he had clipped as many as 120 articles on the subject. Some of this material covered the activities of the Baptists, the Pentecostal Churches, the Jehovah's Witnesses, while others dealt with specific religious problems in the Baltic and Moldavian Republics or in Central Asia (where religious feeling is intimately linked with nationalist or separatist aspirations). Most of the writers, however, attacked the Orthodox Church, of course, since it is the predominant religious group in the Soviet.

[1] I was more curious about the little book than she was, however, so I read through it and was astounded at its weakness. The author begins by stating that the opposition between Communism and Christianity should not prevent believers and unbelievers from living in peace and concord. It only needs a patient and convincing argument to point out the errors of religion to anyone who still believes in God: We Communists believe that faith in God is injurious, that it is a kind of autosuggestion which weakens men. . . . No religious man can understand the interconnection among natural phenomena because he imagines that they are controlled by some sort of mysterious power. Such a man could never become an active member of our society and take his place among Communism's pioneers. Naturally, it is difficult to re-educate old people, but even that can be done. We must take care that 'not a single young worker, not a single *kholkoz* farmer, not a single worker or student continues to believe in these supernatural powers'.

Though they have intensified their propaganda, Moscow and provincial newspapers avoid mistakes made in the past. The tenor of the new approach is obvious in the 23 December 1959 edition of *Partiinaya Zhizn* (*Party Life*): 'Our aim is to help our citizens understand fully the changes which have taken place since the triumph of socialism. It is not enough to point out the contradictions contained in the Bible, or to draw our readers' attention to the fact that the self-interest of the propertied classes tries to justify itself by appeal to the Gospels.'

These facts are true, the article goes on, but too abstract and too removed from conditions in the Soviet Union. We must remember that even Church leaders are trying to persuade their flocks that 'the teachings of the New Testament are compatible with Communism'. Most of our anti-religious articles spend too much time discussing the Churches of the past. They are very interesting historical problems, of course, but the history of religion has no goal of its own; it is merely a means of atheist education and of destroying the vestiges of religion.

Our whole propaganda programme must be revamped; it has to combat certain customs (which are incompatible with the country's vital interests, from the scientific point of view), but it should not fight against religious practices as such. 'It should appeal to everyone and answer any questions about the structure of the universe, the origins of life, and various scientific results and achievements, and, in general, give confirmation of materialist teachings.'

Some newspapers, the article continues, claim that religious celebrations afford the faithful constant occasions for drunkenness and that the clergy benefit financially from them. 'It does no good to write this sort of thing, however, because we must admit that the Church is struggling against alcoholism and is making an heroic effort to raise the people's moral standards. The real point is that the clergy use religious feasts to strengthen their flocks' religious convictions.'

Furthermore, it would be a good thing to open newspaper

columns to renunciations of religion by members of the clergy: 'We should give every assistance to those sincere individuals in various groups who, thanks to the major changes occurring in Soviet life and the influence of public opinion, have finally realized that man does not need religion.' Breaking away from religion is 'a major event in a man's life, a triumph of Marxist-Leninist ideology'.[1]

To what extent—and how—has the Soviet Press actually applied these directives, which are certainly clear enough?

First of all, there is no denying that more and more newspapermen spend time ridiculing religious superstition. In 'Papa, Mama and the Holy Water Font' (*Komsomolskaya Pravda* of 18 August 1959), for example, we are told about a little boy whom the police found lost in a railway terminus; his poverty-stricken mother, who was caught up in fanaticism and, consequently, became the laughing-stock of the neighbourhood, had sent him from Syzran (a large town on the Volga), to get holy water and oil, and blessed bread from the Monastery of the Trinity and St Sergei near Moscow.

Another case described in the same newspaper gives the story of the sorry plight of a young man who had simultaneously applied for entrance into the University and the Orthodox seminary; he admitted that he was torn between two careers, because he did not know which would be most lucrative, as though he were making up his mind about which of two pairs of trousers to buy.

Sometimes, accounts like these are used as an occasion for highly pretentious literary endeavours. One review,[2] for instance, devotes forty pages of closely printed texts and illustrations to tell the story of a young woman called Assia. Entitled 'S.O.S.

---

[1] The programme outlined by another influential magazine, *Voprosy Filosofi* (*Philosophical Questions*), 1959, no. 8, takes almost the same line. It declares that 'in order to raise Communist awareness to a higher level and overcome religious prejudices, we must first of all strengthen political convictions, inculcate moral notions of work in everyone (especially young people) and campaign untiringly for the idea of international friendship'.

[2] *Yunost* (*Youth*), no. 2, February 1960.

(Save Our Souls)', it tells how she meets a young student, goes to the cinema and on walks with him and, eventually, falls in love. Paul, however, does not say much about what he does or about what he is studying. One day, Assia discovers that he is a seminarian at the Monastery of the Trinity and St Sergei. Raised as she has been according to strict Marxist principles, Assia is overcome, as are her friends; the only thing to do now is to bring Paul to his senses and make him give up his ruinous vocation.

Assia goes to the monastery, has a good look at the monks and how they spend their time, and finds them incredibly ludicrous. Paul, too, begins to hesitate; doubt gradually creeps into his soul. Though he does not completely renounce his faith, he leaves the seminary. Assia's friends find work for him in a factory and everything ends with the couple living 'happily ever after'.

Just as characteristic is *The Miraculous Ikon* by V. Tendriakov. A boy finds an ikon, which had disappeared during the troubles of 1929, in a river. His grandmother and all the other villagers go into raptures at his find. But little Rodka, who has had too much of his friends' chaffing, takes a hatchet and breaks the ikon into pieces. His grandmother beats him and he is taken to hospital.

The priest and the village schoolmistress became involved in a lengthy discussion of the whole affair. Who is better able to take care of the boy's education, a fanatical family or the community? The priest points out that the law is explicit and puts the education of children in the hands of their parents. On the other hand, the teacher insists, the boy should be put into an institution to make sure he is protected from bad influences. No one reading the story could have the slightest doubt of what the authorities' final decision will be with regard to poor little Rodka.

Sometimes the Press will take a scientific stand to expose religious superstition. Such an attack on the devil appeared in *Science and Religion*. Origen is cited where he denounces carnal commerce between husband and wife; Tertullian provides a text which describes woman as Satan's branch-officer on earth.

The conclusion is that religious morality prevents a healthy married life and that (especially among Moslems) it nourishes the persistence of medieval attitudes towards women. Reason's triumph is highlighted and the reader is told that 'we are not governed by instincts, but by reflexes'. Cybernetics' achievements are boasted of as giving man 'complete domination over nature'.

Journalists sometimes even give the names of the people whom they accuse. Parents in Magnetogorsk are told that they are responsible for the death of the child after it was baptized by immersion; a woman named Anastasia Arsenieva has instituted divorce proceedings against her husband because he has made remarks hostile to religious belief. The *Literaturnaya Gazeta* for 5 March 1960 lashes out at the teachers of a certain Lida who still has not been able to develop the attitude of a responsible citizen despite ten years of secondary education. Indeed, she herself took the risk of writing to a newspaper and saying that she believed in God with all her heart and what advice could the editors give her.

On the other hand, we are shown the example of Galia Kimtchenko, a young student of Kursk, who has been able to divorce herself from the destructive influence of outmoded religious superstition.[1] Under the influence of religion, she had been encouraged by the example of Chaliapin to sing in the cathedral choir and even to paint ikons. She was admitted into a convent as a novice and was promised Paradise.

Fortunately, she came to her senses just in time; she got help from the police and thus regained her freedom.

We are given the same sort of story in the confession of Nina Deriabin. In appropriate language, she describes her life as a travelling evangelist; for several years, she went from one village to another, helping the women with their work in the fields, always praying and arranging Bible readings for the farmers during the evenings. After four years, she realized her mistake; other evangelists, who were nothing more than drunkards and

[1] *Komsomolskaya Pravda*, April 1959.

card-players, were jealous of her. Finally, she decided to take a job as a construction worker.

That was ten years ago, and now she no longer believes in God.

'A saint's life is becoming more and more difficult,' concludes the author of the article, 'while living conditions are getting better. But so long as church bells ring, there will be living apostles, crafty people who will exploit the faith of the people. The Church needs them, and they are tightly woven into the network of fraud and hypocrisy.'

Every confession like this is catalogued with utmost care. Some of them have even been collected in a sort of anthology.[1] It includes similar confessions by eight Orthodox, three Roman Catholics, eight Baptists, one Old Believer and ten Pentecostals and Seventh Day Adventists. They were all poor people, victims of life's hardships; they had no friends but, after reading natural science texts, they realized that genuine Communist doctrine, being a 'new and more human religion', was not compatible with the teachings of the Church.

But these confessions did not seem particularly impressive for the ordinary readers of Russian newspapers, so editors found a better subject: clerical apostasy.

There is nothing especially Soviet about the phenomenon of the renegade priest. They are found all over the world and some of them have even become famous. In most instances, however, they prefer to remain unknown and withdraw from notoriety to avoid scandal.

Things are handled differently in the Soviet Union, however. Each time a Church worker makes an act of renunciation of religion, the event is given enormous coverage in the official Press. This procedure is still quite recent, having started in 1959, to be exact.

[1] *Why we gave up Religion* (in Russian), Moscow: 1959.

On 14 July 1959 the daily *Sovietskaya Litva* (*Soviet Lithuania*) devoted half a page to a letter written by the former Father Ramasauskas, a Lithuanian:

'I am thirty-nine years old and have spent many long years in the grip of the opium of religion. Not only did I believe in the existence of the "Most High", I was also a Roman Catholic preacher. Since childhood, my conscience has been so clouded by belief in God that I spent all my time thinking about the life to come.'

He goes on to describe his upbringing at the hands of his father and mother, who were poor, simple peasants. The school chaplain was the first person to talk to him about Paradise, where they who believe will be rewarded for their sufferings on earth. The young man thought he had found his vocation; he entered a seminary, was tonsured in 1950, and later, after his ordination, was curate in four successive village parishes.

As he studied the Bible, he realized that 'the idea of a creating God is a product of human imagination'. He declares in his letter that the Roman Catholic Church 'is pursuing its fight against the forces of science and progress and anathematizes everyone who is fighting for peace'.

'After considering all these facts,' he concludes, 'I understood that I could no longer remain a minister of religion and I decided to renounce my priesthood.' He ends by saying that he has completely broken with his past, is now married, has been given a 'very nice flat'(!) and supports himself and his wife 'by decent work in a factory in Vilna'.

A few days later it was the turn of a renegade Orthodox priest.

In a letter addressed to Bishop Sergei of Astrakhan and Stalingrad, Father Nikolai Spasski makes formal renunciation of his priesthood and office as curate, and adds a confession of his errors.

After having spent some time in a seminary, he then made commercial studies and 'served my country sincerely for more than a quarter of a century'. During the German occupation of Ukrainia in 1941, they tried to take advantage of his talents in their supply offices: 'My seminary training saved me, however, and I became a priest.'

As he became more and more engrossed in studying the Bible, he encountered a series of absurdities and legends and soon reached the conclusion that 'no Christ has ever existed, neither at the beginning of our era nor during any other time, neither on earth nor anywhere else'.

He recalls the moment when he first began to doubt the existence of Christ. It was on 11 March 1943, when the Germans killed peaceful citizens of the village of Kozyri (in the Chernigov region) by burning, as they had at Oradur, the school where they had taken refuge. He had defied God then by crying out: 'If you really exist, stop these murderers, otherwise you do not deserve to be worshipped by the people.'

Next, he underlines recent scientific advances which no longer allow any 'reactionary doctrine of a supernatural existence', and cites Engels, according to whom the immortality of the soul is an outmoded notion. He then moves on to attack miracles, pilgrimages and, in a general way, all religious fakery.

Neither does he shrink from denouncing some priests who promoted manifestations of this sort, and specifically cites the Bishop of Smolensk for having spent several thousand rubles 'to celebrate his own feast day'.

'There are honest priests,' he admits, 'but we do not respect them.'

The letter ends with an appeal to believers: 'Do not go on believing in the forces of the supernatural; they do not exist and have never existed; immerse yourselves in a serious study of science and it will help you get rid of your religious superstition.'

Other articles published in other newspapers make it clear that there was an organized campaign underway.

Thus, on 6 August of that year, *Sovietskaya Rossia* printed a letter from a correspondent in the Sverdlovsk region, which recounts the apostasy of a priest of Nizhni-Sergei during the preceding February.

Only thirty-one years old, Father Oplesnin had, for the five years of his ministry, been aware of the clergy's avarice which tricked the people by 'forbidding them to go to the theatre, read newspapers or listen to the radio'.

Now working in a metals factory, the ex-priest devoted all his free time to anti-religious propaganda; he had already given 300 lectures in different centres throughout the Urals, organized an 'Office of Atheist Propaganda' in his home city, and was writing a book to describe the motives behind his breaking with religion in the name of truth.

Another periodical published the statement of the renegade priest Victor Detchko, which included accusations against Archbishop Antony of Stavropol and Baku.

Or, again, we are told about the novice Valentine Pakhomov who, though he remained a fervent Christian even after leaving his monastery, was finally convinced of the unworthiness and hypocrisy of the clergy and made a complete break from the Church. These facts were laid out in a letter to the Bishop of Astrakhan and Stalingrad published in *Komsomolskaya Pravda* on 13 August 1959.

Even the Moslem clergy do not go unscathed, and mention is made of the *mullah* Kadir Rassulev, who was attached to the Astrakhan mosque before he renounced his position, and of Pir Niaz Hodja, a descendant of the Prophet who preferred to become an atheist propagandist.

Towards the end of 1959 a real thunder-clap broke. This time, it was no obscure country priest, but a leading light of Orthodox religious education. Under the heading 'Breaking away from Religion is the only Right Way', *Pravda* published a three-column statement bound to attract attention:

'Yes, it is I, professor of Sacred Scripture, of the Old Testament and of classical Hebrew in the Orthodox seminary and Theological Academy at Leningrad, former inspector of its institutions, master of theology and archpriest—I have broken away from the Church and religion.

I now make public confession of the atheism to which I have concluded as a result of much thought and study, after a long and painful inner struggle, and a complete revision of my idea of the world.

Forty-eight years old, almost twenty-five of which have been spent at intermediate posts of responsibility in the Orthodox Church, I leave once and for all a world of unreal illusion and, sometimes, deliberate lies.'

The statement was signed by Professor Alexei Ossipov, who went on to say that he was perfectly aware of the calumnies which followed the apostasy of two of his former pupils, Fathers Darmanski and Kuzin, who had gone before him on that road. 'I have reached this conclusion,' he continues:

'After earnest and sincere study of the Bible and the history of religions from a critical and historical point of view; after observing the dynamic progress of the natural sciences; after taking stock of the wretchedness of the entire capitalist world and the small, not to say miserable, importance played there by religion: and finally, after imbuing myself with Marxist-Leninist philosophy and our Soviet realism, which beckon us, not without authority, along the path they point out, the only right path.

All of this has led me to the deepseated conviction that there is no God, no world of the spirit or "great beyond", and that every religious system is no more than an illusory reflection within human consciousness of the still unfathomed mysteries of the nature of social law, and of the psychological and physiological peculiarities of human beings themselves.'

He goes on to give us some information about his life. Born in Estonia and member of a working-class family, in 1928 he joined a Russian Christian students' organization in Paris and began a branch of it in his native city of Talinn.

Trained by what he read in the writings of emigré professors, he became a lecturer to youth groups; on the advice of a priest, he enrolled as a student in the theological faculty which was still, in those days, attached to the University of Tartu (Dorpat).

He was, however, beset by doubts: ecclesiastical dress, the 'verbiage' of Orthodox services, and the deep contradictions between religious philosophy and the actual practice of the Church, all repelled him. As a lodger in a presbytery, he became familiar with the 'horrible atmosphere' in ecclesiastical circles and the low level of the clergy's interests.

The arguments of the 'bourgeois philosopher' Berdayev were some comfort to him, however, and helped him distinguish between the worth of Christianity and the unworthiness of Christians.

After completing his studies, he was appointed curate to a Talinn parish, but had still not achieved a solution to his inner personal crisis. Nevertheless, that did not stop him from applying for a post at the Theological Academy of Leningrad which had just opened after the war.

Probably because of the lack of other candidates, he was given a chair and put in charge of inspecting the students. He worked very hard to keep the Church's future ministers free of fanaticism and superstition; he advised them to go to the theatre and the cinema; he arranged literary and political lectures and thus aroused the displeasure of his superiors.

The 'fanatics' also accused him of having contracted a second marriage after his wife (whom he had left at Talinn during the war) emigrated to the United States. The whole business, which is rather obscure, was submitted to the Patriarch, who decided to deprive him of his priestly faculties, but allowed him to remain a professor and to dress as a cleric.

It is surprising to find Ossipov's name listed among the collaborators in the new edition of the Bible and the contributors to the *Journal of the Patriarchate of Moscow* during a period when, at his own admission, studies in the history of religion had given him the last link in his 'chain of atheist convictions'.

'My decision to break with religion was made and strengthened during those days. Why did I not leave the Theological Academy at once? Actually, I was still in the process of breaking away from the Church and was still influenced by the abstract morality she preaches; I had the idea that I could be a help to future priests so that they would not become preachers of the stupid superstitions of fanaticism.'

Gradually, he realized his mistake and began to understand that 'only a complete break with religion would put him at peace with his conscience and give him the right to consider himself a man of integrity'.

One day, in the midst of a discussion with his colleagues and superiors about anti-religious articles which had appeared in the Press, he finally felt 'as though he would suffocate in this scholastic atmosphere' and decided to break his stalemate by openly declaring that he was mistaken 'to preach lying and erroneous doctrines', with the hope that such a sincere admission would open men's eyes.

It was, of course, a serious blow to the directors of the Theological Academy, many of whom were even mentioned by name in their former colleague's indictment.

Ordinarily, the Soviet Press does not intrude into the private lives of its citizens; there is never any mention of domestic affairs in the newspapers nor of the way famous personalities spend their leisure time. Names like Princess Margaret, Princess Grace of Monaco or Queen Farah are completely unknown all over Russia. So the scandal-starved Russian readers fell on the

Ossipov affair ravenously, and the whole country's interest was focussed on it for some time.

On the whole, however, this priest's apostasy does not seem to have been any more effective than any of his predecessors'. There were too many internal contradictions in his statement; it was very difficult to make out during which period he was sincere and during which period he was lying to those about him. The Communists themselves are too loyally attached to their own doctrines to respect a renegade. So far as the Church was concerned, the whole affair ended in a solemn decree of excommunication, pronounced on 30 December 1959, of Ossipov, Spasski, Darmanski, some other former priests, and some laymen 'for having publicly blasphemed the Name of the Lord'.

Nor is it too much to suppose that not a single faithful Orthodox was led astray from Christianity by what had been done by these men, who were all more or less discredited.[1]

The Press, however, continued to make much of the Ossipov apostasy. On 20 December 1959 *Izvestia* published an interview with the unfrocked priests and gave it four columns. Headed 'Reason against Mysticism', Ossipov's interview insists again that science and religion cannot be reconciled.

'At bottom,' he says:

'Protestantism has yielded to science and, out of the whole Bible, is striving to preserve only the general principles put forth in the New Testament. Not even the Catholics agree in their attitude towards these problems: in one of his addresses, Pius XII analysed the means of linking science to religion.'

But Orthodoxy, he goes on, will be the most backward Church in the whole world; she preserves biblical myths intact, categorically repudiates all the scientific discoveries which have contributed to biblical criticism, and constantly gives evidence of

[1] Ossipov, however, was not discouraged by the way things turned out. In 1960 he published two pamphlets, *Reply to Believers* and *The Way of Spiritual Liberty*.

her anti-democratic centralism and totalitarian tendencies 'by frequently moving her bishops from one place to another'!

During 1960 there were some new cases of apostasy, but the Soviet Press did not see fit to give them as much publicity. Thus, for instance, the confession of the 'former priest' A. V. Klimenko was only reported in provincial newspapers.[1]

No one could say that Klimenko's statement was brilliantly original:

'I was a priest between 1942 and 1960, but I stopped believing in God six years ago, because I made an intensive study of religion and became convinced that it teaches only lies.... There has never been a God nor a Jesus Christ, nor an afterlife, nor protecting and interceding saints in heaven.

This is why I have not preached once to my flock during the past five years.... No reader should be surprised to learn that an atheist was the village priest of Sulimovka. There are more atheists than men of prayer among ministers of worship....'

The rest of the statement is about as poor. Klimenko claims, for example, that some of his flock were outraged that the words, 'the servant of God' should be used in the baptism of a child: 'Our nephew will never be a servant; he is a free Soviet citizen!' He also says that 'no one' came to his church, which was the local church for four villages, on Sundays except a half-dozen old ladies between the ages of seventy and eighty.

He finishes his statement by insisting that he does not want to be part of a Church 'which covered itself with shame by supporting the Tsars, nobility, wealthy landowners and the bourgeoisie; anathematized those who were struggling for national security . . . anathematized Tolstoy and organized pogroms'.

[1] It was published in the Kiev *Pravda* on 19 January, and I saw it reprinted in the *Red Dawn*, the official newspaper of the spa at Sotchi, on 8 July.

In the long run the directors of the anti-religious propaganda campaign must have realized that the general public are completely unaffected by this sort of declaration. For some time, they have been using a new method: apostate priests have yielded the limelight to unworthy priests.

Moscow newspapers made a great deal of certain incidents alleged to have taken place in Zagorsk, where seminarians at the local monastery have drawn attention to themselves by their drinking bouts and rowdy behaviour.[1]

There are other, infinitely more serious accusations made, however. On 21 June 1960 *Sovietskaya Rossia* published an article by its Kazan correspondent entitled 'Swindlers in Soutanes'. It recounts the condemnation of 'the swindler Kressovitch' to three years' deprivation of liberty and surrender of personal property by the supreme court of the Autonomous Tartar Republic. The 'swindler Kressovitch' is actually Archbishop Job of Kazan and Tartary, accused of having perpetrated an income-tax fraud of two million rubles during his seven years as head of the diocese by falsifying accounts; certain members of his clergy are involved in the affair and accused of fraud amounting to 600,000 rubles. The Archbishop is supposed to have used the free gifts of the faithful to buy carpets, furniture, expensive paintings, refrigerators and to pay for journeys to visit his children living in a large house in the Ukraine with two motor-cars.

Without knowing the juridic and fiscal details of this unhappy business, we cannot come to an objective judgment. The Soviet clergy's constant difficulties with controllers of revenue are notorious, but this is not surprising in view of the fact that it is almost impossible to keep close account of Church revenues which, aside from the sale of candles, come entirely from parishioners' free gifts, usually very small but very frequent and shared by the local parish and the diocese.

Soviet readers, however, were bound to wonder how a man

---

[1] *Trud (Labour)*, the journal of the workers' unions, published an account of the affair in its issue for 17 April 1960.

on the receiving end of contributions, even though he were a bishop, could swindle two million rubles (about £75,000) if his revenues did not go into hundreds of millions.[1]

Other propaganda methods used formerly seem to have been replaced by this literary and journalistic approach during recent years.

According to experts, atheist lecturers who were sent into rural areas and public debates with ministers of worship were not as successful as had been hoped they might be.

In the Tendriakov article mentioned above, the same remark is made openly about such lectures: 'Only atheists attend them.'

In Literature and Life for 21 February 1960, propagandists in the area about Perm, who are chastized for being less diligent than they should be, are urged to take example from the widespread activities of strenuous local priests who go about the countryside in hundreds, passing on the good word of religion, unintimidated by the freezing weather and terrible condition of the roads.

The most eloquent criticism appeared in the leading Soviet humorous magazine, Krokodil. In its 29 February 1960 number, there is a cartoon showing two men and a woman kneeling in front of the altar in a small church and praying: 'O Lord, send us quickly an atheist lecturer to work in our district.' Judging from the caricature alone, this seems the best way to increase the number of believers in Russia.

Anti-religious museums have also had their day. There was a time when every tourist was taken through them and all Europe discussed them. Now, so far as I know, there is not a single such museum in Moscow. In Leningrad the famous Cathedral of Our Lady of Kazan, which was built in imitation of St Peter's in

---

[1] This is not the only case we know of involving the clergy in financial litigation. The Soviet Press has made similar accusations against Archbishop Benjamin of Tchita and Archbishop Hermogenes of Tashkent and Central Asia, declaring that they have 'appropriated monies belonging to the Church for their own use'.

The tomb of St Sergei in the Monastery of the Trinity and St Sergei

The Superior of the Pokrovski convent at Kiev

Настоятельница
Киево-Покровского
женского монастыря
Игумения Рафаила
11 Июля 1960г.

The village priest with the author and two members of the kolkhoz at Trebukhovo, Kiev region

Rome by a serf of Count Stroganoff, the great architect Voronikhine, is still used for this purpose, but the general public lost interest in it a long time ago.

During my stay in the city built on the Neva, I made a point of visiting the 'Museum of the History of Religion and Atheism', set up beneath the towering arches of this cathedral. The vast nave of the church is partitioned off into dozens of small areas filled with pictures, prints, pamphlets and an infinite variety of other exhibits all primarily intended to give a slanted idea of the history of religion.

One principal section is devoted to China's old beliefs through nature and ancestor worship, Confucianism, Taoism, Buddhism, Lamaism to magic and 'the cult of wealth'.

Another section brings us to feudal times and the origins of the papacy. We are introduced to 'the myths of God the Father, Christ, the Blessed Virgin and the veneration of saints as used by exploiters, and the heroic struggle of the Russian people against the encroachments of the papacy' through old masterpieces of painting, sculpture, crucifixes and images of saints. From this section, we pass on through the Inquisition, the Reformation, Copernicus and his discoveries, Voltaire's writings and Daumier's graphic satires to pilgrimages to Lourdes, the Vatican as Fascism's ally, and the liberating labours of Marx and Lenin.

Other sections laid out in the same way cover the activities of the Russian clergy and the close relations which existed between them and capitalist property-owners, all led by the Tsar.[1]

All in all, the general effect of the exhibition is rather bewildering. Despite the obvious effort to show the misdeeds of the clergy since humanity's history began, the thing that shows up more clearly is the role the Churches have played in the evolution of art. Visitors to the museum are mostly students or people who live in the provinces; whether they believe in God or not, they cannot

[1] Under the aegis of the Soviet Academy of Sciences, the Museum has published several guide-catalogues which give an excellent idea of the collections: *History of the Papacy and the Inquisition*, Moscow-Leningrad, 1959; *The Religions of China*, ibid., 1960; *History of Orthodoxy and Russian Atheism*, ibid., 1960.

help but admire the beautiful paintings and prints without paying very much attention to their subjects.

I was standing before something that looked like a sort of crèche; inside it a bishop was seated in his throne which stood beneath a massive and arched ceiling and had a brazier of burning coals standing in front of it; a heretic with a most contrite expression on his face stood a little way from the throne.

Two teen-agers were standing alongside me, deep in admiration of the scene, which was probably meant to illustrate the Inquisition. One of them nudged the other with her elbow and said: 'Oh my, isn't it beautiful!' If this is the result of an atheist system of education, surely there is something better.

We ought not to forget, nevertheless, that these museums, public lectures, newspaper articles, pamphlets, brochures and historical studies are meant only to complement the materialist, and therefore atheist, education given in all Soviet state schools.

The 'Society for the Diffusion of Political and Scientific Ideas', which now carries on the work of the old 'Union of Militant Atheists', maintains its strong influence in this field and special attention is paid to the adequate training of teachers. 'Atheist' seminaries have been started in most paedagogical institutes (the Press have listed them at Vologda, Pskov, Lvov, Krasnoyarsk, etc.); the Universities of Moscow and of Kiev have faculties of the history and theory of atheism, and other universities probably have them as well. A thirty-four hour course covers the origins of religion, its close ties with the exploiting classes, the position of the Church in Tsarist Russia, various sects, religious feasts and the religious notion of the creation of the world.

In addition to these specialized courses, there is, of course, the ordinary generalized educational programme. The Soviet Academy of Sciences backs up the anti-religious propaganda movement with its authority. In June 1959 it organized a congress for the investigation of scientific atheism. Soviet Russia's most illustrious names in the world of science (Mitin, Oparin,

Pavlovski, *et al.*) participated in sessions and pointed out how advances in physics, chemistry, physiology and astronomy have made it possible to carry on a more effective battle against the modern fideism which underlies all religion.

The Academy of Paedagogical Sciences of the Russian Federal Republic, in its turn, published a manual in 1956, the collaborative work of twenty-five leading authorities, which made available to teachers a long investigation of the scientific and atheist education of youth. The problem is presented as hinging upon, anticipating and eliminating any and all religious influence, spending time on the problem during natural science and history lectures, and underlining the malevolent role played by the clergy in oppressing the working masses and blocking all progressive thought. Such instruction, the manual points out, should, as far as possible, reach not only students but their milies.

With this manual and similar publications as their inspiration, all Soviet teachers, whether they are anthropologists, astronomers, biologists, ethnologists, archaeologists or historians, vie with one another in their explanations of the universe, life and religion in its many forms, always discarding any notion based on supernatural origins.

The ordinary masses of the country are difficult to convert, but the youth are docile. More and more, anti-religious propaganda is being focussed on that quarter in the clearly defined hope that the time is not far off when, all over the Soviet, a negative answer will be given to the question 'Is there a God?'

6

The Churches and the Law

FACED with these intense attacks on religious belief launched by the Party's propagandists, Churches today find themselves in an awkward situation in the Soviet Union.

Article 13 of the Constitution of 1918 recognized that all citizens have 'freedom of religious worship, and for religious or anti-religious propaganda'. But the revised constitutional text of 1929 made an important change in those words; its Article 124 only recognizes the right to 'freedom of worship and of *anti-religious* propaganda'. Thus, any possibility of using the Press lectures and education to rebut the statements and activities of people working to destroy all spiritual belief has been practically removed.

One article (18) of a law issued on 8 April 1924 had already expressly stipulated that 'the teaching of all religious doctrines, allowed in special theological courses only, is forbidden in all educational establishments, whether they are state-operated or private'.[1]

But this restriction is by no means the only one. Article 17 of the same law states that:

'Religious associations [parishes] are forbidden to: a) establish welfare funds, co-operatives, production associations and, generally, use the funds at their disposal for any purpose other than meeting the exigencies connected with religion and

[1] Cf. Gidulanoff, *The Separation of Church and State* (in Russian), Moscow: 1926, for a complete array of decrees, directives and verdicts.

worship; b) to lend material aid to their members, to organize prayer groups of children, young people or women and, generally, to organize meetings, clubs, cells or centres for biblical, literary, trade, professional, religious, etc., studies as also to establish sanatoria or dispensaries.

Only books requisite for worship may be kept in churches and other places of worship.'

The Penal Code, in articles 122 to 126, provides very stringent penalties for all violations of these regulations. Enforced labour in corrective institutions will be the penalty for:

'Religious instruction given to children or young people in educational institutions and public or state schools. . . . any fraudulent activity aimed at arousing the superstition of the people for the purpose of gaining thereby. . . . obligatory collections taken for the support of ecclesiastical or religious groups . . . the usurpation of public functions . . . the celebration of religious services in or on public exhibition in or on any of these institutions or premises of all religious images.'

The *Sputnik Ateista* (Moscow: 1959) recently made a detailed analysis of the legal position the Church has been placed in by this legislation. It is stressed that the only function of religious associations is the celebration of religious services; their activities have nothing in common with the many scientific, cultural, professional, or other, groups established by workers for women, children, sport, etc.; collections are not to be allowed outside buildings assigned for worship and should not be for any other purpose except the maintenance of church buildings, the clergy and various other expenses of this kind.

In one of its issues (Number 5, 1960), *Science and Religion* made a considerable contribution to this problem by giving explicit replies to questions submitted by its readers. The article emphasizes that sermons in churches and mosques are not forbidden so long as they are of a purely religious nature; this restriction is sometimes violated by the clergy, however, and they touch on problems connected with politics or education and sometimes give a false picture of national and international affairs.

Stressing the point that any and all religions or sects jeopardize Communism's progress, it goes on to list the authorized Churches and sects. Furthermore, it argues that charitable works are no longer necessary because Soviet society has done away with poverty, hunger and unemployment and has created conditions in which charity ('a shameful vestige of an exploiting society') has become superfluous, no matter what form it takes.

It strikes out unmercifully against sects which forbid their members to go to theatres or cinemas, but also declares that it is absolutely illegal for religious groups to organize orchestras, choirs, concerts, excursions, and entertainment for children or women, as also are special sermons delivered to children only.

The enemies of the Soviet State have laid great stress on these restrictive measures. One should not forget, however, that not a single one of them touches on the basic right given to all Churches and sects in the Soviet Union once and for all: the right to worship and to form associations to that end. This right is not only granted, it is even protected. Article 57 of the penal code provides that:

'Any propaganda or agitation of such a nature as to arouse religious hatred or religious disturbances, as well as the distribution, publication or conservation of all literature of that nature [are punishable] by a deprivation of liberty for a period of up to two years.'

In the *Science and Religion* article mentioned above it is pointed out that the rights of governmental officials do not extend to closing places of worship and disbanding religious associations. Such associations may be suppressed only if they are hostile to the State; if, for instance, their ministers preach against the acceptance of civil obligations (defending one's country, voting, etc.); or if they incite their members to national hatred or any other manifestation of religious fanaticism; or if they are a threat to the life and health of some of their members (as happens among some of the sects who preach mutilation, for example).

So far as closing a church is concerned, such action could only be taken upon the definite decision of the Central Administration.

Some fanatical atheists were astounded by 'the State's tolerant attitude' and an author whom we have already cited several times, P. F. Kolonitski, made a point of answering in a pamphlet issued by the Ministry of Defence as part of the anti-religious propaganda circulated among the members of the armed services:

> 'Administrative measures taken in our campaign to suppress religion are more than ineffectual; they are completely negligible. Far from helping people who still believe in God to throw off their religious prejudices, they stimulate them to greater fidelity to their beliefs. . . . Religion will never give in to restrictive measures which are, besides, contrary to the attitude of a socialist democracy which must always take into account the wishes and attitudes of all workers.'

Soviet legislation has given religious associations a series of precise rights and privileges. Any group of at least twenty believing citizens who are eighteen years of age or older may form an official association for the satisfaction of their religious needs. If there are too few citizens to form a 'religious association', they have the right to organize a 'group of believers'.

Such associations have the right to rent, buy or construct places of worship; they may have their own means of transport and workshops for the manufacture of candles and objects of worship.

Responsible individuals chosen from among the members of the association are in charge of administering its funds. Competent authorities may put at the free disposition of believers any religious buildings or valuable objects of worship after coming to a suitable agreement with them. Signatories to such an agreement assume responsibility for the administration and management of these buildings and valuables, and for any necessary repairs. If the building has historic or artistic importance, the entire association is obliged to keep it in good repair.

In a case where sufficient people are no longer interested in using the building for worship, local authorities are obliged to affix a notice to that effect on the door of the building in question; if notice to the contrary is not given within a week, the matter is laid in the hands of the authorities of the central government.

Revenues received by churches and religious associations are tax-free, but the clergy are taxed according to the same rates applicable to other citizens. Religious associations have no right to levy taxes or fines on their members.

Outdoor religious processions and ceremonies require the special authorization of local administrative branches; such authorization is not necessary for a religious procession which is not an integral part of the ordinary worship service and takes place around the place of worship. In addition to the ordinary places of worship, cemeteries, crematoria and isolated rooms in hospitals or prisons (in case of grave illness) may also be the sites of religious services.

Religious associations and their clergy have the right to gather in assembly and establish educational institutions for the preparation of ecclesiastical staff; in some cases, this preparation may even be allowed to be made in institutions abroad (Great Britain), for the Baptists; the University Al Ahzar in Cairo, for the Moslems, etc.).

Religious associations may publish literature of a religious character, but in practice this right is restricted to the publication of prayerbooks, calendars and strictly sectarian periodicals.

Finally, these religious groups may set up and control monasteries and may place land and livestock at their disposal.

We shall return to the large Orthodox and Catholic monasteries, but there is also Buddhist monastery in the Autonomous Buriato-Mongol Republic.

．　　　．　　　．　　　．　　　．

After reading through this point-by-point analysis of various existing administrative and legislative provisions, it might seem reasonable to conclude that the Soviet Union has pursued separation of Church and State to its logical end.

This is not the case, however; the integral application of motivating principles should logically end in a complete stifling of all religious activity in a country where the entire economy has been planned. How, for instance, could one religious group get the materials necessary for a new roof on their church if the project was not included in a five-year, or other, plan?

Or how could another group be able to take a young man away from the national industrial effort and let him go to the seminary if he wanted to?

Parish life is filled with a myriad of similar problems which arise daily and demand immediate solution.

On the other hand, unless it had recourse to police methods, which in this case were considered absolutely out of the question, an essentially totalitarian state would obviously be seriously inconvenienced by a situation in which millions of its citizens met regularly on the pretext of worshipping, without civil authority's having the least right to oversee their activities.

Aware of these drawbacks, the Soviet Government did not think it amiss to authorize a slight deviation from the principle of separation, and established (as we have already seen) two special committees attached to the Council of Ministers, one to oversee the affairs of the Russian Orthodox Church, and the other to concentrate on the various other religious groups within the country.

The first of these two bodies has been in operation since 1943 and has closely collaborated with the Patriarchs of Moscow. For sixteen years, its president was G. V. Karpov, a man of enlightened outlook and broad horizons who was able to win the confidence and sympathy of the Orthodox hierarchy while he held the post. His recent resignation caused Patriarchal circles real distress; some people even feared that his successor's appointment was a sign that the Government's attitude was stiffening towards the Church.

It is still too early to decide that Vladimir Kuroiedov will take an approach different from his predecessor's. I have been told that he feels he has the right to address the Patriarch familiarly as 'Alexei Vladimirovitch' instead of using his title, 'Your Holiness'. If the story is true, Mr Kuroiedov is doubly mistaken to address the Patriarch in such a manner; when he was still in the world, the head of the Russian Orthodox Church was called Sergei, and added the patronymic, Vladimirovitch, as is customary; after he entered religion, however, he changed his Christian name to Alexei and renounced his ties with his family; as a result, therefore, he has no patronymic any more.

I have met Mr Kuroiedov on several occasions, during various official functions, and have always found him a man of distinguished courtesy, with a cheerful expression and certainly nothing about him to suggest a 'persecutor of the Church'. In any case, the long talks I had with his aide, Boris Makartsev, struck me as most reassuring.

'Our committee,' this elegantly dressed important official told me, 'has for its first purpose the maintenance of contact between the Patriarchate and the Government by aiding in the solution of problems which arise and need the intervention of an administrative office or a soviet organization.

'We have nothing to do with the Church's internal affairs, which are regulated by canon law. Thus, for instance, we do not intervene in the appointment of bishops, especially since the Holy Synod usually chooses leading ecclesiastics of whose capabilities we have long been aware; in some rare cases, where it is a question of a new man, the Patriarch's representatives may eventually give us the name of the candidate, to avoid future friction with the local administration.

'But even in a case like that we do not wish to interfere with the strictly religious sphere. Our objections may, for instance, be based on information gathered from local sources and indicative of less than desirable moral standards or 'separatist' tendencies demonstrated by a candidate in one or another of the outlying republics.

'The task we have been set up for is completely different. We must facilitate the drawing up of contracts giving the Church free title to buildings for an unlimited period of time. New churches are being constructed practically everywhere in this country; the building can begin as soon as twenty people ask for it and have the necessary means.

'You have pointed out that only a very few churches seem to be being built in industrial centres or in the newly settled areas in Siberia. The answer to that is simple—the predominantly Communist people or youth have not specially asked for them.

'But there is more to do than simply build new churches; old and previously constructed places of worship need permanent maintenance which can only be done with the help of the local administrative office. Candle-manufacture demands sizable allocations of wax and paraffin, and there are a thousand other such things which take our attention.

'As representatives of the State, we must also—and this is the committee's second purpose—see that the laws regulating the activity of the Orthodox Church all over Soviet territory are strictly observed. We have to prevent any violation of these laws, whether by the clergy or by local administrations or organizations.

'Misunderstandings develop here or there; perhaps a priest leads a public procession, or another one finds himself the object of the misplaced zeal of a local official or a group of undisciplined young atheists. In cases like these, we take the necessary steps to clear up the trouble at once.

'There is, however, one area that we stay out of completely. Anti-religious propaganda does not come within our competence at all; it has nothing to do with us and is carried on by various branches of the Party in conformity with decisions taken by its congresses; it is not a Government activity. Lately, this propaganda has been considerably amplified, but you must remember that it has been going on for several generations now; the Soviet regime did not create atheists, there are enough of them in any country.

'No matter how one looks at it, it seems to me completely inadmissible to confuse an ideological conflict with a "struggle against the Church". I myself am a Communist, but none of my friends who is a Party member feels at all hostile towards religious believers. Citizens should not be separated from one another because of religion. So far as I am concerned, I sometimes dream of the future when the coexistence of these two ways of looking at the world will be finally realized.

'Perhaps I should say something about the internal organization of our committee. In our central office, we have very few people, a staff of not more than twenty; but we have deputies in each of the regional districts of the Soviet Union. They handle minor local difficulties and ask us for a decision in more serious cases, which are rare. They provide for parishes' material needs whenever their help is asked and I think I am correct in saying that, generally speaking, the whole organizational system works, and both the government and the Church are satisfied with it.'

On a lower storey of the same building, a handsome but rather old-fashioned villa, I heard the same thing, more or less, from two members of the other committee, Messrs Vodtshikov and Zadorozhski. The only difference between the activities of the two committees is that theirs has to deal with the rather complicated problems which arise in no less than twelve separate religious groups.

According to statistics they have available, the Soviet Union now has 1,235 Roman Catholic parishes, with three or four million faithful; 477 Lutheran parishes, with a total membership of a million and a half, 8,000 mosques to minister to fifteen million Moslems; 1,000 Old Believers' parishes, with their one million members belonging to one of three different obediences; 5,400 Baptist communities, with half a million members; 400 Seventh Day Adventist groups; 96 Reformed parishes; about 100 parishes of the Armenian Gregorian Church; 20 Buddhist communities and 400 synagogues.

Both these gentlemen were kind enough to give me information about each of these groups, information which I found exceptionally helpful during the rest of my investigation, which had only begun.

Having had a close look at anti-religious activity in the Soviet Union, I had now to examine the other leaf of my diptych: the world of believers.

7

The Patriarchate of Moscow

SINCE Moscow became the capital of the Soviet Union its development has transformed it into one of the world's largest urban centres, with a total population of eight million. Constructed on a semi-circular plan, with the Kremlin as its hub, the vast metropolis spreads out over an area of 150 square miles. Great arterial roads fan in towards the centre of the city from its outlying suburbs, and most of the broad and asphalted city streets carry traffic in four lanes.

Old, two-storey houses with baroque decorations are wedged in between lofty ultra-modern buildings, and the towers of skyscrapers soar up towards the sky over different parts of the city.

Construction is constant: huge new districts are rising in some of the suburbs and the whole, almost superhuman, construction campaign is overwhelmingly impressive and reminiscent of what was happening in some American cities not too long ago.

In the Red Square shifting crowds circulate in front of the G.U.M. Stores from morning till night, while, on the other side of the square, an endless queue of pilgrims waits patiently to get into Soviet Russia's national shrine, Lenin's tomb.

Briefcases under their arms, business men hurry along the pavements; telephones ring constantly in the bustling offices of the innumerable administrative branches in the city—the modern world's Moscow throbs with prosperous and bustling activity.

In an old residential area of the city, a few hundred yards away from a street crowded with trams, lorries, taxis and private motor-cars, are the offices of the Patriarchate of Moscow, where they have been since the last war. It is an old and charmingly colonnaded building with its own forecourt and gardens, and used to be the Embassy of the Third Reich.

Every time I have had the opportunity to go in through the building's grilled entry, I have felt a subtle thrill pass through me —as though I had been taken away from the earth and put on another planet. The whole atmosphere breathes contemplation and peace.

The secretariate of the Patriarchate is in an annexe at the far end of the courtyard. In an antechamber one meets old farmers and their wives come to plead that their village priest, to be appointed to another parish, be allowed to stay with them; when a bearded priest, his long hair reaching his collar, passes through the room they block his way, kissing his hand respectfully and asking his blessing.

Within the offices, one is received by clerical or lay officials who have the unctuous manner and affability usually associated with a clerical atmosphere; conversation with them starts immediately, but on subjects infinitely removed from the 'seven-year plan' or national industrialization. The visitor feels at once that he is in the living heart of old Orthodox Russia.

During recent years, a very important role has been played by Metropolitan Nikolai of Krutitsa and Kolomna, the Patriarch's immediate auxiliary and his vicar-general for Moscow. Until very recently, while still director of the Office of External Relations of the Russian Orthodox Church, his duties were somewhat similar to those of a Vatican Secretary of State, and he gained world-wide renown through his direct participation in various congresses and other international manifestations promoting international peace. For Metropolitan Nikolai is not merely an accomplished diplomatist; he is also the Russian Orthodox Church's greatest preacher. The several volumes of his marvellous sermons which have been published have stimulated the religious devotion of countless Orthodox faithful.

Outstanding organizer and zealous defender of the faith as he is, he spent several years close to the late Patriarch Sergei, and was one of the three men who saved the Russian Orthodox Church during the time when she was most in danger. His capabilities have been recognized not only by his flock but also by civil authority, and like the Patriarch, he has received the highest Soviet decorations. He is invited to official receptions given by the Kremlin and foreign embassies and, as the clergy's deputy, holds a seat at the meetings of the Partisans of Peace of the Soviet Union.

Russian emigré circles outside the Soviet have sometimes gone so far as to criticize Metropolitan Nikolai's attitude towards the Soviet Government as too conciliatory. People who make such judgments are completely out of touch with what is actually going on in the Soviet Union.

During the Second World War the entire nation supported the Church, but just as strongly did it support the existing regime; millions of its sons sacrificed their lives while fighting under the hammer and sickle. Whether critics of the Soviet Union like it or not, the present Government can depend upon the unanimous support of its people, even though some of its activities are stringently censured in various élite circles. The fact is indisputable, as I myself found out during many frank conversations with people from different levels of Soviet society.

Because of the many ties he has with the ordinary people, Metropolitan Nikolai is in a far better position to know them than anyone else. Besides, what should we expect of him? Should he be intransigently hostile to the very government which has given his Church legal existence and protects it from all violence? Who could imagine that the Cardinal-Archbishop of Paris or the Archbishop of Canterbury would take an official stand against the President of the French Republic or the Queen of England?

Did not Christ Himself tell his disciples that they must render to Caesar what is Caesar's? Not even the most carping critic could accuse the leaders of the Russian Orthodox Church of

His Beatitude Ephraim II, Katholikos—Patriarch of the Georgian Orthodox Church

Ефрем II, католикос—
патр. вкарх всея
Грузии. 1960 г.
тбилиси

From left to right: His Holiness Patriarch Alexei; Bishop Peters Strod, religious head of all Roman Catholics in Latvia; the Grand Mufti of Tashkent; and Mgr Turss, Lutheran Archbishop of Riga

His Holiness Patriarch Alexei of Moscow and all the Russias, with Vladimir Kuroiedov, President of the Committee on Affairs of the Russian Orthodox Church

At the jubilee celebrations of the Russian Orthodox Church: the fortieth anniversary of the re-establishment of the Patriarchate of Moscow and all the Russias

having given in on even the smallest point of Christian dogma—and is not that what really counts?

An actual encounter with Metropolitan Nikolai would convince anyone of this great prelate's dignity and uprightness. His tall stature, his regular features and neatly groomed grey beard, and his serious, but nonetheless kind, expression all combine to make him almost the archetype of the high-ranking Russian Orthodox clergyman. I had already met him on my visit to Moscow in 1958, and had been told that his health since then had deteriorated because of serious heart attacks and that, as a consequence, he was shortly to give up handling the Church's external affairs. When he was kind enough to receive me again during this last visit, however, I could detect no particular signs of physical weakness as he greeted me in a vast drawing-room, furnished richly in mahogany, and hung with glorious ikons and a painting of St George and the Dragon.

We immediately became involved in a serious but cordial conversation, in which he confirmed the information given in the official publication *The Russian Orthodox Church* (The Moscow Patriarchate: 1958).

'I have not the slightest fear for the Church's future,' he said. 'Battered by waves of propaganda, she remains solid and unshakable as a rock. Hostile attacks do nothing but stimulate the devotion of believers and, instead of schools, mothers themselves are giving their children religious education; liturgical services and reading through the Bible have strengthened the religious faith of millions.

'During the past fifteen years, we have been able to revive a powerful organization which had been shaken by hardships during the preceding period. This organization, which is governed by apostolic canons and the decrees of the ecumenical and national councils, is headed by His Holiness the Patriarch, who is President of the Holy Synod, which is composed of six members, all residential bishops, three of whom, the Metropolitans of Krutitsa, Kiev and Leningrad, are permanent members.

To handle the business of the Church's various branches of government, we have created the Office of Administration of Patriarchal Affairs, the Office of External Relations of the Church, the Directive Committee on Theological Education, a material administrative office, the Committee for Pensions and a publishing service.

'We get no financial aid whatever from the State, but our needs are amply taken care of by the freewill offerings of the faithful.

'To give you some idea of the work done in the material sphere alone, let me mention that, during recent years, the Patriarchate has spent millions of rubles on restoration work connected with the churches of the monasteries of the Trinity and St Sergei, and of the Assumption at Potshaev; the Cathedral of St Vladimir at Kiev; the Cathedral of St Nikolai and the basilicas of the Transfiguration, of St Vladimir, of the Holy Trinity and of the Monastery of St Alexander Nevski, in Leningrad; the churches of the Pskovo-Petchersky monastery; the cathedrals at Kishinev, Zhitomir, Rostov on the Don, Cheboksary and other cities; the buildings used by the Moscow Academy of Theology in Zagorsk and other religious educational institutions.

'New churches are built without any trouble wherever a real need for one exists, which is not the case in Moscow, where their number seems sufficient for the moment. Still, even in this region, a considerable number of churches have sprung up in rural areas during the last few years. Churches have even been constructed in the new large, industrial areas, such as Stalingrad, Murmansk or Magnitogorsk (which recently acquired two new churches).

'The Orthodox Church now has, spread over Soviet territory, 73 dioceses, which are governed by 7 metropolitans, 37 archbishops and 29 bishops. Our parishes number somewhere near 20,000, to which we should add some 3,000 "houses of prayer" or chapels; we also have 69 monasteries and convents which shelter men and women who, even in this day and age, are eager to pursue the monastic ideal.

'It would be difficult for me to give you exact figures for the number of faithful. Because of the separation of Church and State, we do not keep lists of parishioners as used to be done under the Tsars. If you keep in mind the number of parishes, however, you can work from that to some sort of approximation. It is surprising how crowded our churches are today; some parishes even have thousands of parishioners. Even if you count the memberships in these latter as one or two thousand per parish, you will see that you finish with an impressive grand total.[1]

'We are giving special attention to the training of new priests, which is now done in eight seminaries and two theological academies. Some of these young men come from the old clerical class, but many of our present priests are former technicians and doctors. Before a priest can be appointed to a parish in Moscow or Leningrad, he must first pass an examination at the Theological Academy in either of those cities; it is sufficient to have been graduated from a seminary to be appointed to a rural parish.

'Until now, our priests have had no other means of support but the donations of their parishioners, and they have sometimes been accused of having extravagant incomes. To counteract this slander, we are in the midst of setting up a new system; in the diocese of Moscow, half of the curates are paid by the bishop and give him all the revenues of their parishes in return; in some other dioceses, all the priests are already receiving salaries. According to the size and importance of the parish, these salaries go from 800 to 1,500 rubles a month, in rural areas, to between 2,000 and 2,500 rubles in Moscow, a sum which is about enough to support a family decently after taxes have been deducted.

'What has stirred up a lot of jealousy of the clergy is the motor-cars which some of them have at their disposal. The thing to remember here is that they do not own those cars personally; they belong to the individual parish and, when one takes into

[1] Thus, multiplying the 20 to 23,000 parishes by 1,000 or by 2,000 the total would be about 25,000,000, or 50,000,000 believers, this latter total being about one-fourth the total population.

account the considerable distances sometimes involved in a priest's ministry, they are necessary professional equipment. Most of our priests find it very difficult to do everything connected with being in charge of a parish, especially when it comes to the Sunday sermon, which is by no means the least of a priest's duties.

'Present Russian Orthodox Church jurisdiction includes some parishes of the Autonomous Orthodox Church of China, the Exarchate of Western Europe and the Exarchate of the Two Americas, a diocese in Belgium, deaneries in Austria and Hungary, the metoichias of Belgrade, Sofia and Beirut, and missions in Japan and Korea. We are in constant and fraternal contact with the great Autocephalic Churches of Constantinople, Alexandria, Antioch, Jerusalem, Georgia, Poland, Czechoslovakia and the various Balkan countries.

'Our attitude towards the various non-Orthodox religious groups is based on our Lord's wish that there be one flock and one shepherd and is motivated by fraternal love in Christ which, while excluding both proselytism and indifference, impels us towards mutual understanding and co-operation. Recent years have seen our friendly contacts with most Christian groups increased and fortified; among such groups are the Armenian Gregorian Church, the Anglican Church, the Old Catholic Church, the Episcopal Church in the United States, the Coptic and Ethiopian Churches, most of the Reformed and Lutheran Churches, the Society of Friends, the World Council of Churches and its different national branches, the British Council of Churches, the International Society of Friends of Reconciliation (a pacifist group), the English Society of the Friends of Reconciliation, the English interconfessional body known as "Christian Action" and the American Bible Society.

'We have exchanged visits with most of these bodies and I do not feel I need point out that relations between ourselves and the Anglican clergy grow stronger every day.

'I cannot give you any sort of decisive comment on the

Ecumenical Council which the Pope has called to meet at Rome in the near future. We do not expect to be invited to the council, and it has only been through the Press that we have been able to gather even the vaguest idea of the structure, ends and programme of this great meeting. We shall be able to make our attitude clearer when we know more.

'I have learned that Patriarch Athenagoras of Constantinople has given public evidence of his interest in the council; but that interest was strictly personal and, when he was asked if he would send observers to the council, he felt it necessary to reply that he would not.

'The situation will remain as it is now until things have developed more.

'To conclude, let me say a few more words on the point of our relations with the secular authorities. How could we possibly abstain from using every means at our disposal to contribute to a movement which aims at the well-being of the Soviet people? How should we not be proud of the extraordinary progress made in technology, science and education by the present regime and which has transformed the old ignorant and backward Russia into one of the world's most developed countries? How can we refuse to co-operate in propagandizing for international peace? This is no Communist slogan; it is a verse from the Scriptures: "Peace on earth to men of good will. . . ." '

.   .   .   .   .

Leaving Metropolitan Nikolai, I was deeply impressed by his remarks, which were as precise as they were moving. Nevertheless, my doubts had not been quashed. Though the Orthodox Church's position in the Soviet Russia had improved beyond all reasonable hopes during the past fifteen years, would she still be strong enough, in the long run, to hold out against the day by day expansion of materialist and rationalist ideas?

One of the Patriarchate's officials, the very charming and

helpful Mr Buyevsky, who acts as angel guardian to all foreign visitors and is a mine of information about the religious centres throughout Russia, strove to reassure me on this point during an excellent luncheon at a Hungarian restaurant. Our meal consisted of delightful national dishes, accompanied by an excellent Tokay, but, as always happens in similar cases, our attention was on a subject far more sublime than gastronomy.

'What you are afraid of,' he said, 'originates in a false supposition. Religion is not philosophy; the churchgoer believes that the Holy Spirit comes down to men through the sacraments, and our Church boldly declares that that is all he needs. In itself, the liturgy is a richly spiritual experience which leads to a consciousness of God's Truth. The believer steeps himself in solemnity, the language of the service, its symbolism and tone of its prayers; he is enveloped in an atmosphere of mysticism and his recollection leads him to God. The liturgy's influence on souls can never be sufficiently appreciated, especially among a people as intuitive as ours.

'Furthermore, you must remember that Christian teaching is built on belief in the divine person of Christ and no priest could ever be satisfied with a tendency towards a spirituality expressed independently of established forms of worship.

'No one, therefore, could pretend, without running the risk of exaggerating, that we have lost every possibility of spreading accurate notions about religion. If the ordinary people really did not know anything about religion any more, how could discussions between believers and non-believers go on almost everywhere, among old people as well as among our young people, and even behind university walls?

'Usually, Sunday services are followed by a sermon—a practice to which our Metropolitan attaches particular importance. Preachers avoid political and social problems, but give their congregations the basic precepts of Christian morality and the essential points of Christian doctrine. As you know, the Patriarchate also has a publications service and I think that the editor-in-chief of the *Journal of the Patriarchate of Moscow* would be able to give you more information about its activities.'

. . . . .

During the Middle Ages, Moscow was hemmed in by a circle of monasteries, which also served as a defence line against Tartar invasion. Their bells were sounded to summon and alert the people of the city and, as the enemy drew nearer, their crenellated walls became battlements swarming with armed monks.

Even today the New Monastery of the Virgins, though now completely surrounded by modern Moscow, retains its old war-like look and high redbrick walls, behind which its churches' golden domes excite the curiosity and admiration of tourists. Most of this 'little Kremlin' has been made into a national museum, but more removed parts of the buildings are used by various offices of the Patriarchate, especially its publications service.

It was there, in a spacious suite of offices, that I went to meet Anatol Vedernikov. The monthly he directs allows Orthodox all over the world to keep in touch with the activities of the Patriarchate. Separate from the official party, it provides news about religious life in Russia and abroad and also publishes highly interesting articles on theological subjects (the life and work of saints, the Christian way of life, religious music, the apocryphal Gospels, the teaching of Gregory Palamas, etc.).

Mr Vedernikov told me that the Patriarchate also publishes liturgical books, calendars and collections of the sermons of Patriarch Alexei and Metropolitan Nikolai. Recently, for the first time in Russia for almost forty years, a complete text of the Bible, and a separate volume of the New Testament alone, was published. About 50,000 copies were printed and it is being sold by dioceses and individual parishes.

My talk with Mr Vedernikov soon veered off on to a more general line of thought. He was certainly not without arguments to convince me that the Orthodox Church's influence is making itself felt in more and more quarters. There are many former military men among its priests; one priest, for instance, used to be a colonel; the Bishops of Kaluga, Novgorod and Dmitrov all fought during World War II. But he told me something even more interesting: Bishop Luke of Simferopol was a renowned surgeon before taking orders, had been a professor at the Medical Academy, with the rank of general, and was a laureate of the Stalin prize.

'You may be surprised at this,' Mr Vedernikov began, 'but I insist that anti-religious propaganda is useful to us. In a country as immense as ours, abuses among the clergy could easily go unnoticed, but the Church should almost be grateful to those who uncover these wounds and give her the opportunity of healing them. Much fuss has been made about various apostasies; but even the "Godless" have infinitely more respect for a man who remains faithfully to his convictions and can defend them with dignity.'

Before we parted, I was still to learn that the Patriarchate was preparing to publish the first volume of an annual soon; it was to be devoted entirely to exegetical, liturgical and ecclesiological problems.

After I had returned to Paris, I saw a copy of this annual (*Selected Orthodox Studies*, Moscow: 1960) and found its contents highly interesting. Professor N. Uspensky writes about the Vespers service in the Orthodox Church; Father Borovoy discusses the *Collectio Avellana* as an historical source for East-West relations at the end of the fifteenth century; Professor Ivanov examines New Testament texts and translations, and other authors analyse the Old Believers and the Ecumenical Council of Constantinople held in 1156. I was most impressed by the high quality of scientific scholarship of all these studies.

It was also after my return to Paris that I learned that Metropolitan Nikolai had retired.

Worn out by the responsibilities of his office, that great

prelate had given up his post and gone into retirement at Sukhumy, on the sunny shores of the Black Sea, for a well-deserved rest. His place as Vicar-General of the diocese of Moscow was taken by Metropolitan Pitirim of Leningrad.

The direction of the Church's external affairs has been assumed by Bishop Nicodemus, a very energetic and intelligent prelate who is only thirty-one years old and was consecrated Bishop of Podolsk in July 1960. Time will certainly give him the experience he needs. At the moment, however, it seems to me that with the withdrawal of Metropolitan Nikolai the Russian Orthodox Church has suffered a very heavy loss, his merits are too great, and his role of guarantor of good relations between the Church and State for so many years too important, for him ever to be forgotten.

8

Through Orthodox Parishes

THERE was a time when Moscow was called 'the city of forty times forty churches'—but this was an exaggeration, of course. Even including the many private chapels in the homes of the nobility and wealthy merchants would bring the number of Orthodox places of worship to about 600; and among those were the many shaky wooden church-buildings destroyed during the Revolution and the two world wars.

How many are there today? Perhaps about fifty, which is, perhaps, a figure not high enough to meet the needs of all the faithful, but not so extraordinary if we compare it to the number churches in Paris, for example, which is the capital of a Catholic country.[1]

During my stay in Moscow, nothing amused me more than to hear an American tourist say: 'And I thought they were forbidden to pray!' The good lady should rest assured on that point; there is no Government in the world which is likely to 'forbid' praying. And so far as Soviet Russia is concerned, we have already pointed out at length that worship enjoys complete liberty there. Anyone staying at my hotel could have had conclusive proof of that by going to the little chapel nearby, a few steps from the Central Post Office, where continuous services are held before the miraculous ikon of 'Our Lady Searching for Lost Souls'.

[1] In 1960, the official Guide to Moscow published a list of 55 churches used for Orthodox worship. The proportion of churches in other large, urban centres should be almost the same. Leningrad now has 15, as opposed to the 90 it had before the Revolution, and the parishes in its diocese number almost 300.

I went into any number of other churches—the vast patriarchal Cathedral of the Epiphany, the Church of St John the Warrior, and the Church of the Entombment of Christ, where a memorial service is held every morning in memory of the venerated Patriarch Tikhon, whose remains rest nearby in a chapel in the Donskoy Monastery, no longer used for religious purposes.

No matter which church I went into I always found large and devout crowds of people assisting at the services; I met priests who had had the opportunity to visit Paris and London and they told me how astounded they had been to find houses of God in the West so frequently empty.

Nor will I quickly forget the incomparable beauty of the liturgical singing during the Office, done by the two excellent choirs of the Church of Our Lady, Comforter of the Afflicted.

This church stands on the left bank of the Moscova river. In front of it runs the broad street which has been known as the Ordynka ('Street of the Horde') since that time centuries ago when the envoys of the Kremlin set off from this spot to reach the camp of the Mongol Horde which had been set up along the Lower Volga.

During the old regime the parish ministered to many wealthy merchants who had chosen to live in this quiet area.

Its curate, Father Mikhail Zernov, is, perhaps, one of the most intelligent men it was my privilege to meet while in the Soviet Union, and the long conversations he was gracious enough to hold with me are etched deep in my memory.[1]

'My own family,' he said, 'were business people. My parents were educated and enlightened people, as also were their friends. Believe me when I say that the idea of entering a seminary could only have developed in me in an atmosphere as intellectual as our home's, during a time when the clergy were the allies of the police and when the names of His Imperial Majesty and all the members of his august family were printed in our liturgical books

[1] Father Zernov has been recently consecrated bishop.

in capital letters, while God, our Lord, had to be satisfied with lower-case letters.

'Things are different now, however, and worship and religion are no one's slaves. Of course the teachings of religion and materialist dogmas are completely contradictory. But there is room for some sort of agreement. We must never forget that, in the field of morality, atheist Communism's goal is the same as Christianity's. It is not too much to suppose that the precepts of the Gospels would, perhaps, be more easily realizable in a system where people are not swayed, as in the West, by the single-minded desire for lucrative gain—licit or not—and where no journalist or film producer would think of surrounding crime and murders of passion with the rosy glow of romanticism.

'Is not the "man of the future" expected to lead an exemplary private life? Do we not expect him to be unswervingly attached to the ideal of peace? Do we not preach the equality of all races to him? And, as a result, have we not been seeing a new generation grow up before us, eminently balanced, healthy, devoted to their obligations and completely different from any past generation?

'I know that you will make objections to what I have just said. Basing your comments on what you have read in newspaper articles, you may protest that we are also having an outbreak of juvenile delinquency in our cities. That is not true; the only "delinquents" involved are a negligible minority of alcoholics and some young people who have gone astray; they are our society's offscourings, and we are right in taking all possible steps to rid ourselves of them.

'Ordinary people have nothing to do with this unhappy business, and there is really nothing to be surprised about if our young men, taking their example from French students [sic], have started putting their arms around the shoulders of their girl-friends—something which used to be absolutely unheard of in public.

'It is also a fact that, now, no one can "make his way" by using bigotry to bolster up his qualifications. So far as I am concerned, I am very happy to say that I intensely dislike self-centred hypocrisy. Conditions under the new regime remind me of the parable of the Two Brothers: the Socialists *say* that they will not yield to any divine law, but their actions show that they do, while the Capitalist world, which calls itself Christian, claims that it submits to divine law, but its actions contradict its claims.

'At one time, the whole of society lived under the influence of religion and religious ideas. Now, however, we have moved into an era of antithesis in which most people are indifferent to religion. But I am absolutely convinced that a future era of total synthesis is inevitable. Truth is one; the Communists and Socialists are looking for it in their own way, but it was revealed to us by Jesus Christ. The time is coming when they will join us.

'Consider this, for example. The Christian Churches teach a doctrine of divine providence and free will which, we are told, is contrary to Marxist doctrine. But wasn't it Karl Marx himself who discovered the laws of that evolution of human society which is effected over and above the individual will? Take his statement and substitute "divine providence" for "the laws of evolution" and you will see that it matches the Church's teaching completely.

'But we can go a step further. Doesn't materialist philosophy include the principles of infinity and eternity in its notion of the world? And isn't it a fact that the same atom people used to define as an indivisible particle is now considered by experts as a reservoir of energy? And isn't this same energy governed by natural laws which we recognize as having their source in a Creator?

'Our critics say that our churches are just "social centres for old ladies". I am certainly not going to deny that, as in every other country in the world, our "pillars of the Church" are mostly old people. But these so-called "grandmothers" or "babushkas" are not as old as they might seem. They suffered a great deal during the last war, and those hardships have left many of them looking much older than they really are. Actually, most of them are not even fifty years old; they have all, therefore, been educated in Soviet schools and along Marxist lines—but that has not prevented them from remaining loyal to their religious beliefs.

'You yourself must surely have noticed that there are always a good number of grown men, young people and children at the services in our churches. Furthermore, conversions are increasing in every quarter, and have been helped along by our priests' tolerant attitude. A passerby is overcome by curiosity and goes into a church—something he has not done for twenty years, perhaps. Moved by the beauty of the church's decoration and the singing, and everything which reminds him of the traditional splendours of old Russia, he stays until the end of the service to ask for information. To his surprise, he is told that there is no question of "signing on" or of registering, as he would have to do if he were dealing with any of the civil administrative branches. He soon sees that the priest is not at all concerned about his political opinions. And the Church takes one more son to her arms.

'Of course, everything in the Church's life is not sweetness and light. The training given in our seminaries, for instance, does not completely come up to the needs of our times; parochial supervision is not efficient enough, and some of the officials of the Patriarchate still retain something of the spirit of the old, imperialist Holy Synod—but I have seen a new generation of priests coming up, and I am full of confidence for the future.'

Not all Moscow's clergymen share Father Zernov's optimism, of course. Very many of them would be less categorical. They feel, rather, that they are isolated in the middle of a hostile world, and do not minimize the abyss separating their beliefs from materialist theory. They have doubts about the usefulness of discussions with adversaries who are determined to hold fast to their position at any cost; there must, they insist, be other means of helping truth to triumph; no boxer's capabilities can be measured by a dynamometer.

Despite these hesitancies, they are all full of confidence in their mission. 'We have outgrown the time when we had to be

taught by civil wars,' they insist. 'A strongly entrenched governmental authority which has been accepted by the entire nation
recognizes that we are deeply attached to the interests of our
country. It realizes now that it has nothing to fear from the
followers of Christ whose kingdom was "not of this world". On
the contrary, that Government is beginning to see that society's
stability can be otherwise threatened by untrained and uneducated
atheists.'

.   .   .   .   .

My work in Moscow had finished, and I had spoken with the
directors of anti-religious propaganda as well as the leaders of the
Orthodox Church.

Because I wanted to cover as much territory as possible in my
investigation, I decided to set off on a long, meandering tour
which would take me beyond the Volga, into the Caucasus and
the heart of Ukrainia. Wherever I went, I saw open churches with
large congregations and complete freedom of worship.

There is often talk of the 'restrictions' put on foreign tourists
in the Soviet, restrictions which keep them from going 'wherever
they choose'. I think that that accusation is unjustified. Russia
is a country which has always been extremely badly equipped for
tourism. In Tsarist days anyone going for a trip in the country
stayed with friends or relatives and no one, except some rare
commercial travellers or newly appointed minor officials, ever
dreamt of staying at an inn or small hotel. Intourist is putting
forth great efforts to supply this lack of accommodation, and
the itineraries it provides for its clients are so laid out as to satisfy
even the most curious; in fact, a tourist would have to have
almost unlimited energy—and finances—to be able to visit all the
Intourist hotels scattered through Russia's cities and provinces.

With official permission, it sometimes happened that I
wandered off the route of ordinary, mapped-out tours. Every
time I did, I regretted it, because of the difficulty I encountered in
finding lodgings, restaurants and transport. Any tourist who did

not know the language and regional customs would certainly become lost and, at the end of the day, would find himself at the only place where he could get directions—the police station.

People in the Soviet Union do an enormous amount of travelling, especially in the summer. Holidays provide a perfect opportunity to spend the money they cannot spend elsewhere in the crowded, but poorly stocked, shops.

No one is put off by great distances; one can see simply dressed women boarding aeroplanes at air terminals as though they were boarding suburban buses. Trains are always crowded to capacity, and only Intourist can make reservations for trains and they will even guide you through the crowded waiting-rooms to your compartment. There is a special office at Moscow, for less ambitious travelling, where one may reserve a place in one of the special taxis which are public transport vehicles and go to neighbouring cities and towns.

It was in one of these extremely comfortable taxis that I left Moscow for Vladimir one lovely Sunday morning. We drove along a magnificent road which is the first section of a highway, as yet uncompleted, which will probably be the longest in the world and stretch from the capital to the Pacific Ocean. As we drove along through typical Russian countryside, with its rolling fields, clumps of birches and dark forests on the horizon, I saw the belltower of a white-walled church rise up about every fifteen miles, its green or golden domes shining in the sun. Some of them were closed, but I could see men and women going into others to attend Sunday services.

After a journey of about three or four hours, we went in through the imposing Gates of Gold, flanked on either side by towers dating back to 1164, and had arrived at the ancient city which, before Moscow, was, for a time, the residence of the Great Princes of Russia.

The Cathedral of the Assumption has a place of distinction among all its many historical monuments. Built by Prince Andrei Bogolubski towards the end of the twelfth century with the help of 'artisans who came from all over the world', it shows some Romanesque influences and its ikonostasis holds some truly magnificent ikons, some of them the work of Andrei Rublev, the most famous ikon-painter of the Russian Middle Ages.

The service was just ending; hundreds of candles glowed in the dim light and, just as I had noticed in other churches in Moscow, the cathedral was crowded. After the service, I attended the marriage of a young couple in a side-chapel of the cathedral; this is something which is quite rare in present-day Soviet conditions.

A few weeks later, while at the other end of the country in the Caucasus, I watched another religious ceremony of quite another type. It was at Sotchi, the great spa where dozens of 'rest houses' which stretch along in a line about twelve miles long are visited year after year by about 50,000 workers.

The local church stands very near the local railway terminus; no visitor to the city could help seeing its gilded domes.

When I went into the church the choir was singing what sounded like some sort of requiem chant, but I could see no coffin. I discovered that the requiem was being celebrated *in absentia*, a fairly frequent practice when the deceased person has been killed during a war or has died some distance away from his family.

Later, the priest went into a side-chapel, followed by a small group of people. A woman who looked about thirty years old led a little boy up to the font to be baptized. She had come all the way from Barnaul, a city in Siberia, where apparently there was no church. The boy looked rather sullen and did not make the sign of the Cross; eventually, he seemed to relax and his face brightened and he followed the example of his elders.

That was not the first time I had seen a child influenced by the tone of a situation. While I was in Moscow I went to visit one of the churches in the Kremlin with a schoolboy, who did not take the trouble to remove his cap as he entered. He almost seemed defiant. Since the church is no longer used for worship, no one paid much attention to him. As he looked about, however, he noticed two small groups of youths, schoolboys like himself, all respectfully uncovered and with their caps in their hands. He stopped, looked a little reflective and, after hesitating a bit, took off his cap.

Father Gabriel Makutkin, who is the parish priest at Sotchi, explained to me that many people take advantage of their stay in this seaside resort to 'put themselves right' with their religious duties since they are far away from the criticism of friends and neighbours or, perhaps, simply because there is no priest living in their area.

Consequently, his lovely little church is always busy. In addition to the regular services, he performs about 600 baptisms each year, a few hundred requiem services and even two or three dozen religious weddings. Father Makutkin had nothing to complain about so far as the administration or the attitude of the residents of Sotchi was concerned: 'Everybody here respects me,' he declared, and I was sure he was right, because it is not difficult to have deep respect for such a charming and dignified priest.

A few days before, it was in the heart of the Caucasus, I was received in audience by His Beatitude Ephraim II, Katholikos-Patriarch of the Georgian Orthodox Church, which is independent of the Moscow Patriarchate but bound to it by ties of fraternal affection. He is a man of great erudition, and has written widely on religious and literary subjects, including a dictionary of Georgian archaic usages.

The Katholikos has his residence in Tbilisi, a picturesque and lively city surrounded by hills and with wide, shaded streets. It is the capital of Georgia, the country United States newspapermen insist is 'oppressed' but which its natives proclaim as one of the most prosperous and flourishing of the whole Soviet Union.

Georgia's territory is larger than the combined areas of Belgium, Switzerland and Italy; there are a good number of 'millionaire kolkhozes', co-operative agricultural settlements whose yearly outputs bring in millions of rubles. The Republic's vineyards are spread out over about 250,000 acres and its tea plantations supply all the needs of the entire Soviet Union.

I had every reason to believe that the Katholikos of All Georgia was probably not distressed about material needs in a country like that, but surely there must have been other problems, of a spiritual order, which demanded his attention and energy.

I had, of course, been very much encouraged by the impressions I gathered through contacts with Tbilisi's intellectuals. I recalled that Georgia has been a Christian country much longer than Russia has, since the first half of the fourth century, in fact; surrounded by hostile Moslems, these people have always found their greatest moral support in their religious faith. Their clergy have never been influenced by reactionary tendencies.

While sightseeing in the city, I was taken to see the cathedral of Mzhet, which had recently been restored and reopened for worship; it was pointed out to me as an example of the authorities' eagerness to maintain and restore the magnificent religious monuments of the medieval Caucasus.

Furthermore, I could not find a trace of atheist literature in any of the bookshops I visited; it was obvious that the need to combat religious belief was felt less strongly here than in Moscow. What propaganda I did see was aimed at fanatical sects and the shortcomings of the clergy.

On the other hand, the education given in Georgian schools is no different from that in any other Soviet republic; all young people are trained according to the principles of materialism. Did not the Church suffer because of that?

Speaking with Katholikos Ephraim, I was struck by his reflective air and the obviously great wisdom behind everything he said.

'Anyone responsible for the fate of the Church,' he said, 'is constantly aware of the weight of the cross he has to carry. But he cannot allow himself to be influenced by the difficulties presented by any given situation.

'Our tradition goes back more than a thousand years; I am the one hundred and thirty-ninth in a long line of patriarchs. Our Church's autonomy was abolished in 1811 when Georgia voluntarily joined the Tsarist Empire, but it was restored in 1917; for an entire century, therefore, we were governed by a Russian archbishop with the title of Exarch.

'In 1943, the Patriarch of Moscow formally recognized our independence. We have recovered our old independence, but, though we still have seventeen dioceses, we have no more than 150 parishes to serve three and a half million people who used to be ministered to by about a thousand priests.

'Our seminarians currently study at seminaries in Moscow and Stalingrad, but when we have our own seminary at Tbilisi, probably soon, candidates will certainly be numerous.

'The local delegate of the Government committee has shown that he understands our aims and position very well; a mature, calm and thoughtful man, he gave us his support when we wanted to build a new church at Poti.

'We are not particularly affected by anti-religious propaganda, which uses mostly scientific arguments. There is no doubt that many of my countrymen have given up practising their religion. But how can anyone pretend to know another man's real attitude towards religion? Are not all men prey to their friends' and acquaintances' shifting opinions? If the Government's attitude should change even the slightest bit, 99 per cent of the people who are indifferent to religion today would crowd our churches tomorrow. But did not the same thing, or something very like it, happen in France at the end of the revolutionary period?

'People today think that science can solve all problems, but the human soul's interior life will always be genuinely mysterious, no matter how great modern civilization's concrete progress is.

'It was a great pleasure to see very many students at our services last Easter. There had been rumours that there would be trouble that night, but I do not know why. Absolutely nothing happened; no one interrupted the services, and all the young people in the congregation came up to kiss my handcross after the liturgy. I consider that a good sign for the future.'

Because of his high official position, the Katholikos naturally refrained from referring to the sufferings endured by his Church during the civil war, sufferings which were particularly violent in this country of headstrong mountain-people. I knew that, after the re-establishment of the autocephalic Church of Georgia, its first Katholikos died of exhaustion, that his successor, Katholikos Ambrose, was sentenced to imprisonment, and that the Metropolitan of Kutais was assassinated.

I also knew that, under the old regime, there were 2,455 churches in Georgia, and twenty-seven monasteries, most of which were afterwards closed to worship or destroyed.

In Georgia, however, as in the rest of the Soviet Union, no one likes to talk about the past; people who were the victims of reprisals, justified or not, always say, even in conversation with their closest friends, that they were 'involuntary victims of an historical necessity'. I myself have heard the same phrase over and over again, even when talking with friends and acquaintances I have known for many years.

The head of the Church of Georgia was doing what everyone else did: he admitted the surprising improvement in the situation and remained confident that things would get even better.

.   .   .   .   .   .

After a very short flight in an Aeroflot aeroplane, I found myself in the midst of the Ukrainian plains, far from the mountains of Georgia. The Kiev airport is out in the country, about thirty kilometres from the city. As we drove towards Kiev, I felt a genuine thrill at seeing the dozen golden domes of the Petchersky Monastery growing larger and larger, as they towered above the monastery hill on the other side of the Dnieper, in a burst of reflected light beneath a dazzling sun. No matter how often one visits any of Russia's large cities, this breathtaking view always takes one by surprise.

Formerly the 'breadbasket' of Europe, modern Ukrainia is now a highly industrialized country. Eleven and a half million acres of the country's rich, black soil still furnish grain for domestic needs, but the economic centre of gravity has shifted towards industry, whose production is now twenty-two times what it was in 1913 and has been further enlarged during the past three years by 500 new factories of major importance.

Ukrainia's modern iron and steel industry alone has a higher production rate than all the Tsarist empire's had. Secondary schools are twenty times the number they were before the Revolution and there are ten times as many students enrolled in institutions of higher education.

Once again, in different circumstances this time, I wondered what effect this increased economic and educational level had had on religious loyalties.

My first visit after arriving in Kiev was, naturally, to the great monastery, the cradle of Russian Christianity. A thousand years ago, the wooded Petchersky district, now a suburb of Kiev, was a hideout for Varengian warriors and, later, a refuge for hermits who dug cells for themselves out of the region's limestone as shelter against rough weather.

By the beginning of the eleventh century, this settlement had developed into a subterranean monastery 'of the Caves', Petchersky in Russian, whose monks have stood as models of Russian holiness for subsequent generations.

Down through the centuries, the Petchersky Monastery has always been one of Russia's leading religious and cultural centres and countless thousands of Orthodox faithful have gone there on pilgrimage. Its inevitable expansion led to the building of a second section, on a hill overlooking the first.

I must confess that I felt rather depressed after I had gone into the Upper Monastery one fine Sunday morning. Everything looked so desolate. I had just opened the magnificent entry gate, built over a twelfth-century chapel, when I was face to face with a vast heap of ruins, all that is left of the magnificent Cathedral of the Ascension, a masterpiece of old Russian architecture that was destroyed during the Second World War.

Surrounding it are what used to be the monks' cells, now used as workers' homes or for offices and in a state of dilapidation.

The Upper Monastery has been constituted a national museum, but restoration work which is taken care of with great expedition in other places seems to be going very slowly. Only the beautiful Church of 'Christ beneath the Birches' is in perfect condition, and many people visit it to pray before the tomb of Prince Yuri Dolgoruki, the founder of Moscow.

I sat down on a bench in the central court of the monastery to contemplate its ruins and muse over its past greatness. A stranger came up to me and said: 'I can tell that you are Russian, sir, so I feel I can speak freely with you about something which is sad, but all too true. Our Orthodox Church lives in oppression. Here, they have closed the hostel where pilgrims used to be able to stay and rest. If anyone wants to become a monk, he runs into all sort of trouble at the labour registry; there are only about fifty monks left in the monastery. But I suppose the local representative of the Committee for Orthodox Affairs is delighted with the situation—he is a determined enemy of religion.'

At this point, a woman joined us on the bench and entered into our conversation. 'We pray and suffer in silence,' she said. 'They say that our beautiful cathedral was destroyed by "Fascist barbarians", but the real truth is quite different. It was deliberately burned down before the war so that people could not use it to pray in. People stood sobbing and in tears as they watched it burn. I often think about it now, but I find some comfort in going to services in other churches and was very moved when the priest at one of them gave a sermon in which he told us about the undying strength of fraternal love.'

Afterwards, I was able to check this woman's tale, and discovered that there was not a word of truth in it. The claim that the monastery cathedral was deliberately burned down by the civil authorities in 1938 or 1939, as she insisted, though she admitted she had not been there, is simply a lie. According to the most authoritative witnesses, among them the members of the Ukrainian Exarchate, the disaster took place during a bombardment of Kiev during the war, and no one can say with certainty whether it was the result of Russian or German bombs, though it seems most likely that these latter were responsible.

Despite this discrepancy, my meeting with these two people was most symptomatic of what some people in Kiev felt. It was the first time since I had been in the Soviet Union that I had heard anyone bewailing 'religious persecution', real or imaginary. Obviously, at least some people in Kiev were upset at their situation. I wondered why. Was it because local authorities were stubbornly unsympathetic? Did it grow out of the separatist feelings which have always been strong in Ukrainia or out of a religious spirit which is stronger than any other regions?' I could not say.

On the other hand, I had only to go into the Lower Monastery to see for myself how inaccurate the information I had just been given was. The part of the monastery open to worship was far from deserted. People strode across the forecourt to the little cathedral and dozens of women were praying in the porch because they were unable to get into the church, already crowded to bursting.

I made my way through the crowd—not without difficulty— and once more was able to join in the chanting of the Creed which the whole congregation sang with great fervour and feeling. A boy lay in prayer on the altar steps beside me and he seemed to be in a trance, so immobile was he. I was on the point of thinking he had fainted, but he rose from his knees and his face was so bright with ecstatic joy that I wondered how I could have thought he was ill.

From what I saw, it is far easier to destroy a piece of architecture than uproot faith from men's souls.

I was no less reassured on this point by what I was told by Bishop Nestor, the Superior of the monastery, who received me

THROUGH ORTHODOX PARISHES

after the service. Like every other clerical official in the Soviet Union, he had sometimes encountered difficulties, but had no particular complaint to make. Life was going on in its ordinary course, and faith would conquer all obstacles.

I had still another evidence of this while going through the caves beneath the Church of St Antony. With an old monk as guide, I had gone down beneath the church with about twenty women, all wearing white headscarves, and obviously come from some distance to make the same pilgrimage which thousands of others have made down through the centuries.

There are two or three small chapels in the crypt of the church, and numerous cells which are the tombs of monks of the monastery who lived in the eleventh century; their bodies have been miraculously preserved from corruption.

In less than half an hour we brushed past forty coffins, all open. Peering through the half-light, I could make out the monks' shrivelled bodies through the pieces of glass now used as covers for the coffins; their hands were completely without flesh, like skeletal hands covered with parchment. One of them was a prince, another was a priest, still another was a monk who had died with a reputation for holiness. Their heads were covered with violet silk veils embroidered in very pale gold, and their bodies seemed to be wrapped in blue shrouds. Each of them was an individual in life, but death made them all look alike; only bishops could be distinguished by their episcopal crowns. With the light of the candles they carried flickering on their faces, the pilgrims kissed each of the coffins and signed themselves.

But a most extraordinary demonstration was waiting for me in one of the small chapels where, without the direction of any priest or monk, all these women broke out into song, chanting hymns antiphonally.

Here at last I had seen the 'Church of the Catacombs' that Western journalists like to write about. But there was nothing sad or afflicted about the scene; on the contrary, these pilgrims had not come down into this dark chapel to hide from Government persecutions. They were simply manifesting their faith and devotion in one of the most sacred places in all Russia.

.   .   .   .   .

During the next few days, I became acquainted with Kiev, most of whose central part was almost completely destroyed during the Second World War. I was struck by the beauty of the broad streets, with a double row of chestnuts planted down the middle of each, and lined with six- or nine-storey buildings decorated in the Ukrainian style—according to a general plan absolutely unique in all of Europe.

I came upon the Cathedral of St Sophia which was built between 1037 and 1046, and is now a national museum. The Church could not afford to undertake the restoration of the cathedral's frescoes and mosaics, so the work is now being done under the supervision of the Academy of Sciences, with a substantial subsidy from the Ukrainian Government. It will still take several more years to restore the frescoes, which were buried under three to five layers of paint, but the mosaics are already visible to visitors who are overwhelmed by the astonishing variety of their 130 tones, green, brown, yellow and gold.

The neighbouring Cathedral of St Vladimir is open for worship. Not a very old building, it is decorated with glorious paintings by Vasnetzov, Nesterov and other famous painters of the nineteenth century. This magnificent cathedral is the church of the Metropolitan of Kiev.

I had occasion to attend services there, surrounded by a great congregation which included many men; I had never heard as fine a choir anywhere else.

I did not have time to do more than merely have a hasty glance at the superb Church of St Andrew, a baroque building constructed by the great architect, Rastrelli, and also open for worship, as are several others.

I had a very interesting talk with Father Skoropostizhni, secretary of the Exarchate of Ukrainia and administrator of the diocese of Kiev's 600 parishes.[1] We had a long discussion about the situation of the local clergy and he admitted that not all of them were sufficiently well equipped for an ideological battle against the defenders of atheism. On the other hand, the apostasies which attract so much attention in his area left him absolutely unperturbed. He told me that renegade priests do not number more than one per cent of the entire clerical population. They are generally men of dubious background who became priests to avoid being sent to work in Germany during the occupation of Ukrainia. Men like these are no threat to the convictions of the people.

When I visited the Pokrovski convent, which was reopened in 1942, I felt particularly reassured. Notified beforehand that I should be arriving, the superior of the convent, Mother Raphaila, met me at the door and very graciously invited me to take some refreshment. She took me round to see the convent's two churches, its gardens, its cemetery and the workshops, where many of the nuns make the bedquilts which are sold by co-operatives for twenty-five rubles apiece. Other nuns paint ikons and sew and embroider sacerdotal vestments.

There are 245 nuns in the convent, about 100 of whom are still novices, since a woman may not take vows as a nun until she is fifty years old; half of the novices have entered the convent during the past ten years and almost all of them have had at least a secondary education. Many of the nuns are graduate nurses and took care of wounded during the last war.

As we passed them, I noticed the respect with which the nuns greeted their superior. The convent was like a quiet island of peace and contemplative recollection in the midst of the great city of Kiev.

One lovely summer evening I went for a stroll through the

[1] There are as many as 8,000 churches in Ukrainia's seventeen dioceses and 700 of them are in the diocese of Vinnitza alone.

gardens which overhang the banks of the Dnieper. There is an avenue which goes along the embankment and is lined with restaurants and cinemas, screened by willows and chestnuts.

A loudspeaker poured music out over the paths where people were taking the evening air and strolling along quietly. Suddenly, everyone stopped and a crowd of a hundred or two people gathered; interrupting the musical programme, the announcer reported that an American aircraft had been shot down over Soviet waters on the Barents Sea. The announcement was repeated once, and then again, but no one moved; people listened in complete silence. When the report had ended, the crowd dispersed, still silent and with looks of consternation on their faces. It was obvious that the idea of an international conflict, even far away, held absolutely nothing for the people of Kiev to rejoice about.

High above us on the top of a hill, stood a huge monument. I walked up to it and a panorama of a vast plain, many kilometres in area, stretched out before me, while above me stood the gigantic bronze statue of St Vladimir holding a cross in his hand, as though he were still blessing the country to which, over a thousand years ago, he had first brought the light of Christ.

.   .   .   .   .

On the next day a powerful motor-car took me to the kolkhoz of Trebukhovo, about forty miles from Kiev. I have never understood why Intourist guides seem so reluctant to take foreigners to these collectives which should now, rather than anything else, be a source of legitimate pride to them.

I chose this village rather than any other because it was the only one in that area where I would be able to attend a church service during the week; Trebukhovo was celebrating the feast of the patrons of its church, SS Peter and Paul.

It was by no means a wealthy kolkhoz; its 1,200 families had to support themselves on the produce they grew on its sandy, clayey soil. Despite this, I found nothing reminiscent of the old poverty of rural Russia; there were 1,700 head of cattle, 400 horses, a garage which held fifteen tractors, twelve harvesters and thirty-one private motor-cars, two doctors, a dentist, four nurses, an amateur theatrical group and a secondary school for 800 pupils. The community was scheduled to receive a nursery for 450 children, a hospital with thirty-five beds and a 'house of culture' during 1961. I certainly never expected such obvious prosperity.

Still, I had not come to the village to study Soviet agricultural progress. My attention was focussed on the many-domed church from which liturgical singing was echoing.

The large wooden building, decorated in the style of the Kiev cathedrals, is large enough to hold a thousand people. On this week-day, however, there were only about three or four hundred men and women in the congregation. Many children were in the church with their parents, and others played outside. The service was unusually long, but the whole congregation was attentive and fervent.

At the end of the service I introduced myself to the priest, an old man whose eyes were full of kindness and love. He asked me to come to his presbytery, a modest little wooden house. Like his parish, Father Peter was celebrating the feast of his own patron saint and had invited some of his parishioners to join him in a simple but, like all country-meals, copious luncheon: *paté*, chicken, salad and tart, with some small glasses of vodka. Times had changed: we were far from the days in 1935 when a foreign visitor summed up the weekly parish collection as five loaves of black bread, four green apples and one egg,[1] but the rooms of the cottage were narrow and the furniture scanty.

For once, I was able to see for myself just how far from the truth are those allegations that the Orthodox clergy are being gradually corrupted by the luxury which surrounds them.

Soon, a very lively conversation began around the table. The priest boasted of the kindly attitude of his parishioners and the local authorities, with whom he lived in perfect accord. The

[1] Paul B. Anderson, op. cit.

conversation next swung round to topics of the day's news, especially the shooting-down of the American aircraft.

One old farmer who had fought in the Second World War offered his belligerent opinion: 'We can't take the provocations of our enemies any longer without striking back.' Father Peter immediately began to bring all his efforts to bear on calming our fellow-guest's enthusiasm and ended by getting the upper hand; at his suggestion, we all drank to peace among men of good will.

Could I give a more conclusive proof of the beneficent influence exercised by Orthodox priests in the thousands of parishes spread across Russia?

9

The Seminarians

A S I TRAVELLED through Orthodox parishes, only rarely
did I meet a young priest. White hair and grizzled beards
showed that most of the priests I met were older men.
How was this age-gap to be filled? What steps had been taken,
and what progress made, to form new ranks of the clergy? These
were questions that inevitably arose in the mind of any investi-
gator.

There are now two theological academies in the Moscow
Patriarchate (one at Leningrad and the other at the Monastery of
the Trinity and St Sergei, near the capital) and eight seminaries
(at Moscow, Leningrad, Kiev, Minsk, Odessa, Saratov, Stavropol
and in Volhynia).

In view of the present and inevitable future needs of the 20,000
parishes, the number of seminaries seems quite small. On the other
hand, that there are so many operating is already considerable, in
view of the fact that for twenty-five years, and until 1944, all
institutions of religious education were closed, except for a theological institute which operated for a time at Leningrad after the
Revolution, and some clandestine schools which were able to
keep going elsewhere.

It was extremely difficult to fill the gap created during the
time-lapse; many professors and experienced priests had died, and
others had given up their ecclesiastical vocation altogether. The
work done by the men responsible for reviving religious education after the inauguration of the Theological Institute at Moscow,

in June 1944, was all the more remarkable in view of the fact that the level of candidates for the priesthood had fallen considerably.

'Professors at the Institute,' we read in the life of Patriarch Sergei, 'were no longer faced with classes of students of the old type, but with young, up-to-date young men who, in many cases, had come to the seminary without the slightest understanding of what religion really meant.'

Two streams of thought immediately sprang up in religious educational circles. One of them, directed by Bishop Gregory (later to become Metropolitan of Leningrad), insisted that it was absolutely necessary that seminarians absorb the rich theological heritage of past centuries, while adapting themselves to the conditions of modern life; the other group accented the immediate need created by the many parishes which had no priests.

Gradually, the two attitudes balanced one another off and a compromise was arrived at. It has been formulated by the information services of the Patriarchate in these words: 'The principal task facing schools of theology, whether secondary or more advanced, is to provide for the training of future Orthodox priests who will be well instructed and imbued with religious principles, men who will be shepherds of souls because they are convinced such is their vocation, and will be able to stimulate men's moral resources to new energy and life, and thus promote the country's spiritual advancement.'

During the first few years after religious education had been revived, many of the seminarians had been admitted to the schools without preliminary examination and were obviously too poorly equipped to keep up with the course of studies; a good half of the students at the Theological Institute found themselves forced to leave after having failed the first set of examinations.

It was no less difficult to find professors for the schools. In 1947 there were only nineteen at the new Theological Academy at Moscow, and it was not until 1954 that there were twenty-four. At first the Leningrad institution had to struggle along

Old Believers attend the funeral of Archbishop Irinarchos at the Rogozhski cemetery in Moscow

Mgr Flavian, the Old Believers' Archbishop of Moscow, surrounded by his clergy at the celebration of the golden jubilee of his ordination

Old Believers at the parish church of the village of Strelnikovo, Kostroma region

After service at Strelnikovo: two Old Believers in traditional costume

with thirteen professors, and there were twenty of them in 1954.[1]

Present candidates for seminaries must be at least eighteen years old and have a secondary school certificate; be able to read Slavonic texts with ease and recite a large number of prayers; have a letter of recommendation from their parish priest which has been countersigned by their diocesan bishop. In order to be admitted into one of the Theological Academies, a young man must first complete four years of advanced studies and must sit for special examinations in all his seminary studies and receive at least honourable mention for his performance in the examinations.

The subjects studied in the seminaries are: ecclesiastical history and Sacred Scripture; dogmatic, moral, fundamental and comparative theology; pastoral methods; homiletics; typology; liturgical studies; history of the Church in general and of the Russian Orthodox Church in particular; critical studies of schismatical and heretical teachings; the Constitution of the U.S.S.R.; Church Slavonic; Greek and Latin; three modern languages of individual choice; Church music.

The curriculum at the Theological Academies is, of course, more extensive. In addition to the subjects taught in the seminaries, students at these academies also study patrology; pastoral and ascetic theology; the history of Christian art, of the primitive Church, and of Byzantine and Slavic church architecture; historical and critical surveys of Catholicism and Protestantism; Canon Law and Hebrew.

In addition to their ordinary classes, seminarians are expected to carry on some individual project about which they are responsible for periodic reports during their classes. During each scholastic year, they must submit four or five papers on assigned topics and students in the last two years must also give one sermon.

[1] For a more detailed account of the situation, cf. the Rev. Alexander Schmemann, 'The Revival of Theological Studies in the U.S.S.R.', which stands out among many other, more aggressive, articles in the collection *Religion in the U.S.S.R.* published by the Institute for the Study of the U.S.S.R., Munich: 1960.

If there is no canonical impediment to their doing so, seminarians work in parishes as deacons or sacristans during their last two years of study. At the end of their fourth year of training they may be ordained and assigned to the parochial ministry.

Students in the first three years of study at the Theological Academies must submit a dissertation each quarter and the written text of a sermon. Fourth-year students must submit a specially written paper for their diploma as candidate in theology.

Students ranking at the top of their class are given first-class diplomas. They may submit a thesis (but only three years after concluding their studies) for the degree of Master of Theology, which they must defend publicly but without having to take any accessory examinations. If they seem capable of more advanced studies, the most successful holders of first-class diplomas may be named to the Theological Academies as aspirants; after a year of preparation, they become members of the academy's teaching faculty.

Western ecclesiastical circles have sometimes complained that, though they are interested in the life and activity of the Russian Orthodox Church, they never get any information about the subjects covered in the theses and dissertations written by young Russian theologians. Their interest can be satisfied now, by reading through the April 1960 issue of the *Journal of the Patriarchate of Moscow*, in which appeared a detailed report of the dissertations submitted to the Theological Academy at Moscow since 1949.

The list of these subjects is very wide and includes biblical studies, dogmatic theology, morality, liturgy, hagiography, Church history, Canon Law, and the history of Christian art. Rather than go through the entire list, we give a sample of the actual titles: 'The Doctrine of the Priesthood according to the Old Testament'; 'The Eschatology of St Paul'; 'The Dogma of the Redemption in Russian Theological Writings'; 'St Theophanos the Hermit's Doctrine on Grace'; 'The Teaching of the Fathers of the Church on the Human Passions'; 'The Dogmatic and Ethical Doctrines of St Irenaeus of Lyons'; 'The History of the Orthodox Church in Latvia'; 'The Christian Doctrine on Man's Destiny'; 'Pastoral Obligations according to St John Chrysostom'; 'The Orthodox Palestinian Society and its work in the Near East': 'The Realization of Theological Concepts in the Paintings of Andrei Rublev'. As can be seen, these studies give evidence of a rather wide horizon of interest, though it would be difficult to make any judgment of their intrinsic worth without knowing their contents.

This is, of course, the real problem: Is the intellectual level of Russian seminarians, to say nothing of their moral level, high enough to enable them to accomplish all the work waiting for them with dignity and effectively?

.   .   .   .   .   .

To put my mind at ease on this point, while I was in Leningrad I spent a whole day at the Theological Academy at the Monastery of St Alexander Nevski, and I did the same thing at Moscow, at the Theological Academy at the Monastery of the Trinity and St Sergei, about forty miles out of the city.

The conversations I had with Professor Pariiski, the Dean of the first academy, and Father Ruzhitski, the Rector at the second, were very instructive indeed.

I made no attempt to hide from either of these men that it seemed to me, as a layman, that the philosophical training given the seminarians lacked something, especially so far as modern ideas in the field are concerned.

Nor did I neglect to mention the opinion expressed by various foreign experts that biblical studies in Russia are too narrowly confined to the actual text of the sacred books.

'We are not Protestants,' Professor Pariiski replied, 'though I have a wide acquaintance among them and have the utmost esteem for them. As a matter of fact, I delivered a series of lectures at the Theological Faculty at Bonn in 1956 and have a great deal of admiration for Karl Barth.

'But we Orthodox people do not use the same methods.

Though we are perfectly aware of the recent discoveries in Egypt and Palestine, and though our own Professor Ivanov has written a thesis on textual criticism of the Gospels, going all the way back to Professor von Soden and his school, we are less interested in the origin of each sentence in these texts than in their moral interpretation. Our real teachers are the Fathers of the Church, and we do not consider a rationalist like Adolph Harnack one of our authorities.

'We have read through the recently discovered apocryphal Gospel of Thomas very closely, but do not see how it can be much help to us.

'What we are most eager to do is prepare young men to be priests capable of spreading the "Good News" of the Gospel to their flocks. We sorely need spiritual guides for the millions of souls which are searching for salvation, for all those so-called "grandmothers"—who must be immortal, by the way, since we've been hearing about them for the past forty years.'

Father Ruzhitski's reaction to my remarks was just as explicit. Indeed, his predecessor, Father Shepurin, had declared in September 1946, touching on current tendencies in theological education, that: 'When they modelled themselves on similar institutions in the West, our old Theological Academies paid too great a tribute to human rationalism which must not be suffered to make any claims on the truth of dogma. . . . It is time that we discarded the German fetish for meticulosity and volume-long collections of references since methods like these merely conceal a lack of creative ability. Our Orthodoxy's history constrains each of us to creative work, in conformity with the Church's tradition aimed at revealing the vital mysteries of that tradition with religious experience as our basis.'

Father Ruzhitski's remarks were made along the same lines. 'Our teaching programme,' he said, 'has been outlined in accordance with a principle of positive exposition of doctrine based on Revelation and the writings of the Fathers of the Church. We are constantly aware that theology's role is to be an introduction to the spiritual life; that is why we consider it the highest of the sciences and the most important of the arts.

'In our course in fundamental theology, of course, we introduce the students to the essential stages which human thought has passed through. We do this to the extent to which a familiarity with these notions is absolutely necessary if a man is to consider himself at all cultured. But we are not an institute of higher theological studies; we are a school established to train priests for their ministry. We live in another world, the world of religious experience and faith.

'The things our students must know before anything else are the Scriptures, the dogmatic and moral teachings of the Church, Canon Law and all the aspects of the liturgy.

'We apply ourselves with ardour to study of the Biblical text, giving it a patristic interpretation, and not an historico-critical one, as Western scholars usually do now. When a textual point arises, we give preference to the Hebrew, and not to the Vulgate, as the Catholics usually do. Also, unlike the Church of Rome, we do not admit the Books of Judith, Esther and the Macchabees as canonical and do not, therefore, include excerpts from them in our liturgical books.

'As it stands now, our programme is already very sweeping and only by hard work can a seminarian assimilate it all. We should make it far too top-heavy by introducing considerations of modern ideas—which disappear so quickly anyway. Isn't Bergson already part of a period which has passed and gone? Isn't Sartre's day as the idol of the West's disenchanted young people pretty well over?

'Even our own nineteenth-century lay theologians—Khomiakov, Kireevski and other lights of the Slavophile school—have lost all pertinence to conditions in the modern world.

'There is no room for the writings of all these thinkers in our educational programme, just as we have also had to give up teaching a course in elementary medicine, which we used to teach when the country was without nurses and midwives.

'Our priests today have a very precise set of duties to accomplish and I am of the conviction that the teaching we give them provides them with everything they need to know.

'You would be mistaken to accuse us of a narrowness of outlook. Our Orthodox Church manifests greater tolerance today than it ever has before. We attack neither Catholics nor Baptists; it is not in our character. We are in sympathy with the Ecumenical movement and encourage all Christians to join in the fight for peace.'

On this point Father Ruzhitski repeated the exact words Professor Pariiski had used to me.

Accompanied by my hosts, I went through the dormitories, refectories and other rooms in each of the academies, and found everything remarkably neat and tidy. I spent a long time looking through the stacks of the two libraries and noticed about twenty Soviet periodicals spread out on the tables in the reading rooms.

Theological literature of Russia's nineteenth century is represented by an almost complete selection of titles, but works written after emigration by an author as famous as Berdayev were missing.

It seemed to me, on the other hand, that the selection of Western theological literature was extremely poor. It amounted to only a few Protestant studies (including several by Karl Barth), which had obviously been sent by the German universities responsible for their publication.

The stringent exchange control in the Soviet does not allow Church educational institutions to buy enough foreign books. But I felt that this lack could very easily be made up for by donations from Christians all over the world; I know from my own experience that scholarly books addressed to officially recognized institutions of the Soviet Union arrive at their destination without the slightest difficulty.

.   .   .   .   .

I had intended to establish some sort of contact with the students at the seminaries I visited, but they were already on holiday. Most of the young men had gone to their families or off to the provinces where they would have to serve their time as apprentice deacons. About twenty or more of them stayed behind, however; some of them were finishing up their theses and others had been asked to stay because they were needed to sing in the choirs or to assist during the services.

I had long talks with them and was able to come away with a good approximation of their attitudes.

There is an opinion rather widespread among the enemies of the Church in the U.S.S.R. that young men enter the seminary to avoid military service and ensure themselves a comfortable life in the future. There is no basis for the first allegation. Priests only, and not seminarians, are exempt from military service and civil authorities are especially watchful nowadays to be sure that this law is most carefully applied.

Nothing quite so decisive can be said about the 'easy life' indictment, however; because they live on the fringes of the working and productive community, priests are, to all intents and purposes, more protected from the harrying of the administration than most of the people and their parishioners' generous gifts make it possible for them to live more comfortably than the ordinary Soviet citizen does. But are these small advantages enough to lead a man to renounce the world and devote himself entirely to serving God?

The impression I got at the seminaries would lead me to say no. All the young men who shared their tea and cakes with me in their refectory told me about the inner voice which had called them to the priesthood. They were all neatly dressed, straight-forward and radiated health and sincerity. They certainly did not seem like budding 'profiteers'.

No matter what happens, they are going out to face the enmity of atheists and the indifference of their poorly instructed flocks. No one could say that a bed of roses was waiting for them.

I was face to face with the fledgling eagles of the Orthodox Church. Members of a generation born and raised a long time after the Revolution, these young men have not been influenced by the political ideas history has condemned; they did not suffer the hardships of the civil war; free citizens of a country which daily becomes more prosperous, they have chosen the way their conscience pointed out. With priests such as these, the Church can be sure she will survive.

10

The Old Believers and New Sects

AN OUTSIDER casting a glance over the thousand years of the Orthodox Church's history could easily conclude that she is monolithic. Actually, however, her past has been far from quiet; like every other large religious group, she has had her share of violent shocks. An important schism once threatened to shake her steadfastness, and other sectarian movements have since developed within her.

There is no need, here, to go all the way back to the fourteenth century to make the catalogue complete and discuss how sects like the *Strigolniki*, who repudiated the clergy and the sacraments, or the 'Judaisers', who denied the divinity of Christ and the dogma of the Trinity, caused trouble in the cities in the Novgorod province for a long time.

The case is different, however, when we come to a religious drama which flared up in the seventeenth century and whose consequences are still felt in the Orthodox Church.

In 1652 Tsar Alexis, father and predecessor of Peter the Great, named Archbishop Nikon, wilful and ambitious man of remarkable intelligence, Patriarch of Moscow. For many years, members of the Russian Church's higher clergy had been distressed about many errors which had crept into their liturgical books over the centuries, as these books were copied from the Greek by careful, but uneducated, scribes.

No one seemed better equipped to direct a revision of these texts than the new Patriarch who, as a matter of fact, immediately set to work at the task with all the enthusiasm of his fiery temperament.

But neither he nor the Tsar could have foreseen the storm of opposition that their projected reforms would stir up among the people. As far as the ordinary Orthodox layman was concerned, everything connected with his religion was somehow sacred; fanatically devoted to tradition, he could not suffer the slightest change to be made in the texts which had come down to him from his forefathers.

A ferocious battle started between the reformers and the traditionalists as soon as the revised texts were promulgated. The essential basis of the quarrel was the spelling of the name 'Jesus' but, even more, the proper way to make the sign of the Cross, a custom still widespread in Russia. Patriarch Nikon insisted that the sign of the Cross should be made with the thumb and first two fingers; his adversaries, on the other hand, wanted to hold on to the traditional way—alleged to date from apostolic times—of signing oneself with two fingers. They claimed that these two fingers symbolized the two natures of Christ, while the other three fingers which were folded back against the palm signified the Trinity.

Other, though less important, points of controversy were whether the *Alleluia* should be sung twice or three times; the retention or exclusion of a word in the Creed; the number of hosts to be used during the liturgy, and whether the priest should walk round the altar during the liturgy with or against the sun.

Patriarch Nikon was not a man to be hindered by trifles. He decided to take a firm stand and break down any resistance to his reforms, unconscious of the situation's tragic element: his most stubborn and determined opponents were some of Russia's most fervent believers, the Church's most devoted flocks. They were not without arguments for their position: there was no conclusive proof that the Greek texts the Patriarch used for the revision were less corrupt than the already existing Russian texts. Besides, the brutal means he used to bend the entire Russian Church to his will were certainly not demonstrative of any attitude which could be called Christian.

The religious history of the Russian people was moving into one of its darkest periods. Patriarch Nikon's authoritarianism was beginning to be a threat to the Tsar and he was deposed and exiled to a monastery. But the Nikonian attitude endured and reprisals against recalcitrants continued and grew in intensity and cruelty.

This is not the place to go into all the critical events and turning points in what was a genuine war of religion and which Russia endured for several generations.

After the textual and liturgical reforms instituted by Nikon had been given definitive approbation by a Church Council, persecution focussed on recalcitrant members of the clergy. Four of them were accused of rebellion and *lèse majesté* and were burned at the stake on 1 April 1681.

One of these victims was Archpriest Avvakum, a man possessed of outstanding polemic talents and indomitable courage. He remains an outstanding figure to this day; he is the subject of a lengthy study by Professor Pierre Pascal, and his own autobiography, written in a colourful and vivid style, was lately republished in Moscow.[1]

Among the other outstanding martyrs of this time, Theodosia Morozova, the wife of a boyar, and Princess Eudoxia Urusova are usually singled out. Four hundred monks of Solovetsk, in the White Sea, were executed in 1676 after they had withstood an eight-year-long siege on their monastery by Government troops.

And there is no way of counting the many victims amongst unimportant and unknown people. During the regency of Tsar Alexis' daughter, Sophia, the reprisals took on new rancour and the position of the schismatics, who were henceforth to be known as 'Old Believers', soon became analogous to that of the early Christians in ancient Rome.

---

[1] Pierre Pascal, *Avvakum et les débuts du raskol: la crise religieuse au XVIIe siècle en Russie* (Paris: 1938); *The Life of Archpriest Avvakum, written by himself* (in Russian), Moscow: 1960.

Their tongues were cut out, they were whipped to death, their property was confiscated, they were imprisoned, their heads were beaten in and some of them were burned alive. Flight into the vast forests was the only alternative left to the ones who stubbornly refused to submit to the official Church. Even then, however, government pursuivants hunted them down in their hiding-places and no alternative was left them but suicide. Hundreds, if not thousands, of the fanatical Old Believers voluntarily hurled themselves on to the burning pyres they themselves had built at the approach of the imperial police. Mussorgski immortalized their sacrifice in his opera *Khovantschina*.

More tolerant than his sister Sophia, Peter the Great finally put an end to these atrocities. He was satisfied to double the Old Believers' taxes and to forbid them, as he had all his other subjects, to be bearded. This last was another point on which the tradition-alists were not ready to give in. They considered their beards somehow holy, because they made their wearers look like God and His saints. J. Perry, a contemporary of Peter the Great and English observer in Russia, claims to have met an old man leaving the barber with his shorn beard beneath his coat; the old man was going to keep it in a safe place until his death, so that he could appear before St Nicholas, his patron, as a good Christian should. 'All his friends,' Perry adds, 'did the same thing.'

In any case, the Old Believers were now able to live without their lives in jeopardy, though the Orthodox higher clergy and hierarchy remained as stubbornly opposed to them as before. The Government, urged on by the Holy Synod, treated them with extreme severity and turned their communities, which had sprung up round several provincial monasteries to which they had fled for refuge, into sources of revenue for the local police.

The Old Believers fled from this oppression and settled be-yond the Volga, in the Ural Mountains and as far east in Asia as the Mongolian frontier, drawn to the borders of China by the old legend of the mysterious kingdom of 'Prester John'.

They had to wait two centuries before their rights were com-completely restored. Catherine the Great's clemency gave them only a brief respite; the reigns of her grandchildren Alexander and Nicholas I saw reprisals break out afresh.

It was not until the first revolutionary movement, in 1905, that the Old Believers were allowed to establish parishes and schools, ring their bells and organize processions. Their clergy, however, were still not officially recognized and conversion to the schism was sanctioned by severe legal penalties. It was only the Revolution of 1917 which, paradoxically, gave back to the Old Believers the complete religious liberty which they had been denied for so many years.

One question which immediately arises after rehearsing the long suffering and martyrdom of the Old Believers is how they were able to survive all this persecution. There are more than one million of them today; many of them were extremely prosperous and held a leading position in the world of commerce and business during Tsarist times.

The miracle of their survival has an entirely reasonable explanation; they survived because of the strength of their belief, the purity of their faith. Not only did the Old Believers insist that they should be allowed to make the sign of the Cross with two fingers and grow beards, they were also, and this is the real point, determined to obey *all* the teachings of religion and to live as they felt true Christians must. Surrounded by people who were given to drinking and licentiousness and whose word of honour was not worth much, the Old Believers lived exemplary family lives, had a reputation for temperance in food and drink, and always met all their commitments. And, like the Anglo-Saxon Puritans, they were surprisingly rewarded with material success. Banks gave unlimited credit to the Old Believers, who were responsible people by definition, and Old Believer cotton merchants and manufacturers amassed vast fortunes.

Their material prosperity, however, was balanced by the rather heavy price they had to pay because of their religious tenacity. Because it was impossible for the community to ordain priests after the bishops they initially had had died off, they were forced to go outside Russia, to the monastery at Bela Krinitza in Bukovina, for help. Some groups of Old Believers repudiated these ordinations which they considered irregular and preferred to go on without priests or sacraments. Still others made their submission to priests of the official Church though they were allowed by the Holy Synod to keep their old texts.

Thus, the Old Believers were divided into three groups, the most important of which is the Bela Krinitza jurisdiction. It is vigorously organized under an archbishop who is titular of Moscow and All the Russias, and has authority over four other dioceses; it takes part in all the various meetings for world peace, and maintains contact with Old Believers who fled Russia during Tsarist persecutions and went to Rumania, Canada, China and other countries. The group's religious centre is at the Rogozhski cemetery in a Moscow suburb.

It was there that I went to meet Mr Cyril Abrikossov, the civil administrator of the archdiocese. I knew, of course, that the Old Believers prefer to remain slightly aloof and rarely unburden themselves to anyone whom they have not known for a long time. Fortunately, however, I had been able to secure letters of introduction before leaving Paris; besides, any fears I had on that score were dispelled as soon as I met Mr Abrikossov.

This charming man, descendant of an old Moscovite merchant family and now highly esteemed in modern Soviet official circles, was not content with showing me the most generous traditional Russian hospitality. He went to great lengths to give me complete information about his community's past and present condition, escorted me through the church grounds and did everything he could to make it easier for me to establish contact with leading members of the Old Believers in provincial areas.

The very old Rogozhski cemetery, where so many of Arch-priest Avvakum's followers lie beneath white crosses, breathes an atmosphere redolent with the poetry and quiet charm of days gone by. Nineteenth-century writers constantly referred to it, though few people visited it during the long years when the Old Believers were more or less under interdict.

As we entered the vast cathedral standing at the entrance of the cemetery, Mr Abrikossov said: 'You may not believe me, but the altars in this church—the largest in Moscow—were sealed for half a century, between 1854 and 1905. The church was completely closed under Pobedonostsev and one of our gardeners, still a young man then, who had left his coat in the building, did not find it until twenty years later, still lying in the corner where he had left it.

'But this history of our hard times goes back much farther. When we began construction on the cathedral, after the great epidemic of 1771, we were only given permission to build one dome on the church, instead of the five provided for in the plans; that is why it still looks more like a large barrack than a church.

'Napoleon's troops paid us a visit—but, luckily, we had taken the church's treasures away beforehand. Our liberator Platov, the famous Cossack general, was a co-religionist of ours, and he presented us with his camp chapel.

'Today, we are slowly coming back to life. Our parishes are getting close to the 300 mark; and in Moscow alone we have 50,000 members. People still respect the Old Believers for their discretion, reserve and the fact that, as always, we "keep our own counsel". We are universally esteemed and well thought of in every area of life; our people are given important posts almost automatically. We no longer need fear the civil authorities and the official Church has stopped sending missionaries to win back our flocks. Our relations with the Patriarchate are cordial, or at least entirely correct. Gifts of the faithful are largely responsible for our revenues, as also is the sale of candles which we not only provide to our own churches but even to other religious bodies.

'During the Civil War, of course, things went rather badly with us. Many of our faithful put their valuables in our safekeeping during those days. You know, of course, that the Old Believers have always been enthusiastic collectors of old ikons dating from before the schism; they have never felt that any price was too high for an ikon in which some of their old symbols (such as a saint blessing himself with two fingers) appeared. Before that period, the church was already gorgeously decorated, but by now it has become what can only be considered a museum of old Russian painting, the like of which exists nowhere else.'

I was certainly awestruck by what I saw on the walls of the cathedral. They were closely hung with a succession of master-pieces of the fourteenth, fifteenth and sixteenth centuries; all the great schools—Novgorod, Pskov, Tver and Moscow—were admirably represented, and all the fervour of the pious monk-artists shone through the pictures of Christ, the Virgin, the Nativity and the Ascension.

Apart from all these ikons in the nave of the cathedral, the sacristy held other old treasures: countless parchments, sacerdotal vestments, sacred vessels, etc. Mr Abrikossov presented me with an album of photographs, in which he had collaborated, illustrating the most glorious pieces in the cathedral's collection, which is without a doubt unique of its kind.

After our visit to the cathedral, we had a long talk about my journey through the provinces. I had wanted to visit a 'skit', one of those hermitages hidden far away in the forest which the novelist Melnikov-Petcherski has so marvellously described;[1] while still at school, I, like all friends, had been flooded with tenderness at reading the story of the lovely Flenushka who, raised by her mother, the superior of one of these convents, was torn between the yearnings of her heart and the rigid precepts of her faith.

Sometime before going to Moscow I had read in a Soviet magazine that there are still similar hermitages in the immense virgin forests of western Siberia. Old Believers were still living there, the article said, and bartered the nuts and mushrooms they

[1] Melnikov-Petcherski, *Dans les Forêts*, Paris: Gallimard, 1957.

At the Monastery of Etchmiadzin, religious centre of Armenia

After a service at the monastery: Archbishop Saak stands to the right
of the author

Mgr Strod, Archbishop of Riga and Rector of the
Catholic seminary

Ill-mo Rev-mo
Domino Professo
Constantino
de Grünwa
D. D. D.
+ P. Strody, Epp̃us
Rigae,
22. VI. 1960.

A procession at the Catholic monastery of Aglon in
Latvia

gathered in the forest for grain at the neighbouring villages. They were also supposed to be making converts locally.[1]

Mr Abrikossov's comments disillusioned me, however. He said that no one knows where these last remaining hermitages are now; they have no officially recorded existence, and their inmates are wanted by the Government as 'deserters from work and military service'.

As a compensation, it was suggested that I cross the Volga, to the area to which generations of these defenders of the old ritual had taken refuge for many long years. There are still many Old Believers' parishes there, and I was assured that they would welcome me hospitably.

Thus it was that, after spending the night on a train, I stepped off on to the station platform at Kostroma on a bright Sunday morning. I had made the journey in the Soviet version of our sleeper, and my travelling companions struck me as the same type of people I should have encountered in Chekhov's day: elderly women with resigned expressions on their faces; minor officials; and obviously bored young military officers.

Scarcely had I arrived at Kostroma when I was struck by the contrast between the old and the new in the city. The streets, which were once so quiet, were now crowded with housewives bustling in and out of shops, their arms laden with parcels; young people on bicycles wheeling in and out of traffic in every direction; crowded trams going out towards the suburbs.

In the centre of the city, there are several merchant galleries,[2] single-storeyed buildings painted white and probably dating from Gogol's time. Directly opposite these stores, however, stands the superb modern building used to house the offices of the Council of National Economy. The old fire brigade's tower is still standing on Revolution Square, but a gigantic television transmitting mast dominates the countryside beyond it.

Swarms of small boats and skiffs ran about on the Volga, while

[1] *Science and Religion*, 9 December 1959.
[2] Galleries of small shops owned by individual traders.

its banks were throbbing with activity: metal industrial factories which make excavators, a shipyard, linen mills (Kostroma produces more than ten and a half million yards of linen cloth a year) and plywood mills (which is sold by Kostroma to all the countries in Western Europe).

Once having crossed the river, however, one is taken back centuries. Beyond neat and tidy blocks of workers' flats, rise the white limestone walls of the Ipatiev monastery, to which the delegates of the national Diet came in 1612 to find Michael Romanov and offer him the royal crown of Russia.

Now a national museum, the monastery is currently undergoing complete restoration work. A very old church of the neighbourhood has been moved there on wooden rollers; the Romanov house, cradle of the fallen dynasty, is being repainted and the decorations in the old cathedral are being refurbished.

After a journey of several more kilometres, I finally reached my destination, the large village of Strelnikovo, most of whose inhabitants are Old Believers. Beyond fields of hemp and flax, I could see the village's lovely wooden church, its twelve or more domes flashing in the sun.

I had arrived in time for the end of the liturgy and found that the Old Believers are as devout during services as members of the official Orthodox Church are. Their liturgical music, however, struck me as being older in composition, and I noticed that all the women had small cushions on the floor in front of them, on which they touched their heads at the times during the liturgy when they bowed to the ground.

After the service I had all the time in the world to observe the parishioners, and I was taken by surprise to see that all the men, young and old, were bearded. Many of them wore long kaftans and flat hats, such as one sees in Russian coloured engravings of the beginning of the nineteenth century. Several women carried babies swaddled in blankets and shawls in their arms; the children had been brought to the church for baptism.

The old parish priest invited me to have luncheon with himself and some of his leading parishioners; it was a day of fasting, and we had to be content with vegetables and fish.

Before sitting down to the meal, all the guests turned to face the ikons hanging in a corner of the room and sang a brief prayer together; the simple luncheon finished in the same way.

In this presbytery, too, this simple loghouse, or *isba*, the furniture and decoration were kept to the barest minimum, and one would have looked in vain for any sign of 'external evidence of wealth'. The priest apologized for not being able to stay with us very long, because he had to go to a neighbouring village for a funeral. I asked if I might accompany him, but learned that the journey would mean walking seven kilometres each way, and my courage failed me, despite my curiosity.

During the meal, I had a fine opportunity to have a good look at my fellow-guests. These obviously pious people impressed me by their dignity and reserve; they were certainly not the endless talkers most of their compatriots are. Through the room's tiny windows, I could look out on the fields stretching across to the horizon and growing green for the approaching harvest.

The whole situation—the old, wooden presbytery, the simple, frugal meal, the pious Old Believers, the green, rolling fields— was reminiscent of times past and gone, the days of Holy Russia.

I finished my day in town with a visit to another Old Believer. Already very advanced in age, he has been living on a pension for many years, in a small house where he passes time by working in its garden.

The furnishings of the house seemed comfortable enough, and there was an attractive hanging on the wall. Two kolkhoz farmers were with us, and they seemed as eager as my host to extol the excellent material conditions in which they lived and the freedom they were allowed to fulfil their spiritual obligations. Once again we began and ended our meal with a prayer, a faithful loyalty to the customs of past centuries.

·　　·　　·　　·　　·

In the religious life of the Russian people the Baptists are at the opposite pole from the Old Believers. Bold innovators, they have nothing to do with ritual, and go as far as repudiating the priesthood and the sacraments. Their whole aim is that each Christian will build his own church within his own soul.

There is one point, however, which the Baptists hold in common with the Old Believers: both groups claim to have originated in the old, national Orthodox Church. This is an important point, since it gives a conclusive lie to anyone who would insist today, as others did in the seventeenth century, that the fundamental energy and drive of this great Mother-Church is channelled towards conserving traditional rituals and forms of worship. Naturally, any innovating religious tendency—rationalist or mystical—could hardly have shown signs of life in the old Moscovite Tsars' Russia without being instantly stamped out. Peter the Great had scarcely opened 'a window on Europe' when various sectarian movements began to exercise their influence on the souls of the Russian faithful.

At the beginning of the seventeenth century, appeared the first evangelists of the 'Khlysty' ('Flagellants') sect, whose members held a bizarre doctrine supposed to have been inspired by the Holy Spirit and which ended in extravagantly disordered sexual rites. (Indeed, some people claimed that the famous Rasputin belonged to this sect, certain splinter-groups of which still survive today, despite efforts at suppressing them.)

In the second half of the eighteenth century, the 'Khlysty' were succeeded by the 'Skoptsy' ('Eunuchs'), who went as far as preaching a mystical self-mutilation.

Though these two movements, and others like them, only succeeded in winning the loyalty of a small number of unbalanced and fanatical people, something far more worthwhile was accomplished at the end of the eighteenth century by several gifted Mennonite preachers who had come to Russia with German colonists at the invitation of Catherine the Great.[1]

[1] Cf., on this whole subject of sects within Russia, P. Miliukov, *Essay on the History of Russian Culture* (in Russian), 2nd rev. ed., Paris: 1933, II, part I.

As soon as the new colonists had settled, the Russian peasants in the Taurida and the province of Samara were amazed at the order, cleanliness and prosperity of the new villages. The natural conclusion was that the newcomers' religion was the basis for their prosperity. Zealous ministers worked among the neighbouring Russians and southern Russia was soon dotted with a series of sectarian communities of 'Stundists' (from the German *Stunde*, 'hour' devoted to prayer and Gospel reading).

Afterwards, German Baptists became very active in the same regions and adult baptism by immersion became more and more popular.

Government authorities were powerless against these pious and inoffensive people who just read the Scriptures in common and tried to live up to their teachings. Local tribunals had to acquit any member of the new sects who had been indicted before them.

Towards the end of the nineteenth century, part of the aristocratic society of St Petersburg was thrown into a flurry by the arrival of an English apostle of 'spiritual renovation', Lord Radstock, who had already been in Russia as an officer during the Crimean War.

In those great families, one could always find a number of restless souls in the throes of religious anguish; had not the Jesuits been able to make fervent converts, during Joseph de Maistre's time, among the princely Gagarin, Golitzin, Volkonsky, etc., families?

Now, the new herald of the 'Good News' became the cynosure of all eyes; leaders of society such as Colonel Pashkov, Baron Korff, Count Bobrinski, Princess Lieven and General Chertkov put their lives and their wealth at the service of the new faith.

The combination of these two currents, one aristocratic and the other basically popular, gave rise to Russia's large Baptist community.

In 1884, the authorities became alarmed at the growth of the movement, interdicted the 'Society for Spiritual and Moral Reading', and disbanded a 'Union of Believers' organized by Col. Pashkov at St Petersburg.

Pashkov himself went into exile with his friend Baron Korff. By one of those contradictions which were so frequent during the Tsarist regime, however, while this group was being dissolved, southern Russian Baptists were allowed to hold meetings at a village in the Taurida province and form an association which was to be the nucleus of their future organization.

During the entire nineteenth century the Baptists were aided by Protestant ministers whose names they still hold in great esteem: the Lutheran Pietist Wust; the Reformed Bohnekempers, both father and son; the Mennonites Willer and Unger; Baedeker, the missionary; and the Scottish evangelist Melville, who is better known among the Caucasian Stundists as 'Vassily (Basil) Ivanovitch'.

These educated and enlightened men facilitated the elaboration of a solid and coherent system of doctrine—something which another sect connected with the Evangelicals, the 'Molokani' ('Milk Drinkers', i.e. during the periods of fasting), lacked.

They kept their followers loyal to the Government and prevented them from straying off into eccentricities such as those indulged in by the 'Dukhobors', a sect who, among other things, refuse to do military service and still behave rather extravagantly in Canada, where they emigrated with Tolstoy's help and now have several communities.

Russia was fertile soil for evangelism. It gave the profoundly Christian peasants the one thing they lacked: a knowledge of the Old and New Testaments. The commendable, but shortlived, efforts along those lines by the Biblical Society, which was created at Tsar Alexander I's initiative after the Napoleonic War, were, unfortunately, never followed up.

After it had lived through and survived the rather ineffective reprisals of Pobiedonostsev, the Baptist evangelical movement came into full bloom after the first Revolution in 1905. It succeeded in having its congregations in Moscow and St Petersburg given legal status; it held assemblies at Kiev and elsewhere; it began to publish its own periodicals. Like the Old Believers it, too, achieved complete religious freedom—paradoxically—when the new regime proclaimed the separation of Church and State. In October 1944, the Baptist Union and the group of Evangelical Christians merged into a single unit, which the Pentecostal Churches joined in August 1945.

There are now 5,400 communities in the new Union, with more than 540,000 members, two-thirds of whom live in Ukrainia. Evangelical Baptists have made quite large numbers of converts during the past twenty years; if official anti-religious propaganda has turned people away from Orthodoxy, it has unwittingly put their feet on a new path to truth. After the fall of Tsarism the Baptists also benefited by the rather unsettled state of affairs in the country; in those days, they used to preach in the streets and even in cinemas.

The present Council of Christian Evangelical Baptists of the Soviet Union is composed of ten members, three of whom are its presiding board. It directs the work of sixty provincial superintendents; in 1956, it published a hymn-book and issues a periodical, *The Fraternal Review*, with a circulation of 3,000. In Moscow, finally, its offices are in a handsome building which also houses a large prayer-hall.

The first time I went into that prayer-hall, I felt as though I were in a Lutheran church: the walls were absolutely bare of decoration, and there were an organ, choir and galleries lined with pews for the use of the faithful. But there was no altar, only a severe pulpit in which the lay preacher stood to read the lessons. Although it was a week-day, the congregation was rather large and included, as everywhere else, many women in white headscarves. I did notice, however, that the proportion of men was larger than I had seen in Orthodox churches. The congregation sang the hymns to an organ accompaniment. It was very strange to hear hymns translated from German or English and put to music by Bach or Handel being sung in a typically suburban Moscow accent.

As usual, I was invited to share a fraternal meal. Here, again, we sang prayers before and after the meal. The guest of honour at the luncheon was Mr J. Zhidkov, President of the Committee and Vice-President of the World Union of Baptists. To my left sat Alexander Karev, the Secretary-General, a balding man with a mischievous smile and eyes crackling with intelligence and wisdom.

'You should not be surprised at the solidity of our organization,' he said to me. 'The Russian soul is still as eager for truth as it has ever been; there are no "lukewarm Christians" here. Religious indifference, which is on the increase in the West, is unknown in our country.

'Though everyone cannot be satisfied by the ritualism and dogmatic rigidity of the Orthodox Church, our people are now too well educated and cultivated to accept the doctrines of the "Khlysty" or the "Skoptsy". Our community's rationalist approach seems particularly well adapted to the needs of our time, as do our doctrine and form of worship, which are rather similar to those of the Reformed Churches.

'Our opponents are wrong in claiming that most of our members belong to the most uneducated levels of society; if that were the case, we would not be able to point with pride to the young people, 20 per cent of our total membership, who have already benefited by obligatory secondary education. The fact is that there are now half a million Baptists in Soviet territory, as opposed to 100,000 in Tsarist times.

'All our people become members of the community with a clear-headed attitude, since we baptize—by immersion—only those candidates for membership who are at least seventeen years old (and not nine or ten years old, as Baptists in England and the United States do). Besides, every candidate must first go through a preparatory period which lasts from two to three years. Many of them are naturally members of Baptist families, but others come to us from the Orthodox Church and some have even left the Communist Party to become Baptists (one of our deacons is an ex-member of the Party).

'You have just seen the result of all this: every Sunday several thousand people come to our church; we have services two to four times a week, and we all take Communion together once a month, without a minister of course. Last year, we even received 150 new members in Moscow alone, and some years have seen that figure go as high as 250. We do everything we can to give them a modern outlook, and we encourage sports.

'Atheist propaganda does not bother us at all; as a matter of fact, it helps us to purify ourselves and get rid of our short-comings. When one pamphlet[1] accused us of obscurantism and reactionary tendencies, we used as our best argument our activi-ties as loyal and energetic citizens; when anyone preaches to us about leading a "decent life", we suggest he look at our com-munity to find the best example of right living.

'Far from complicating our existence, the Council for Various Religious Groups actually facilitates it, through its watch-ful control, by being our intermediary in our relations with local authorities and other countries, and by ensuring us religious liberty all over the country.

'We are also able to keep up and increase our contacts with other countries. The Orthodox have most of their co-religionists in the peoples' republics; ours are in the United States, but there are also some in Scandinavia and Western Germany. We ex-change visits with them and, as a matter of fact, we now have delegates attending the tenth World Congress of Baptists in Rio de Janeiro.

'People frequently offer us financial aid, but we refuse it because the gifts of our own members are enough for our need.

'I am sure I need not add that we are intensely interested in all the various movements towards world peace; our president gave

[1] L. Serdobolskaya, op. cit.

a remarkable address during the second world conference for peace at Prague.

'We are watching the activity of the World Council of Churches with great interest and are sure that its co-operation in the cause of world peace and understanding between nations will be most constructive.'

. . . . .

Is Mr Karev's optimism fully justified? There is no doubt that the Russian Baptists' horizons are far broader than the Old Believers', the other large group which has grown out in diametric opposition to the great axis of the Orthodox Church. Stymied by two centuries of official repression of their efforts at proselytizing, the Old Believers have finally achieved religious liberty, but too late for them to be able to acquire new members. The few new members they have received (among whom, I was told, is Tolstoy's grandson) have joined the sect for family reasons, because they have married women belonging to the group, and these new conversions cannot be considered a sign of a widespread swing towards the Old Believers. The best they can hope for is to keep their membership figures and present organization at their present level, unless their hierarchy decide—and the possibility cannot be excluded *a priori*—to reunite with the Orthodox Patriarchate.

The Baptists' situation is entirely different. Their doctrine has the attractiveness of novelty; it arouses curiosity. Recently, the *Literaturnaya Gazeta* expressed surprise (not without some justification) on learning that there is a community of 500 Baptists at Magnitogorsk, the large industrial city in the Urals which has developed only within recent years, has an entirely worker population, and which has been the arena of an all-out atheistic propaganda campaign.

But I am far from sure that this headlong progress of the Baptists can continue indefinitely. There are many things against it. Behind the Council for Various Religious Groups unswervingly proper attitude towards them lurks a blind hostility which is sufficiently justified by the Baptist Church's American ties. The name of Adlai Stevenson, whose signature I saw in the visitors' book at their Moscow centre, is certainly not what the present Government authorities would consider a good reference.

As far as the Patriarchate is concerned, it cannot possibly show the Baptists the same tolerance it does the Old Believers; it obviously cannot be sympathetic to a group which denies the sacramental system and wins over many of its own flock.

The telling argument against the Baptists is none of these however. The real point is whether a religious community which originated outside Russia, and continues to maintain contacts with foreign influences, has enough in it to attract the masses of a nation whose religious sentiments are so intimately bound up with national feelings and traditional customs.

Religious Minorities

RUSSIA had no problem about less important religious groups until the beginning of the eighteenth century. Before then, neither the Tartars in the old kingdoms of Kazan and Astrakhan, nor the pagan tribes in Siberia, nor the few hundreds of foreigners who lived in Lutheran or Calvinist communities in Moscow's 'German' suburb had enjoyed the slightest importance in the country's spiritual life.

The situation changed radically, however, when Peter the Great conquered Esthonia and Latvia, with its Lutherans and Roman Catholics; when Poland was partitioned and millions of Roman Catholics came under Tsarist domination; and when Armenia and the Moslem khanates of central Asia were annexed during the nineteenth century.

Generally speaking, the Tsars were reasonably tolerant towards all these religious groups. Lutherans, reputably diligent and punctilious, were extremely well thought of in court circles, in the civil service and in the army; neither the Armenians nor the Moslems were harried, and persecution of the Jews, who lived in their ghettoes, did not really crystallize until the latter half of the nineteenth century, at the same time as the first legal obstacles were thrown up against marriage between members of the Orthdox Church and of any other Church.

Catholics, however, were in a somewhat different position, which was complicated by the fact that most of them were Poles. Twin branches of the single great family of Slavs, the Russians and the Poles have developed along different lines from the outset; their varying evolutions were bound to bring them into opposition to one another during the course of time, and led them into irreconcilable conflicts of interest. The inevitable result was that, as Prince Wiazemski put it, there grew up between the two nations a 'genuine incompatibility of temperament'.

At the beginning of the seventeenth century, the Poles sacked Moscow and tried to put their own King Sigismund's son on the Russian throne; at the end of the eighteenth century Warsaw's streets echoed with the clattering boots of the Cossacks.

The Polish revolt in 1830–1 and its subsequent cruel repression inevitably revived all the old rancours and the enmity spread into the field of religion.

During the dramatic days when his sovereign powers were shaken by the unexpected turn of history, Tsar Nicholas I saw in the Catholic clergy the revolutionary movement's strongest supporters. After that, the imperial Russian Government confused the cause of Catholicism with the cause of Polish nationalism. This attitude was hardly surprising, however, in those areas of eastern Europe where national frontiers had almost always coincided with religious boundaries.

It is an interesting fact that, until the eve of the 1917 Revolution, Polish servants asked their nationality by their Russian employers would usually answer: 'I am a Catholic'.

The stiffening of Russo-Polish relations after 1831 could hardly help be reflected in the situation of the Catholic clergy, who were henceforth submitted to countless annoyances. Their position was further complicated by an old, unsettled account between the Orthodox Church and the Roman Catholic Church: the affair of the 'Uniates'. Those former Polish-Lithuanian and Ukrainian Orthodox had submitted to papal authority while under Polish rule and been allowed to conserve their own rituals; after the partition of Poland, they began to return to the Orthodox Church and after World War II they corporately submitted to the jurisdiction of the Moscow Patriarchate.

But an ideological conflict of infinitely greater proportions has developed between the Kremlin and the Vatican since 1917. As we pointed out in the preceding chapter, the Roman Catholic clergy were particularly afflicted by the upheavals brought on by the Civil War. Since that time, the Government's change of attitude, which began during the struggle against Hitler and which has been gratefully acknowledged by all other Soviet religious groups, has not satisfied the Roman Curia. Essentially totalitarian, as she herself admits, the Roman Catholic Church needs more than freedom of worship alone; she insists that her influence extends to education, the instruction of the masses and, even, into political life—all things which it is absolutely impossible for the Soviet Government, no less totalitarian than she, to concede her.

Out of this atmosphere of unconcealed mutual enmity, the slogan 'Church of Silence' developed, and legends spread throughout the entire West which claim that there are no longer any practising Catholics (or even believers of any kind) in the Soviet Union since all their churches have been closed.

Any tourist passing through Moscow, however, can visit the famous Church of St Louis of the French, near the centre of the city. Built in 1830 by members of Moscow's French colony, it has remained open until today and did not even close during the revolutionary troubles.

While having a walk about the city one day, I went into the church, attracted by its striking Empire façade which rises up beyond a small garden. It was a week-day, but I was fortunate to have come into the church while Mass was being celebrated in honour of a saint. Ten marvellous Ionic pillars formed the frame for the congregation of several hundreds. As in the capital's Orthodox churches, they were mostly women, all wearing white headscarves. Another similarity to the Orthodox churches I had visited lay in the congregation's singing with a fervour unknown in the West. The *Opus Dei* was sublimely beautiful. A large number of the congregation knelt in the aisles during the entire service.

After the Mass I went to the sacristy of the church, where Father Witold Bronicki received me with the greatest kindness and did not hesitate, even though I was a complete stranger to him, to give me very detailed information about his work.

'Like all property in the city,' he said, 'the ground our church stands on is nationalized, but the building is lent to the parish without charge. There is no presbytery, but I have been given the small flat in town which my predecessor used.

'In the days when there were three Roman Catholic parishes in Moscow, two of them were Polish, but they are no longer in operation because there are far fewer Poles here now. The Church of St Louis, which used to minister to the foreign colonies and the diplomatic corps, has never been closed, as you know; most of the people who come here now are Poles, while the diplomatic corps have as their chaplain a priest attached to the United States Embassy. The French priest who served the church at the beginning of the present regime was first replaced by a Pole, and then by Father Brown, who was, at that time, the French Embassy's chaplain, assisted by a Polish priest. The church was constituted a parish, and Father Buturowicz was alone, and I have succeeded him.

'I am a Soviet citizen, of Polono-Lithuanian nationality. I studied for the priesthood at the Vilna seminary and was ordained a priest in 1946. I am fortunate that I am able to preach in Polish, the language of my parishioners, whereas one of my predecessors, who was a Frenchman, had to preach in Russian, of which they understand little.

'Parish affairs are directed by a committee of three members aided by a control commission. Both groups' members are almost always retired professors, engineers, etc. Unlike Orthodox parishes, we do not sell candles, which we buy from the Old Believers at the Rogozhski cemetery. The church's revenue comes entirely from our parishioners' free offerings.

'There are about 3,000 people in the parish; about a thousand of them attend Sunday Mass regularly. Every child born in the parish is baptized, and their parents teach them their catechism, using little booklets I provide. Before receiving their first Holy Communion, they must pass an examination which I give them. Last year, we had fifteen first Holy Communicants.

'Religious marriage ceremonies are becoming more and more rare; I officiate at only seven a year, perhaps. On the whole, however, the parish's level of morality, which fell terribly during the war years, is now rising at a satisfactory rate. Our real scourge is alcoholism, which we are doing everything we can to fight.

'There is no friction between ourselves and the civil authorities; the municipal delegate and the regional delegate of the Council for Various Religious Groups are obliged to see that Soviet laws are rigidly obeyed, but they never bother us and are content with approving the periodic elections of members of our committee.

'Our spiritual superior is Bishop Stepanavicius of Vilna and Ponevezha. We receive the decrees of the Holy See through him and have no difficulty putting them into effect; thus, for instance, we have been able to apply the various liturgical modifications recently prescribed by the Holy See.

'Regulations prohibiting contacts with Communists do not apply to Socialist countries, according to the Vatican's interpretation. It would obviously be impossible for us to refuse Holy Communion to a member of the Komsomol [Communist Youth Organization].

'Naturally, I am one of the many who regret that there is no concordat between the Vatican and the Soviet Union, and I hope that there will be one some day. The future depends on circumstances completely unconnected with religion.

'Looking at the situation from every point of view, what have we to complain about? In Lithuania there are as many as 1,000 Catholic parishes, divided into five dioceses. There is also a considerable Catholic community in Latvia; that is the place you

The minister of the Moscow Baptist Church, A. Karpov, baptizes a new member

Confirmation by Mgr Turss, Lutheran Archbishop of Riga

In Moscow's chief synagogue:
prayers on Yom Kippur

Mufti Ziautdine Babikhanov
addresses believers in Tashkent,
Uzbekistan

should visit to meet Catholics, since it is not very far from Moscow.'

.   .   .   .   .

On the face of it I could hardly avoid a great deal of travelling if I was going to form any sort of clear and precise idea of all the religious minorities in the Soviet Union, all of them concentrated in frontier areas. The task struck me as indispensable; though the Catholics, Protestants, Armenians and Moslems are only playing a minor role in the spiritual evolution of the Soviet Union, I nevertheless felt that their present situation would be of great interest to their co-religionists in other countries of the world. With that end in view, then, I used the railways and Aeroflot aircraft to travel through the Baltic countries, Armenia and Central Asia to gather the information and facts I considered essential to my investigation.

If I were asked to sum up my impressions, I could not omit some comment on the economic and cultural changes which have taken place in these areas since the establishment of the new regime and which have, naturally, influenced the people's religious attitudes.

I had never set foot in Armenia, but had long been familiar with Central Asia and the Baltic countries. In my student years, I had crossed Turkestan from one end to another; my family were originally from Riga and when I returned there I was still able to see my grandparents' house, in the centre of the city, which is now used as the municipal archives and has been given a new façade. Once more, memory helped me to make comparisons.

Founded in 1205 by Albrecht von Buxhoewden, Bishop of the Order of Teutonic Knights, the old city of Riga was part of the Hanseatic League, then fell under Swedish domination before becoming Russian territory under Peter the Great, and is now the capital of the Republic of Latvia and has kept numerous traces of its medieval background.

Many architectural monuments dating from the thirteenth and fourteenth centuries were destroyed during the last war, but the Gothic steeples of the Domkirche and other Lutheran churches still rise above the central quarters of the city. The old walls of the fortress, the massive Powder Tower, the picturesque Swedish Gates and the castle (formerly the citadel of the Teutonic Knights but now the Young Pioneers' headquarters) are still places which catch the visitor's admiring eye.

But these are the only things left to testify to the city's many hundreds of years of foreign association. Hitler destroyed Riga's vestiges of Germanic culture with his own hands when he ordered the repatriation of everyone he considered the 'German race'. The tall, boney silhouettes of the Baltic barons and of the more sturdy merchant-princes have disappeared from Riga's streets, as have also the German shop signs. One seldom hears Russian spoken except by tourists who have come from other parts of the Soviet Union. The Latvians, who were until recently still considered an 'inferior race', are now the masters of their own country; they have got back on to their feet now, and one sees nothing but Latvian books and periodicals in bookshop windows.

There must be some former business men or landowners, now hidden away in their modest flats, who regret the still not-too-distant past. But the men and women I saw all over the city seemed to me decently dressed, well fed, self-confident and content with their lot.

How could they feel otherwise, though, when Latvian industrial production has increased tenfold during the past twenty years and traffic in the port grows larger every day? Attractive public buildings and homes are under widescale construction.

I saw an incredibly large, bustling crowd at the railway terminus, where people were rushing this way and that, after a hard day's work, to catch trains to take them to the marvellous beaches at Maiori, Dubbulti and Tzindari where there are countless rest hostels for workers, private homes and lively restaurants.

At the other end of the Soviet Union, I saw the same sort of development at Erevan, once an obscure prefecture but now the capital of the Republic of Armenia. Though it is more than a thousand years old, Erevan looks like an entirely modern city.

In 1926 its population was more than 65,000, and had grown to 385,000 in 1956. A tiny quarter of the old town has been preserved on the curving banks of the Razdan, but everywhere else one sees asphalted roads, large, shaded parks and imposing public buildings. Talented local architects surpassed themselves when they designed the municipal square; it is surrounded by large governmental buildings, constructed of pink or golden tufa with highly decorated façades and combining an Eastern approach with a classical Renaissance style to create a pleasing and harmonious unity.

In forty years, industrial production has grown to fifty times what it was. Armenia has put the electric energy from its mountain rivers and streams to good use and now has the most important chemical industrial plants in the entire Union; one of its synthetic rubber plants alone has more than 10,000 workers.

The country's 1,200 secondary schools teach 280,000 pupils, and there are 30,000 young people receiving higher education. The number of doctors has risen from 1913's seventy-three to 4,000. All this progress is in striking contrast to the conditions prevailing in Turkey, just thirty kilometres away from Erevan.

Through the window of the Intourist hotel I was able to look out at the snow-covered peaks of Mount Ararat, which is outside Soviet territory and is sometimes visited by parties of U.S. officers searching for Noah's ark. The countryside is beautiful, but I was told that the ignorance and poverty of the Armenians living beyond the chain of mountains is beyond all imagination. Besides, Soviet Armenians are not likely to succumb to the influence of separatist propaganda spread among them by their relatives, who come in great numbers to visit them from the United States. They know all too well what could happen to them if they were to lose the protection of the Soviet army and the enormous capital invested in their industry by Moscow.

It was not until I had got to Central Asia that I saw the most sweeping and overwhelming transformation, however. At my first visit, Tashkent was nothing more than a dusty hamlet in the middle of an oasis. Besides a few army barracks, some administrative offices and several simple country homes, there was nothing of interest in the city, except the small 'palace' of Grand Duke Nicholas Constantinovitch, who was exiled here years ago for some scandalous peccadillo. Eccentric though he may have been, the Grand Duke had the laudable idea of putting his immense income to work at setting up the first irrigation projects in this arid territory.

Later, the Tsarist Government decided to resume the work at its own expense, but it has only been under Soviet rule that Uzbekistan has regained the rich and fertile look it had before the Mongol invasions.

Hydraulic operations are being carried out on a gigantic scale; cotton plantations cover hundreds of thousands of acres and the most modern methods gives them a harvest double that of the United States and Egypt. Three million tons of raw cotton are harvested each year in Uzbekistan, and its textile mills (the vast spinning mill at Tashkent is one of the largest in the world) supply all the needs of the entire Soviet Union.

Natural gas deposits are being developed in the Bokhara basin, where the reserves are as large as those in the Sahara. Factories are being built for the manufacture of earth-moving machinery, tractors and other farming equipment, and Uzbekistan's generating plants furnish more electricity *per capita* than similar operations do in some western European countries.

The number of Uzbek students has reached 1,327,000 (as opposed to 17,000 in 1913); there are now 10,000 doctors (there were 128 before the Revolution), and 200,000 technical specialists. Illiteracy has completely disappeared. The country's artistic life has developed tremendously and I was literally overwhelmed by the superb production I saw at the National Opera, which rivalled some things I had seen at Moscow.

Transformed into a leading cultural and industrial metropolis, Tashkent, a city of 800,000, has almost completely changed. Because of the danger of earthquake, no skyscrapers have been built, but the old clay buildings have yielded to constructions in reinforced concrete, and vast new areas are being built alongside the old city. Here, too, the municipal centre is circled by attractive public buildings; it is the hub around which city life revolves, and the inhabitants visit it in the evening to enjoy the refreshing beauty of its sparkling fountain.

Tashkent people, like those in Bokhara and Samarkand, used to look completely Eastern, with the women veiled and the men wearing billowing robes and, many of them, turbans. Now, they have all completely adopted European dress; the little, embroidered skullcap is the only distinctive sign of the Uzbeks or their neighbours, the Tadzhiks.

Yesterday's nomads are today's factory workers or office clerks. They have kept their own language, but Russian is very widely used; many Uzbeks have married Russian women and walk along proudly with their wives on their arms.

Outside the city, the panorama is the same as elsewhere in the U.S.S.R.: asphalted roads which stretch for hundreds of kilometres, flourishing kolkhozes with neat little houses, and cotton harvesters dressed like any western field-worker.

.   .   .   .   .

The changes which have taken place in the attitudes and religious beliefs of these people demand a deeper analysis. Situations vary according to the historical and cultural background of each area.

When I arrived at Riga, my first stop, I immediately went to call on the delegate of the Council for Various Religious Groups, Paul Pizan, a very friendly and cultivated man. He claims that his name is a corruption of *paysan*, and that one of his ancestors, a coachman, was brought from France by a local nobleman.

His field of operations is particularly interesting because there are many rival religious groups in the Latvian Republic. There are relatively few Orthodox, who have only about a hundred rural parishes. In Riga the immense Orthodox cathedral which was built in the centre of the city as a symbol of Tsarist power is almost deserted (I can testify to this myself; I encountered a certain number of visitors there, but they had come as sightseers, to see the magnificent ikonostasis).

Latvia has seventy-five Old Believers' parishes and eighty Baptist congregations; these latter are growing more and more popular. According to statistics provided by the clergy (who based their figures on the number of families), out of two million inhabitants in Latvia there are 300,000 Roman Catholics and 600,000 Lutherans. Easily a hundred churches of either group were destroyed during the Second World War, but only thirty have not yet been reconstructed

Lutheran clergymen are all Latvians, while the Catholics also have a good number of Polish and Lithuanian priests.

The civil authorities only rarely have to intervene in either group's activities. Thus, for instance, a Lutheran minister once ventured to organize an important ceremony out of doors; the municipal authorities had not been previously advised and complained; their complaint was brought to the attention of the Lutheran bishop so that he could reprimand the offending minister. There are no particular difficulties with the Roman Catholics, though they are not always kept in touch with the prescriptions of the Holy See because, as Mr Pizan said, 'They are not capable of understanding them properly'.

My next visit was to Bishop Peters Strod, religious head of all Roman Catholics in Latvia. I found myself seated opposite a broad-shouldered prelate of great dignity and gentleness; his face shone with energy and candour. He told me about himself and his position with the utmost sincerity, beginning, at my request, with a brief sketch of his ecclesiastical career.

'I was born in Lativa. Ordained priest in 1916, I had to

interrupt my studies at the Theological Academy at St Petersburg because of the Revolution. After teaching catechism in Latvian schools for a while, I went to Innsbruck, where I studied philoophy for three years and was awarded a doctorate.

'After that, I taught philosophy in the seminaries at Kaunas and Riga. Consecrated bishop in 1947, I was named apostolic administrator of Riga and Lieppala, while the Ordinary, Bishop Antony Strengowics, was still living. Upon his death, I informed the Holy Father of the event and he replied by telegram, confirming me in my post and sending his blessing to my flock.

'I am the only Latvian prelate of my rank, but, as you know, in 1955 and 1957, the Pope named Archbishop Stepanavicius to head the diocese of Vilnius, and appointed Bishop Majarlis to the Telsiai diocese, both in Lithuania. A third bishop named to a Lithuanian diocese at the same time has not been allowed by the Soviet authorities to take up his duties and lives in the country, far away from his diocese and its activities. The diocese of Kaunas is governed by a vicar capitular elected by the chapter of canons there.

'Although we are in contact with the Vatican, as you can see, we know absolutely nothing about any prohibition of contacts with Communists, which, in any case, would be entirely unenforceable as things are in this country.

'My diocese includes 170 parishes [out of 1,235 in the entire Soviet Union]; many of these parishes used to be no more than mission stations.

'Religion is alive and thriving all over the country; on Sundays, our churches are literally packed with people, and we are not in France [sic] where agnostics go to Mass to let their neighbours see them. Atheistic propaganda has caused a certain number of disaffections among intellectuals, about 15 per cent of whom are unbelievers. But the country people are still faithful to their religious duties and the problem of marrying with a civil ceremony only does not arise here. Couples all over the country have

their marriages blessed by their parish priest. Every parish in the
country receives enough from its parishioners to support itself
and maintain its activities.

'You say that you consider my philosophical knowledge more
advanced than that of the Orthodox higher clergy. I am sorry to
have to tell you that you are wrong. My studies were very
complete, but you must remember that the programme of
philosophic studies approved by Pope Pius XI is essentially
scholastic and only lightly touches on modern schools of
philosophic thought.

'Tomorrow, I shall begin my "visitation" to eight parishes;
last year I visited twenty, but I have to curtail my visits this year
because we are in the midst of a great national celebration, the
twentieth anniversary of our republic.

'I shall confirm young people in every parish I visit and give
my blessing to at least a thousand people. But even that does not
compare with the great pilgrimage to the convent of Aglon at
Lieppala [in Lettgalia, on the Lithuanian frontier]. Great crowds
of pilgrims go there in buses which come from all the neighbouring villages. I celebrate Mass out of doors and I can tell you that
the fervour of the people is enough to touch the heart of even the
most demanding priest.'

Probably not all of Riga's Roman Catholics would share
Bishop Strod's optimism. As I left the episcopal residence, I
encountered a Latvian who seemed eager enough to talk with me
and give me his opinions.

According to him, the systematic propaganda programme of
the 'Godless' was having a growing influence on Latvian minds,
which are very individualist by definition; young people
especially are taken up with the new doctrines; it is a fact that first
Holy Communions are numerous in rural areas, but not in cities;
finally, he said that there was a great difference between the
situation of believers in Moscow or Leningrad and the situation
in which they would find themselves in a provincial city like Riga,
where a teacher or minor official would, justifiably or not, be

afraid of losing his post if he indicated that he was an active member of any religious group.

It is always difficult to arrive at the whole truth in any matter. Despite varying opinions, everyone in Riga and elsewhere knows that Catholicism, which is stronger because of its organization and the training it gives its members, is at a greater disadvantage than other religious groups in the Soviet Union because of the bitter enmity between the Kremlin and the Vatican.

This is a problem which cannot be fully understood unless one takes into account the social and political environment in which Soviet citizens live. What must the Soviet authorities have thought when they read this appeal made by Cardinal Spellman just before Mr Khrushchev visited the United States: 'We must guard against complacency weakening our defenses, permitting the enemy's promises of peaceful negotiation to blind us. . . .' Or at the words of Cardinal Richaud, when the head of the Soviet Government was about to visit France: 'Catholics cannot forget the Church of Silence in which, under the oppression of the Communist regime, so many Christians, so many priests, and so many bishops are being imprisoned and tortured, if not killed, because of their faith'? How can we expect high Soviet authorities to react to Cardinal Ottaviani's statement just before the President of the Italian Republic left for Moscow: 'The days of Tamburlane have returned. . . . It is no longer possible to talk of genuine peace, nor even of coexistence, with the unpunished murderer'?

It is not up to me to pass any judgment on these statements of high-ranking prelates of the Roman Church. But I do wonder if the men responsible for them have taken into account the effect such words must necessarily have in Moscow and the consequences they will entail for all Christianity in the Soviet Union.

In upper Kremlin circles, they must be saying: 'That is the way the representatives of religion really think; if we were to allow our Orthodox bishops to make public speeches on political matters inside this country, they might follow the same line as our foes in the West. We do not need any more proof; the clergy are our sworn enemies.' And if once they catch wind of what their superiors are saying and thinking, minor local officials will consider themselves justified in refusing materials for rebuilding a country church or in inflicting some petty annoyances on the men they see as the 'enemies of the nation'.

A very well-informed Orthodox priest told me one day: 'I am less afraid of anything that all the renegade priests may do than I am of a single papal encyclical.'

It was the same priest, however, who was obviously saddened to hear me say that, in the present situation, the Russian Orthodox could hardly depend on moral support from the Church of Rome, no matter how badly they may seem in need of it. And that is the really tragic side of the situation.

Can we foresee—or even imagine—a change? Everyone knows that Roman teaching rises above contingencies and that it is applied always with reference to eternity. But, working as it is in this world, the Roman Curia should, no less than anyone else, take all the facts into consideration. There have been many occasions when political arrangements have made it modify its attitude. Without going back too far into past centuries, it is enough to recall that it finally and definitely came to terms with the French Republican Government against which it had struggled for so long. Though a compromise between Christian faith and atheism is impossible by definition, must the Vatican's condemnation extend, for all that, to a Socialist structure of society?

Despite allegations to the contrary, the Soviet regime has never laid hands on its citizens' private property; what it did do was abolish the right to hold production equipment as private property. The Vatican's condemnation of this step is still in force. On 1 September 1944 Pope Pius XII declared: 'The Christian conscience cannot recognize as just a social order which denies in principle or makes practically impossible or vain the natural right to property either of the benefits of usage or of production.'

Is this point of view unchanging? Is a Christian forbidden to accept the nationalization of any—or all—branches of industry?

The answer to this question was given on 10 June 1927 by Metropolitan (later Patriarch) Sergei: 'If the State demands that one renounce his property, if he must sacrifice his life for the common good, if it is a question of denying oneself in the service of society—all this is taught to the Christian by his faith.'

Is the controversy insurmountable? At this point it might be well to cite a passage from a pastoral issued to all the Catholics of the diocese of Riga by Bishop Strod a short time after my visit to him:

'Since the men who are united into States and Churches are the same, there must be loyal coexistence between the Church and the State. Faithful to this principle, we Catholics of the Soviet Socialist Republic of Latvia strive to accomplish our civic duties honestly, and we strive at the same time to be loving children of our Holy Roman Catholic Church, in conformity with the principle laid down by Our Lord Jesus Christ, "Render unto Caesar the things that are Caesar's, and to God the things that are God's".'

If the text of this pastoral came to the attention of a certain large Vatican periodical it would probably discount it with the same 'lie' with which it contradicted recent declarations of the Hungarian Catholic Action group: 'These are, unfortunately, false statements made by men who are perfectly aware of the reality of their situation but forced to hide this reality and misrepresent it, under governmental pressure.'

As far as I am concerned, I had the opportunity to talk with Bishop Strod (of whose premature death I have recently, and much to my regret, learned), and one hour with that magnificent prelate was enough to help me understand his character; I testify on my soul and conscience that he was not a man to submit to any pressure whatever when composing messages to his flock.

Will the day come when the voices of Soviet Christians reach the lofty places of the Holy See? The attitude of Pope John XXIII was defined in *Informations Catholiques Internationales* on 1 November 1959: 'The Holy Father has not, of course, done or said anything which might increase the tension already existing between Communist powers and the Church. . . . But neither has he said or done anything which would lead anyone to believe that Rome's attitude towards Communism has changed in any way.'

Perhaps a development of international contacts will lead to a clearer manifestation of the feelings of understanding and good-will which, from every indication, motivate that former representative of the Holy See in Bulgaria. The latest Encyclical of the Holy Father appears already as an important move in that direction.

Some newspapers recently reported the visit to Moscow of Father Antonio Messineo, director of the Jesuits' review, *Civiltà Cattolica*. The reason for this journey was said to have been to explore the possibilities of an agreement which would amplify the rights of the Catholic clergy in the U.S.S.R., and permit them to exercise their apostolate, open seminaries and make journeys to Rome without hindrance. The Church, the article continues, could reciprocate by contributing to a relaxation of international tension. Let us hope that this news is a sign of good things to come; millions of Russian Christians would be overjoyed if the project should be realized.

Compared with Catholicism in the Soviet Union, Protestantism is in an entirely different situation.

There is no political problem bothering the ninety-six Reformed parishes which are concentrated in the Carpathian mountains in recently annexed eastern Ukrainia, nor the 447 Lutheran parishes. Elsewhere, the disappearance of the German colonies in Moscow and Leningrad, however, was responsible for the closing of Protestant churches in those cities; the excellent schools which they owned and directed have also disappeared and the last Latvian church in the former capital, a wooden building which was destroyed during the siege of the city, could not be rebuilt because there were not the twenty parishioners which the law demands as the basis of a religious association. The last German republic of the Volga, formerly a leading centre of Protestantism, no longer exists.

In Latvia and Esthonia the disappearance of the Baltic barons, the traditional protectors and benefactors of the Lutheran parishes, as well as of the German-speaking intellectuals, from among whom most of the pastors, organists and professors of theology came, naturally weakened the influence of Protestantism. It is also equally possible that the hatred of the people for Hitler's sackers fell indirectly upon religious groups whose most eminent representatives were of German descent.

On the whole, however, Protestantism has been able to hold its ground, as I learned from the extremely reassuring details outlined for me by Pastor Klepperi, who was acting for the Lutheran Archbishop of Riga in his absence:

'Our activity is carried on under perfectly normal conditions. We always have large congregations; there are two services each day at Christmas time. Sermons are given in Latvian only and everyone understands them, which was not the case when our ministers frequently used to preach in German.

'We are not, naturally, as wealthy as we used to be; we have not been able to gather together the three or four million rubles necessary for the reconstruction of our old Domkirche. The State has taken the restoration work into its own hands, and we have been assured that, once the work has been completed, we shall be able to use the church, now classed as an historical monument, once a month.

'Contributions from our congregations are enough for our own needs, however; my income as pastor of the New Church of St Gertrude, for example, is altogether comfortable [4,000 rubles a month]; I have no car, nor has the Archbishop, though pastors in outlying parishes are generally able to buy one.

'Many of our churches were destroyed during the Second World War but we have been able to restore about ninety per cent of them. The three churches which used to be in Ielgava were all destroyed, and we have built a new church there, and have done the same thing in three other places. At Riga, however, we had to close the Peterskirche when its parishioners, who were all Germans, joined Hitler in 1939.

'We confirm young people every year, after they have gone through a period of preparation and studied the catechism and the Bible. In 1954 we issued a hymn-book (*Dziesmu gramata*) in an edition of 5,000 copies and are now preparing a new edition of it. In 1960 we published a psalter (*Jauna Deriba Psalmi*) and have been selling its 1,500 copies at the very reasonable price of eighty-five rubles.

'Since the war, there has been no theological faculty as the University of Tartu [Dorpat], but we have instituted theological courses for the training of future ministers, and twenty-eight men, whose ages range between twenty and forty, are now enrolled in them. Not many changes have been made in the programme of studies, except that we no longer teach classical Hebrew, because we consider it useless from the practical point of view. Textbooks we need are sent us from Germany and England. Any student who wants to make further studies has every opportunity to go to either of those countries; as a matter of fact, one twenty-five-year-old student recently left for Oxford, where he will prepare his doctoral dissertation.

'We are in permanent contact with our co-religionists abroad. Mgr Turss, our archbishop, has already visited Sweden, Czechoslovakia, England and the United States and, at this moment, he is attending a meeting of the Christian Union of Lutheran Churches at Berlin. Archbishop Kiivit of Talinn also makes many journeys. We shall soon be taking part in a theological conference held at Bièvres, near Versailles, by the Puidoux Movement.

'I cannot deny that we are often the object of attacks originating in atheist circles, and that our young people are not always impervious to this sort of propaganda; my three daughters, who are medical students and convinced Christians, prefer not to discuss religion with their friends. But if you ask me if I think there is any possibility that Christianity in our country will completely disappear, I can only make one reply: the idea is laughable.'

.   .   .   .   .   .

Several thousand kilometres from Riga, in the magnificent monastery at Etchmiadzin, I was standing in the religious centre of one of the earliest countries converted to Christianity.

The teachings of Christ were brought to Armenia in A.D. 34 by the Apostle Thaddeus, who was followed by the Apostle Bartholomew. Since that time, it has survived invasions and every other kind of political and social upheaval. In recent years, during the first few decades of the new regime, it underwent particularly difficult trials. At least a thousand churches were closed; a movement modelled on the 'Living Church' group in Russia was organized under the same name and stirred up trouble among the clergy; Patriarch-Katholikos Khoren was assassinated in 1938, and no successor could be elected until 1945.

Today, however, the position of the Armenian Church has improved beyond all reasonable hope. Long-standing racial enmity which steeped the Caucasus in blood for so many generations and had so many Armenian victims has finally abated.

In a country such as Armenia, where religious feelings are so intimately bound up with nationalist attitudes, the extraordinary development of the young Republic of Armenia has been an essentially contributive force in rehabilitating the prestige of the Church, the traditional guardian of native culture.

The head of this Church is rightly called the 'Katholikos of all the Armenians', because his countrymen all over the world recognize him as their spiritual leader and are unfailingly generous in supporting his needs and projects; one of his most important benefactors is supposed to be the petroleum millionaire, Mr Gulbenkian.

Residence of the Patriarch-Katholikos, the monastery of Etchmiadzin is an historic site whose origins can be traced back to the second century of our epoch. There has been a cathedral on the place since the beginning of the fourth century, and the present building was erected at the end of the fifth century, but has been reconstructed several times since then. As it stands now, it is a remarkable specimen of the old Armenian architectural genius for combining Byzantine influence with Romanesque style. Constructed in grey stone, the cathedral at Etchmiadzin remains impressive today with its cruciform outline, its dome and square towers topped by arches and pointed roofs. All around the church grow venerable old trees, their trunks grey and gnarled, but their leaves a fresh green, shading the old church building which gleams in the golden sunlight. The thick lawns of the enclosure are dotted with long slabs of stone marked with epitaphs and Armenian crosses.

As I assisted at the liturgy and, later, walked in the lovely cathedral gardens, I did not consider the people more fervent than others I had seen in various holy places throughout the Soviet Union—contrary to reports of some foreign visitors, such as the great Italian novelist Alberto Moravia. Perhaps there were more young men and women present, and perhaps the gay colours of the women's dresses and the bright noonday sun made the crowd leaving the cathedral at the end of the service seem more picturesque. The only thing which I could single out as singularly impressive was the liturgical singing—I have never heard anything as beautiful.

I was told later that the music was written by the great national composer, Vardapet Comitas, who died in 1913 and is buried in the monastery. He studied music in Paris and Germany and succeeded in ridding his country's religious music of all the old Byzantine influences.

When I arrived at Etchmiadzin, Katholikos Vazgen I had left for a visitation of the Armenian communities in the United States (New York, Boston, Detroit, Chicago, Los Angeles and San

Francisco), and I was very warmly received by his vicar, Archbishop Saak.

We had luncheon together in the Katholikos's quarters, and the
table was presided over by a charming white-haired old lady, the
Katholikos's mother. Afterwards, we went to sit in the shade of
the old trees with Archbishop Aprahamian of Jerusalem and
Bishop Vartam of Kara Bey. During the long conversation which
followed, Archbishop Saak outlined an extremely reassuring
picture of his Church's present situation. I found him no less
optimistic than the other qualified representatives of religious
minorities with whom I had talked.

'We are Gregorians,' he said, 'which means that we recognize
the Councils of Nicaea, Constantinople and Ephesus, but not of
Chalcedon, and we have remained loyal to our doctrines for more
than a thousand years. On Soviet Armenian territory we now
have five dioceses, of which the Ararat jurisdiction, which has
thirty churches, ten monasteries and about a hundred priests, is
larger than the other four together. In Turkey and other countries,
naturally, there are more Gregorians. I should say that there are a
good two million Armenians living all over the world, in
addition to those still living here.

'The community at the Etchmiadzin monastery includes fifty-
five clerics, over and above the forty students at the theological
academy who are given a very thorough six-year training after
finishing their secondary education. It would take too much time
to go through the list of subjects taught, but perhaps you can get
some idea of it when I tell you that, in addition to the various
branches of theology (pastoral, dogmatic and ascetic), the history
of dogma, biblical criticism (Protestant and Catholic) and
Biblical commentary, the seminarians also study logic,
psychology, history and philosophy (which the Katholikos
teaches himself), national and religious music and a variety of
languages (classical and modern Armenian, Greek, Russian,
French and English).

'As for convinced believers, there are more of them now,

believe me, than there were under the Tsars. And you may be surprised to learn that a large number of them are Communists. I cannot deny that anti-religious propaganda has had success in some quarters, especially in rural areas, where baptisms are very rare now, while the churches in Erevan, on the other hand, are always crowded. I have no idea what the next twenty years will bring, but feel I am justified in being confident now and saying that it will take infinitely longer than that for anyone to see the end of our ancient Armenian faith.'

.   .   .   .   .

As I was flying across Central Asia over the bluish Caucasus range, the Caspian Sea and the arid Tadzhikistan desert, I wondered if the opinions I should hear expressed by the heads of the Soviet's Moslem communities might not be entirely different.

Though it is now a model city and the most striking example of everything the Soviet system has to offer the people of Central Asia, Tashkent has nevertheless retained its old native quarter with its narrow, dusty streets, its tiny mud houses all whitewashed, its *tchai-kane*, or open-air tea-rooms, and all the strange attractiveness of life in the East.

It was in this quarter, in the flowering courtyard of a superb *medresse* (theological seminary), which seemed brand new and is the seat of Moslem religious jurisdiction in Central Asia, that I introduced myself to the Secretary General of the institution, Mr Fakhrudinov, who kindly gave me details about the Moslems' present situation.

'There are four Moslem "directorates",' he explained, 'in the Soviet Union: ours, the one in Ufa (at the foot of the Urals), the one at Baku and the last, which is at Bunaisk and controls the northern Caucasus and Dagestan. The heads of these directorates, called *muftis*, are appointed by local Moslem religious authorities. Each of them has local representatives (*mukhtasibs*) who are superior in rank to the *imams* (the officials in charge of the mosques) and other ministers of worship.

'We put all this operation into effect in our own region in October 1943, when we called a congress of Moslems living in the five Soviet republics in Central Asia. During the meetings, the 1,115 delegates elected the Grand Mufti Abdul Madjid Khan; he has been succeeded by Grand Mufti Babikhanov, who is now away on holiday.

'Despite the fact that many of our places of worship were suppressed after the Revolution, Moslems in Central Asia now have 178 mosques (of which thirty-five are in Kazakhstan), to say nothing of the many little local houses of worship called *Makkalin*, whose ministers are appointed by the local Moslems.

'Our mosques used to be supported in large part by wealthy landowners who appointed the *imams* themselves. Now our own people provide for whatever needs their religion may have. It was because of this revenue that we were able to build two new, imposing mosques at Tashkent and take up complete restoration work in other areas whose mosques were almost all in very bad repair. The Government is taking care of restoring our historical monuments (such as the tombs of Kussam Ibn Abbas at Samarkand, Sheik Bakhodin at Bokhara, Palva Ata at Khiva, etc.) and has put them at our disposal. Other historic monuments of this nature, such as the famous Gur Emir at Samarkand, have been made into national museums.

'Our directorate's activities are very broad and include the maintenance of mosques; the appointment of *khatibs* and *imams* and the supervision of their religious ministry; and direction of its various delegates, through its intermediary, the *mokhtassid*. It publishes *fatva* (explanations of the Koran), the most recent of which condemned the superstitious veneration of false holy people which has grown up in some areas. In 1959 and 1960 it published the text of the Koran (in two impressions of 4,000 and 5,000 copies respectively) and is having them distributed through local mosques at the modest price of sixty-three rubles. Finally, it maintains contact with Moslems abroad through correspondence and an exchange of visits; it organizes annual pilgrimages to

Mecca in an aircraft chartered by the Government for that purpose. Several dozen Moslems go on the pilgrimage each year.

'We have two *medresses*. The one here is called Barakkhan, and the one at Bokhara, called Mir el Arab, was built in 1535 by Khan Ubaidullah. Students come to these institutions from all over Central Asia, and their ages vary between twenty and forty. The nine-year course of studies includes: the Koran (reading and commentary), Koranic doctrine and tradition, the history of Islam, Arabic (conversation, morphology and syntax), Persian, Russian, arithmetic and geography. There are now about thirty-two students here at Tashkent.

'Islamic regulations make no provision for a census of the faithful and it has never been done before. The most I can say is that our mosques, in which our people pray five times each day, are always very well attended; two to three thousand men, and about fifty women, attend services on Friday in the mosque across the road. On feast days, we have two or three times as many in attendance.

'We cannot complain of losing large numbers of our faithful to atheist propaganda which, on the whole, has spared Islam; newspaper attacks are usually directed against the *makkalin*. Though there are not many young people who come to the mosques, that is not very significant because our religion does not demand regular attendance at services. Looking at it from several angles, the changes effected during the last generation or so have had a salutary effect. Religion is no longer at the service of the wealthy; there are no more *mollah* to establish mosques for their own purposes as they used to do. Our sole source of doctrine now is the Koran.'

After leaving my host, I crossed the street, walked through a broad courtyard and stopped at the door of the mosque. It was an hour for prayer; small groups of Moslems crossed the threshold and went into the interior of the mosque which was forbidden to me. I could see them kneel and bow their heads (here they all wore turbans) to the ground, all the while devoutly murmuring their prayers. Afterwards, I saw them leaving, looking serious and reflective, and speaking in hushed voices. Most of them were rather mature men.

I had been given incontestable proof that Islam enjoys complete liberty at Tashkent. But was that the only place involved? The fleeting impressions I had gathered during a long meeting with a ranking official were not enough to give me an exact idea of the religious situation in Central Asia.

In this region, I felt exactly like the tourist who lands at Moscow ignorant of the country's language, customs and mentality. I had never lived in a Moslem country for very long, and Islam remained a closed world to me. I did not know to what extent this religion could be adapted to the life of modern people who have been Europeanized and industrialized. I thought I had found the answer to that question in a little book written by a young American Catholic priest who recently travelled far and wide through Central Asia:

'Everywhere I went, it was obvious that Islam's heyday in Central Asia had passed. There is no persecution of the Mohammedans, of course, but it is not necessary. Contrary to Christianity, Islam cannot survive for very long without some sort of political activity and, if possible, a society which is governed entirely according to its principles.

The Communists have succeeded in having Islam accept the same legal existence they have offered the Orthodox Church and though, judging from my, granted limited, observations, Orthodoxy will survive, I cannot say the same for Islam.'[1]

But generalizations are always dangerous. The conditions under which Islam is living in the modern Soviet Union ensure it

[1] G. Bissonnette, *Moscow Was My Parish*, London and New York. Attached to the United States Embassy in Moscow, the author never had a 'parish' in the Soviet Union. He considered himself the 'only priest living in Moscow' [*sic*] and admits that he never had any contact with the Orthodox or Catholic clergy in the capital. Nevertheless, his observations on Central Asia seem useful and quite interesting.

every opportunity to survive. What seems more doubtful, however, is the possibility Mohammedanism has of exercising a genuinely effective influence on the spiritual life of the some fifteen million men and women scattered throughout the various Soviet Republics whose populations are principally Moslem. The transition from a medieval social structure to modern society's economic and social condition took several centuries in Christian countries; in Moslem countries, on the other hand, we see it happen in a single leap. In the Soviet Union the old framework of Moslem society, far less solid than in the Middle East or North Africa, is now a thing of the past; the bazaar has given way to the factory or the kolkhoz office. Women in Islam do not play the role of guardian of ancestral beliefs which they enjoy in the Christian world. Islam has no religious centre comparable to Rome or the Patriarchate of Moscow. Can the same religious faith and zeal which once motivated the Arabs of the desert retain its hold on the souls of the Russified Uzbeks, Tadzhiks and Turkmans? Only the future will tell.

·   ·   ·   ·   ·

I did not travel into Siberia and China to visit the Buddhists in the Buriato-Mongol Republic and the regions around Irkutsk and Chita. Their registered communities hardly number more than about twenty in a population of 250,000. They have a lamasery in the Aginsk district, and their religious leader in the Soviet Union is called the Bandido Khambo Lama. There is no doubt that, when the last vestiges of feudalism disappeared from amongst the Buriats and Mongols under the Soviet regime, it took with it much of the influence once enjoyed by the lamas.

In view of these conditions, it seemed to me that a journey to this area would be completely useless.[1]

·   ·   ·   ·   ·

[1] There are some interesting facts about the history of Buddhism in the Soviet Union in an article by Nicholas N. Poppe included in the collection *Religion in the U.S.S.R.* Cf. *supra.*

There was no need for me to make a journey to gather information about the Jewish religion in the Soviet. There is a synagogue in Moscow. No matter where one goes in the capital, especially in university, literary or artistic circles, one meets men and women with Jewish-sounding names. I spoke to many of them and some of them did not hesitate to pour out their grievances to me, with the frankness which is so habitual in that country.

Basically, their complaints were social or political, and as such did not come into the scope of my investigation. I make a brief mention of them, here, however, because race and religion are so intimately connected in the Jewish community.[1]

Antisemitism was unknown in medieval Russia for the simple reason that there were no Jews. It was not until Ukrainia was joined to Russia and Polish and Lithuanian provinces were annexed that the Tsars had a large number of Jewish subjects. For a long time, most of them were left to shift for themselves in the poverty and ignorance of their ghettoes. Official antisemitism only developed when some of the more advanced elements of the Jewish population began to study and accumulate some wealth.

Officially, discrimination was based on religion alone; a Jew had only to convert to Christianity to enjoy full civil rights, and it is curious to notice that in the long list of imperial chancellors there were three non-Aryan statesmen who directed Moscow's foreign policy for several decades.

But no quarter was given the overwhelming majority of Jews who preferred to remain faithful to the Mosaic law. During the last few decades of the regime, an entire body of fiercely anti-semitic legislation grew up. Restricted to the eastern provinces of the Empire, every Jew was denied the right to live beyond an unbending line of demarcation (and especially in capital cities) unless he had graduated from a university or paid the steep sums demanded for commercial licences. A *numerus clausus* (five per

[1] For a more detailed study, see the highly documented and objective work of François Fejtö, *Les Juifs et l'antisémitisme dans les pays communistes*, Paris: Plon, 1960.

cent of the pupils) regulated the number of them allowed to attend secondary schools and universities. Though they had to do military service, they could not rise to the ranks of officers; they were banned from civil administrative posts.

Not content with these restrictive measures, the Government set to work at stirring up the country's hatred for the Jews, to distract the people from the growing revolutionary feelings in the country. At the beginning of this century, this persecution was to result in those tragically infamous pogroms during which the lowest levels of the population were allowed to murder and pillage the ghettoes of some southern cities, under the benevolent eye of the police and the authorities.

'Pariahs' of Russian society, the Jews were naturally in the front ranks of the fighters for the Revolution. There were very many of them about Lenin, and they felt that their final victory was assured with the establishment of Soviet power. The October Revolution knocked down the walls of the ghettoes and gave the Jews access to all of Russia which, for the first time in her history, now became their real homeland. She purged her legal codes of all traces of the old discrimination and pilloried antisemitism as an attitude of reactionary minds.

Under these completely new conditions, Soviet Jewish culture, based on political and economic equality, evolved rapidly and reached a level previously unknown. About 1927 the Jewish Press had three large dailies and several small literary and scientific monthlies. Besides these, there were many local dailies in Odessa, Kiev, Berditshev and other cities. Institutes and sections of Jewish culture were attached to the Academies of Science of Ukrainia and of Byelorussia, and Moscow had a Jewish learned society. In those days the Soviet Union was the site of the largest network of Yiddish scholars in the world. A chain of sixteen theatres, with the Moscow State Yiddish Theatre at their head, was spread throughout the country. In Ukrainia and Byelorussia there were even Jewish courts and several dozen Jewish local Soviets, both in urban and rural areas.

The good times were not destined to last long, however. As the level of the Russian nation's culture rose, the need for a Jewish collaboration in the country's new organization was less strongly felt. Mr Khrushchev himself put it very clearly in 1956 when he was addressing a group of French Socialists:

'At the beginning of the Revolution, we had many Jews in top-level offices of the Party and State. They were better educated and, perhaps, more revolutionary than the average Russian. Afterwards, however, we educated a sufficient number of specialists. . . . If Jews wanted to hold the highest positions in our Republics now, they would, naturally, be resented by the indigenous populations. It is not difficult to understand that there would be jealousy and hostility if, in Ukrainia for instance, a Jew were named to an important post and surrounded himself with other Jews as his aides.'

Besides, when they saw that the Jews were more and more involved in the nation's economic and cultural life, the authorities recognized that the moment had come to encourage their total integration into the country. As early as 1913, Lenin had said that 'only the Jews of the *petite bourgeoisie*, the ones who would like to turn the wheel of history back, hold out against assimilation'. For the Jews who remained stubborn and intransigent the Government created the eastern Siberian 'Autonomous Jewish Republic of Birobidjan', a strictly artificial organization which in 1956 had a population of only 157,000, of whom 30,000 to 35,000 were Jews. The hope was that other Jews would gradually allow themselves to become absorbed into the vast Soviet community. At Stalin's direction, all specifically Jewish institutions and organizations were then closed, including the theatres and periodicals, which were considered incapable of covering their operating costs. A single Yiddish daily, *The Birobidjan Star*, is still in operation.

Another thing which, in its turn, was to have a deleterious effect on the position of Soviet Jews was the evolution of international politics. At the time when the 'cold war' was raging at its strongest, some circles thought they were right in accusing the Jews of 'cosmopolitanism', because they had connections with the whole world, especially with the United States. When Israel (which the Kremlin was the first to recognize) came into open conflict with the Arab powers, the Jews were suspected of 'nationalism', because they showed signs of sympathy and concern for the people of their race in Palestine.

It is completely impossible to root out racist feelings in forty years, especially after Nazi propaganda revived them in occupied territories. One expert in the subject, J. Isaac, has written: 'Spread for hundreds and hundreds of years by thousands and thousands of voices, Christian antisemitism is the powerful, thousand-year-old trunk, with its many and strong roots upon which (in the Christian world) have been carved the many varieties of anti-semitism—even those most opposed to nature and most anti-christian.'[1]

In the light of all this, can anyone affirm, as some have done, that antisemitism is raging in the Soviet Union today? 'While I was in Russia,' writes Father Bissonnette, whom we cited above, 'it must have been dormant. Of course, Judaism gets no more official protection from the state than any other religion does. But most Russians I met demonstrated no open hostility towards the Jews. They do not look very kindly on their success in minor businesses, but that is merely the envy of an unsuccessful man towards a man who has made his mark.' It seems to me, however, that our American observer has once more oversimplified the case.

It is an easy matter to understand the indignation Mr Khrushchev and his aides felt when a malicious press accused them of 'following in Hitler's footsteps'. Allegations of this sort must strike them as monstrous.

[1] J. Isaac, *Génèse de l'antisémitisme*, Paris: 1956.

Soviet legislation on the point is precise. Paragraph 123 of the Constitution openly affirms:

'The equality of all citizens of the U.S.S.R., on all levels of economic, governmental, cultural, public and political life, independently of their race or their nationality, is an irrevocable law. Every direct or indirect restriction of racial or national rights or, conversely, the direct or indirect existence of racial or national privileges is tantamount to the propagation of racial or national discrimination and is punishable by law.'

This constitutional law is far from a dead letter to the Soviet people. I myself had a clear proof of this during a very curious incident I witnessed on a bus on the outskirts of Moscow.

A rather drunk passenger (a worker, judging from the way he was dressed) played a few songs on his accordion to the delight of the rest of us. Then, he broke out into a 'racist' harangue: 'I'm a *real* Russian,' he said, 'a Russian from Tula. You can tell that because I play the accordion. Jews play the piano; you only have to take a look at my chief engineer, he's a very clever chap. He made me pay a fine the other day and . . . he plays the piano!'

This naive and, actually, inoffensive remark provoked another worker, much older than the first, into replying indignantly that 'it is not allowed in our country to make remarks like that because there is no difference between the Jews and the rest of us, and because all discriminatory propaganda is strictly forbidden and punishable by law.'

The passengers seated around me nodded their heads in approval and the unfortunate drunk could do nothing but fall asleep, blushing with confusion, in his place.

A few statistics will make the situation even more eloquent. How can anyone make comparisons with Hitler's methods when referring to a country where there are 24,620 Jewish scientists out of a total of 223,000: where more than 60,000 Jews received medals and decorations for their part in the war, and fifty-nine of them proudly wear the star of a Hero of the Soviet Union; where there are 500 Jewish lawyers at the Moscow bar out of a total of 1,190 and the proportion of Jewish doctors is as impressive; where eighty Yiddish writers are members of the Writers' Union of the Soviet Union; where virtuosi like Kogan and the two Oistrakhs are the country's pride and glory; where Jewish machinists, mechanics and engineers are employed in all branches of industry, and where the launching of the Lunik was made possible by the direct co-operation of a leading Jewish scientist?

To be impartial, however, we must admit that numerous groups of Soviet Jews still feel some resentment. They are the first to recognize that there is no individual racial discrimination in the Soviet, but they claim that they are the victims of a rather intangible 'collective' discrimination.

How can we reproach these people, of whom Péguy said that 'there is no place on their bodies which is not suffering', with being hypersensitive?

The Jews in Russia—and in Poland—have broken all records for suffering and humiliation, in the past. They cannot forget the brief renaissance which Yiddish culture enjoyed. And they still have bitter memories of the trial held a short while before Stalin passed from the scene involving a group of doctors, most of whom were Jews and all of whom were innocent, as it was soon shown.

They put much store on the fact that out of the 2,268,000 Jews listed in the Soviet in 1959, 472,000 (20.8 per cent) gave Yiddish as their national and mother tongue, and argue that they should be able, therefore, to use it in their Press and theatres. Above all, they emphasize the inconvenience they are put to by having their nationality listed on their identification papers. The fact is, of course, that there are two entries on these papers which are the same for everyone; the first concerns citizenship, which is 'Soviet' for everyone, and the second lists the bearer's 'nationality' (the famous classification 'number 5'): Russian, Ukrainian,

Georgian, Armenian or . . . Jew. The Government has found that an excellent way to resolve the problem of 'nationalities', a task the Tsarist regime was incapable of settling.

The Latvians, Uzbeks, Caucasians, Lithuanians and all the other national groups fought against complete assimilation, and today they are proud not to be 'Russians'. The Jews, on the other hand, are the only group not to share this feeling because they think they are 'suspect' and because they have no national territory like the others (no one takes the Birobidjan republic seriously). I was told that a Jewish candidate for a position need only take out his passport and show it to be told: 'Thank you. We'll let you know. . . .' Some people even claim that the passport entry has made it more difficult for young Jews to gain entrance to the university; on this score, however, it seems more likely that the Jews are simply being inconvenienced in the same way as other groups in Soviet society are, and are obliged to put up with the growing crowded conditions in the country's institutes of higher education.

In none of the many conversations I had with Jewish intellectuals did the question of whether they enjoyed sufficient freedom to worship arise. This was the problem on which I was concentrating, but it seemed to leave them obviously indifferent. I had to go elsewhere to get the complete information I needed.

After I had asked at my hotel and obtained the address of the major synagogue, I went there one Saturday. The street to which I had been directed was very near the centre of the city, but I had no luck in finding it; a policeman came to my rescue, in a very friendly way, but he did not know where the street was either. Finally, he said that he would go and ask 'a Jewish workman who lives in this neighbourhood; he probably goes there often to pray'. It struck me that this was a far cry from Nuremberg.

When I finally walked into the main auditorium of the synagogue, it was crowded to bursting. Every bench was lined with men, each of them with his black-and-white prayer shawl about his shoulders, while the women sat in a gallery on an upper storey.

At the front of the congregation, I could see the Ambassador of Israel, who very solemnly mounted the steps up to the small platform at the front of the hall to participate in the readings from the Bible. Someone made room for me in one of the pews, and I sat down. My neighbours were overwhelmingly gracious and attentive; they told me how happy they were to meet a foreign visitor, and to show him that nothing and no one prevented them from assembling in their synagogue.

I asked someone to tell Rabbi Loeb Levine that I was in the synagogue, and I was immediately taken into his study. It struck me how like an old Rembrandt sketch he looked, his sharply defined profile, with its bushy beard, outlined against his library's shelves, each of them filled with old tomes. I took down word for word the information he was kind enough to give me, and I repeat it here in full:

'We are separated from the State, but are in no way in submission to it. The Council for Various Religious Groups limits its activities to providing the raw materials we need for the upkeep of the synagogue or for our publications.

'In 1956 we published a large book of prayers and had 4,000 copies printed, especially for our faithful in Moscow; we sell it at 100 rubles a copy for the benefit of our *yeshiva* (religious school). Other Jewish communities are collaborating with us in the preparation of a new edition.

'We are training future rabbis and specialists in ritual slaughtering, and currently have eighteen students whose course of studies lasts five years. We used previously to have many more.

'In the Moscow area we have four synagogues, two in the capital itself and two in the suburbs.

'Besides these, we also have a number of houses of prayer which have been established, in accordance with Soviet law, with a membership of at least ten Jews each. Since we have no central organization to unite all the believing Jews in the country, I could not tell you how many congregations of Jews there are on Soviet territory, though I do know that there are synagogues in the large urban settlements such as Kiev, Odessa, Kishinev, Krementshug and Dniepro-Petrovsk.

'In private conversations with the authorities we have already brought up the question of creating a religious centre, but we have not yet instituted official proceedings on the subject. Our people get their *matsoth* [unleavened bread] during Passover from State bakeries. This year "Bakeshop No. 9" provided three tons a day between 20 February and 10 April, and people could buy it at several stores for about seventeen rubles a pound. No one complained of not being able to get any, especially since many people make their own *matsoth* at home.

'There is no reason for our religion to consider itself oppressed. During the summer months our synagogue is open between six o'clock in the morning and half past ten at night; each morning, the faithful relay one another in groups of ten to read the Bible and certain prayers. During the week about 300 people are present, and the figure jumps to about a thousand on the Sabbath. On religious holidays the whole street outside the synagogue is crowded with our overflow. Twice a month a cantor comes to enhance our ceremonies by his singing talents. Members of our synagogue belong to all walks of life; we have doctors, engineers, and commercial and co-operative employees.

'If you want my opinion on the extent of antisemitic tendencies, I cannot help comparing it to our situation in Russia under the Tsars. I know I need not remind you of all the annoyances various laws inflicted on us in those days. Just to give you an idea of something of what it was like then, however, let me recall two isolated incidents.

'One day Grand Duke Michael, the Tsar's brother, was being driven in his carriage along a great road which passed near our synagogue. Noticing the steeple that was on its roof in those days, he made the sign of the Cross; his *aide de camp* explained his error to him and the authorities immediately decided to have the steeple removed. It is a harmless little story, but there were other incidents which were far more tragic. For instance, Grand Duke Sergei, the Tsar's uncle and Governor-General of Moscow, decided to expel, in a single week, the 25,000 Jews of all ages and conditions who were resident in the capital.

'Things like that are unimaginable today. The era of pogroms and of the so-called "patriotic", but actually antisemitic, organizations has passed. All this sort of activity was directed from above, by the authorities in power at the time who were, perhaps, under some German influence or other.

'In our time the Constitution guarantees the rights of all the people and all religious confessions. Our Government is working to establish friendship between all races. If anyone tried to treat you like a "Yid", he would be severely punished by the local tribunal. Antisemitic tendencies are restricted to the older generation, who have not yet been able to throw off the old prejudices.

'Recently there was a disturbance in a school when one boy, insulted for being a Jew by one of his schoolmates, answered the insult by hitting the other one with his fist. The director of the school began enquiries immediately and discovered that the insulter's grandmother was an inveterate antisemite.

'We are living in an atmosphere completely bereft of hostility. We worship in freedom; although many of our synagogues were closed between 1924 and 1940, this one has always remained open under the new regime. It was under the Tsars that our doors were sealed from 1891 to 1906.'

In his rabbinic wisdom my respected host did not refer to conditions in other areas outside Moscow. It was not until I had returned to Paris that I learned from the highly documented publications of the International Jewish Congress that Soviet Jews in the provinces are not always in as favourable situations as their co-religionists in the capital.

Indeed, in the very outskirts of Moscow, hooligans set fire to the synagogue at Malakhovka in 1959, around the same time that similar incidents were happening in Germany and other Western countries.

In many cities with a large Jewish population (Kishinev, Czernovitz) people had difficulty getting *matsoth*. Synagogues were reported to have been closed during recent years (about forty out of ninety, according to some accounts), at Czernovitz, for instance; for several years, not a single synagogue has been built and none of the closed synagogues has been reopened for worship.

At Kharkov, where there are 70,000 Jews, they have no place of worship. The Press indulge in violent attacks against the Jews, just as against other religious groups.[1] Two rabbis are said to have been arrested in Lithuania on charges of having appropriated funds and given religious instruction to children.

All these questions were examined at length during an international conference held at Paris during the autumn of 1960.

To conclude this chapter I feel I should cite a passage from the resolution passed by the delegates at the conference; it was resolved:

'That, in conformity with the nation's Constitution, practicing Soviet Jews should be given authority to practice their religion without impediment, to publish their religious literature, and to maintain the central and local institutions necessary for the satisfaction of their religious needs and for the maintenance of theological schools.

Furthermore, that Soviet Jews should be authorized to maintain contact with Jewish institutions abroad, in the same way other religious groups in the Soviet do.'

In my opinion, it would not be difficult to remedy most of the

[1] Cf., especially, the pamphlet of T. Ketchko, *The Judaic Religion, its Origins and its Essence* (in Russian), Kiev: 1957.

abuses singled out, since there is nothing which allows us to believe that the present state of affairs is final and permanent. Authorization has been given quite recently to start a publication of a literary periodical in Yiddish. At bottom, would not the answer lie in making some sort of official declaration which would restore to the unassimilated Jews in the Soviet Union their feelings of self-respect?

12

A Final Picture: With the Patriarch

THE last mental image I took away from the Soviet Union was of fervent crowds at the convent of the Trinity and St Sergei. On the very eve of my departure I was taken there for the services celebrating the 538th anniversary of the discovery of the relics of the monastery's founder, and to be received in private audience by His Holiness Patriarch Alexei of Moscow and All the Russias.

The monastery is about forty miles outside Moscow, and is linked with the capital by a fine roadway which passes through industrial suburbs and a cheerful countryside.

During the fourteenth century, while Russia still groaned under the heavy yoke of the Mongols, the whole area was covered by vast forests which stretched farther than the eye could see. It was in the shade of these birches and firs, and on the banks of a small stream, that a young nobleman, Bartholomew of Radonezh, the future St Sergei, came to live as a hermit and consecrate himself entirely to worshipping God.

Keeping himself alive on dried bread brought to him by pious folk from neighbouring villages, he passed his days reading the Gospels and clearing the forest. Wild animals prowled all about him; he tamed a young bear, and it came back every day to share his frugal meal.

News of the young nobleman and the life he was leading soon spread throughout the countryside; a few fervent souls joined the hermit and shared his way of life. In 1340, or thereabouts, about twelve huts, surrounded by a palisade of logs, were built in the

211

forest; the renowned *Laura* (monastery) of the Most Holy Trinity had come into being.

Like another great figure of Christianity, the 'Poverello' of Assisi, St Sergei of Radonezh played an immense part in the moral restoration of an oppressed nation. He revived Russian monasticism and gave an example of true Christian living to all his contemporaries. He was peacemaker in many feudal quarrels, and his blessing fired the zeal of the warriors who went out under Dmitri Donskoy to free Russia of the Tartar yoke on the battlefield at Kulikovo.

Down through the generations, his monastery has become a veritable national shrine, and its glorious destiny has always been an integral part of the history of Russia.

Centuries have rolled past, but pious pilgrims have never stopped coming to St Sergei's tomb in tens of thousands, despite the radical changes which have developed in the structure and attitudes of Russian society.

'The figure of an historic person sometimes transforms itself into an abstract idea,' wrote Klutshevski, the greatest of Russian historians, 'and that is what happened in the case of St Sergei. By invoking the name of St Sergei, today's people affirm yet again that political strength is not unshakeable unless it rests on moral strength. And the flickering candles on his tomb will only go out when we have gone through the spiritual treasure which has been left us, without taking care to replace it.' Judging from what I saw at the monastery, I feel sure that such a danger is not imminent.

Approaching the industrial hamlet of Zagorsk, one can make out the entire outline of the monastery on a little rise in the distance. Framed in their crenellated white walls, the buildings painted in pastel colours and pale gold stand out brilliantly, almost like something from a fairytale. Over all of them, rise the five domes of the Cathedral of the Dormition, each painted dark blue with golden stars. A Baroque belltower five storeys high and painted in pink and white lends an almost whimsical note to an essentially Russian panorama, worthy of an old ikon-painter.

St Sergei's relics lie in a large silver casket, the gift of Ivan the Terrible, under the vault of the small Church of the Trinity and St Sergei, built in 1422. A square building, the church (or rather chapel) is beautiful in its simplicity and has no other ornament except the six images on its ikonostasis, which is the work of the great medieval master, Andrei Rublev. It was behind this ikonostasis that, as is his custom, Patriarch Alexei was to celebrate the liturgy.

I had already had several opportunities to visit the monastery of the Trinity and St Sergei. I had visited its many churches and museums as a tourist; I had stopped before the simple gravestone of Boris Godunov resting in the shade of a few birches; I had had long conversations with the Superior and the Rector of the seminary; I had taken Communion in the Cathedral of the Dormition; I had even had the surprise of seeing groups of school-girls in the white blouses and red ties of the Communist youth movement strolling round the holy buildings a little disconcerted.

Never before, however, had I been in the midst of such a crowd. At least 15,000 people had come to observe this solemn occasion from Moscow and every corner of Russia. Old women and husky farmers, smartly dressed young women and townspeople in felt hats—all of them were pressing on towards one or another of the churches, from which liturgical singing floated out. They overwhelmed the courtyards and the gardens; they formed queues to fill small bottles with the water which is said to be miraculous and flows from a spring discovered by St Sergei (even doctors have recognized its curative qualities); one after another, they came up to the young monk who was accompanying me to ask his blessing and kiss his hand.

One would have to have the talents of a great poet to reproduce the atmosphere which filled the church where the Patriarch was officiating: the casket containing the saint's relics lighted by countless candles; the clergy in their resplendent vestments; the closely packed pilgrims deep in prayer; the endless flow of banknotes being given to the monk in charge of the collection; and those marvellous singers, of whom Berlioz said, after his visit to Russia, that 'to compare them with the choir of the Sistine Chapel is like comparing the orchestra of the Paris Conservatory to a little group of scrapers in some third-rate theatre. . . . The incredible accents of this music make one tremble with thrills which are almost painful, and which one cannot control.'

When the Patriarch raised the Holy Gifts it was like being taken to another world. The Earl of Bessborough, one of the invited foreign guests, who was standing beside me, leaned towards me and whispered: 'It is an extraordinary sight. The whole world should know about it.'

After the services the cathedrals, the churches and the chapels emptied and a hymn of thanksgiving was sung out of doors in the monastery's main courtyard, in the presence of at least 10,000 people. The new President of the Council for Orthodox Church Affairs was standing very near the Patriarch.

After the Patriarch had withdrawn to his quarters, he came out on a balcony above the crowd standing beneath him and gave them his blessing. Members of the higher clergy made their way to an immense refectory, decorated with superb ikons, to which I was escorted for a luncheon whose party included, in addition to other ranking ecclesiastics, eighteen archbishops and bishops.

After a short rest at a hostel reserved ordinarily for the clergy, I was finally summoned to the Patriarch. I was eminently aware of the great honour I was being accorded: contrary to ordinary custom at the Vatican, the head of the Russian Orthodox Church only receives laymen on very rare occasions.

Patriarch Alexei is of an imposing appearance, rather like a great nobleman transplanted from old Russia to the new Soviet Union. He is an aristocrat by birth; his father, Vladimir Simanski, was a Chamberlain at the Imperial Court. But he is also—and above all—an aristocrat of mind and heart.

While still an adolescent and a student at Moscow's most select college, he discovered his vocation. Bowing to his family's wishes, however, he obtained a university degree and submitted a thesis in international law before entering the theological academy. He then went on an extended tour abroad and still has the most vivid memories of his short stay in Paris.

He finally became a monk when he was twenty-two. His career in the Church since that day has been brilliant: successively Inspector of the seminary at Pskov, and Rector of the seminaries at Tula and Novgorod, he was consecrated Bishop in 1913. After serving as Vicar-General in two dioceses, he was named Archbishop of Novgorod, member of the Holy Synod and Metropolitan of Leningrad, before finally being elected to the Russian Orthodox Church's supreme dignity, in which post he was to follow the same historically oriented course already charted by his two great predecessors, Patriarchs Tikhon and Sergei.

A man of profound culture, endowed with broad intellectual horizons, and possessed of a rare appreciation of actualities, to say nothing of his exquisite aesthetic tastes, Patriarch Alexei has had wide spiritual and administrative experience. He is unwavering in his firm defence of dogma, but does not shrink at showing tolerance for the opinions of others while remaining faithful to his own ideas. His uprightness and sincere Christian love have won the admiration of all around him.

The governing principle motivating all Patriarch Alexei's activity is to preserve intact the teaching of the Church; he wants to purify her and marshal her forces. But he also wants to maintain normal relations with the State, in order to be able to direct the lives of his flock in the most effective way. He has sometimes been accused of being too lenient with his clergy, and some people have felt that he should be a little more strict with them. It is by no means a simple thing, however, to administer the re-established clerical organization of his Church; 10 per cent of the present episcopate previously headed dioceses in Germany and Poland; some of them were sympathizers of various monarchistic organizations, if not of the Living Church Movement. And advanced age has made the venerable old prelate more understanding of human weakness.

Widely respected in every quarter, he is regarded with positive veneration by all the Orthodox of the Soviet Union. Civil authorities accord him the highest esteem.

Besides his offices at the Patriarchate in Moscow, he has a house in the country near the capital, and a villa on the Black Sea, close to Odessa. His official residence, however, is a two-storeyed 'palazzino' at the Monastery of the Trinity and St Sergei. It is decorated in the elegant, but slightly old-fashioned, style of the large Russian archiepiscopal residences: a broad, main staircase, large red carpets and reception rooms hung with ikons.

Patriarch Alexei received me in a very large room, seated behind a vast table covered with a green cloth. He rose to greet me. The superior of the monastery and a bishop made themselves comfortable in armchairs placed against one wall and, in the background, I could see the outline of the Patriarch's personal secretary.

During my life I have had the opportunity to meet a good number of the great people of this world. But I admit that I had never before been so awed as I was face to face with that august old man whom I considered the embodiment of the undying traditions of Holy Russia. To put me at my ease, the head of my Church began by recalling the names of some people of the old St Petersburg society and of the Imperial Guard whom we both knew. Encouraged by his manner, I gathered up courage to ask him various questions.

The statements made by the highest prelate of the Russian Orthodox Church were not meant for publication. Perhaps it will be enough, however, if I say that we touched on some points connected with the major problems of Russian religious life. When I referred to the religious indifference which is widespread among the Russian people, the Patriarch replied: 'That indifference has never been confined to any one era or any single environment. Not during my whole life have I ever lived in an atmosphere more indifferent to religion than the one at the Katkov college where I studied with young men from some of old Moscow's best families.' And when I asked him if the people had not lost some of their respect for the clergy, he smiled mischievously and said: 'On the contrary, I rather feel that it has noticeably improved since the days when one of my aunts, an elderly noblewoman, used to send a servant with a three-ruble note to the parish priest who had come to call on her.'

It was not for the Patriarch to comment on the great council which will shortly be opened at Rome by His Holiness Pope John XXIII. That is an internal affair of the Catholic Church; the Russian Orthodox Church has not been invited to attend. As a true Christian, however, nothing could be closer to his heart than the unity of all Christendom.

He expressed his sentiments on the subject in a message addressed to the delegates at the meeting of the Central Committee of the World Council of Churches at St Andrews, Scotland, on 29 July 1960:

'Examining the various levels of your movement's activity, we can compare it to a veritable human surge eager to explore all the avenues towards reconstituting the once-lost unity of the Church of Christ. No one can help rejoice at seeing Christians united to find a unanimous solution to the problems which not only divide them among themselves, but have rent all modern humanity. By this activity, they freely confess that they are guilty of this disunity. . . .

Motivated by Christian love, the operations of the World Council are gradually erecting a platform for an effective and fraternal reconciliation of Christians united in Christ. . . . Today, as never before, Christians need to be united to concur in humanity's highest endeavours and to fight against the threatening evil of a destructive war . . . whose dangers have never been so real. Christian unity has it within itself to be a power strong enough to break down barriers dividing the world.'

A man whose whole life has flowed from his ardent faith, the Patriarch cannot doubt the perennially enduring nature of religion. He expressed this conviction in a passage of his address before the disarmament conference held at Moscow in the beginning of 1960; 'With what importance can we credit all the efforts of human reason against Christianity, when its 2,000-year history speaks for itself, and when all hostile attacks against it were foreseen by Christ Himself who assured us that His Church is indestructible when He said, "and the gates of Hell shall not prevail against it"?'

My audience had ended. I knelt and received His Holiness's blessing. I was driven to the railway terminus at Zagorsk in a car provided by the Superior of the monastery.

. . . . .

The day's emotions had not ended yet, however. Seated in the electric train, I leafed through the album of superb photographic illustrations of the monastery's monuments which the Patriarch had graciously given me, along with some religious medals.

A group of women with whom I was sharing the compartment immediately became curious. When I told my neighbour, a very portly lady of about fifty, where I had got the album and the medals, she was visibly moved with emotion and enthusiasm, and cried: 'But you have seen His Holiness? He spoke to you? Good heavens, I wish I were that fortunate.' Touched by her obvious emotion, I offered her one of the medals, and she broke into tears.

When she had regained her composure, she told me about her life. She was a worker in an electro-mechanical plant outside Moscow; in a few years, she would have reached retirement age; her husband was working in another branch of industry; they were very happy together. She asked my Christian name, and my late wife's, so that she could remember us both in her prayers. It was plain that I was talking with another survivor of Holy Russia, filled with a humble and touching 'simple peasant's faith'.

The next day, a powerful TU104A aircraft carried me over thousands of miles and in a few short hours I was once again on the banks of the Seine.

13

A Glance at the Future

I HAVE come to the end of my investigation, and it remains now to draw some conclusions from what I saw and heard.

By looking at the situation objectively, I feel that I have drawn an adequately clear picture of the present religious position in the U.S.S.R., and the reader of the preceding chapters will have arrived at some conclusions of his own.

The constitutional law which affirms and guarantees freedom of religious worship is now applied in all its vigour all over the Soviet Union. About 10,000 churches and places of worship of all the country's religious groups are open and millions of the faithful attend religious ceremonies more or less regularly.

On the other hand, this freedom of worship is interpreted in the strictest sense. The law places no obstacles in the way of religious services or the training of ministers of religion, but this liberty does not extend to education nor charitable works, nor does it afford any possibility of spreading or defending religious ideas by means of the Press, radio or public lectures, nor, finally, does it grant the right to own real estate.

The ruling Party looks on religious belief as a survival of the past; it fights against this belief by means of systematic propaganda which it alone controls and directs.

What is the result of the intense ideological struggle now going on in the Soviet Union between believers and unbelievers? How do things look for the future? As we look for answers to these questions, we can see difficulties arise which are almost insurmountable.

The very first thing to be noted is that, because there are no statistics kept, it is almost impossible to give the numerical force of both sides engaged in the struggle. As far as believers are concerned, the most one can do (as we have already done above) is begin by taking the number of parishes and multiplying it either by the approximate number of families in each or by the approximate number of individual members of the religious group. Thus, according to the pessimist camp, there are about twenty million believers, or, according to the optimists, about fifty million, which would represent, at best, a quarter of the entire population.

There is no need, of course, to say that there are no figures for the number of convinced atheists or freethinkers, though, hypothetically, one could say that they are at least equal in numbers with the believers, and certainly no fewer.

Between these two more or less cohesive groups stands the great mass of the genuine, or self-proclaimed, indifferents. They would make up, according to our calculations, about half the population. It is from among these uncommitted people that the weight will come to swing the pendulum towards one or other of the two ideologies. They are the ones who will tip the balance in favour of religion or anti-religion, once they have come to grips with the internal crisis now tearing them apart.

In order to make predictions, we should have to look into the hearts of the Soviet's citizens, and examine their most secret thoughts. Klaus Mehnert, the German author of a very interesting report written after thirteen consecutive visits to the U.S.S.R., declares that 'it is almost impossible to discuss the question of religion freely with Russians. . . . The average Soviet citizen has his own reasons for prohibiting foreigners access to his most intimate life. . . . Anyone who shows the slightest interest in religious matters places himself outside the pale of materialist ideas and is thus numbered among the politically suspect.'[1]

My readers will see that I was in a more favourable situation; recognizing me as one of their own, my believing and unbelieving

[1] Klaus Mehnert, *l'Homme soviètique*, Paris: 1960.

fellow-countrymen did not shrink from letting me share their confidence. But how many people did I have open and frank conversations with? About a hundred, say, which is rather a lot, but certainly not enough.

A Gallup poll is not very effective in the areas where the innermost life of the human soul is concerned.

Having made these reservations, I venture to formulate a very summary and approximate judgment of the opportunities the future may hold for believers in Russia.

Before anything else, the thing I feel we must do is put aside the widespread Western idea that the Russians are a more religious people than any other. Dostoyevsky and the Pan-Slavists promulgated the idea with great vigour, underlining especially the Russian's unmatched attachment to his Orthodox faith.

But as early as 1848 the famous critic Bielinsky held a contrary opinion: 'Mystic exaltation is not in our people's nature. All they have is a lot of common sense, clearheadedness, and positive mental attitudes.' At first glance, recent events seem to prove he was right.

V. Rosanov, a writer of basically religious inspiration, went as far as to write that: 'The transition to socialism, and from there to atheism, has taken place among our peasants and soldiers with disconcerting ease; it is as though all they were doing was having a bath.'[1]

In those days Rosanov's observations did not go beyond the revolutionary masses of 1917. But even today, now that things are stable, we may suppose that the proportion of churchgoers among Russian factory workers is not more than 10 per cent, proportionately the same as the number of Parisian workers who go to Mass (according to figures amassed by the Roman Catholic clergy).[2]

Aside from certain national idiosyncrasies, the Russians are

---

[1] V. Rosanov, *The Apocalypse of Our Times* (in Russian), Sergeev Possad: 1917–18.

[2] The fact remains, however, that the diocese which includes the mining areas in the Donetz basin is recognized as the wealthiest in the whole Soviet Union.

not so different, so far as religion is concerned, from other people of the white race. They are, perhaps, slightly more rationalist than the Latins and, even today, a little more attached to traditional ways and customs. But it must be remembered that they also belong to a young nation which is vigorous, full of energy, capable of the most generous, and sometimes mystical, outbursts, and endowed with great capacities for assimilation and a creative strength which has not yet been tried to its limit in the spiritual domain—a valuable talisman for the future.

On the other hand, we should not forget that religion is not *en vogue* in the Soviet Union; on the contrary, it is almost 'bad form'. Situations like this have arisen in other countries, especially in France after 1789 and, up to a point, during the days of the Combes Laws. Minds seethe with ideas and prevent people from giving open demonstration of their real thoughts.

This fear of 'what the neighbours will say' is behind a phenomenon in the U.S.S.R. which I have already touched on— the contrast between the rarity of religious marriage ceremonies and the frequency of baptisms. A foreign diplomat, conversing with Mr Khrushchev once, ventured to ask him why, in an atheist country, almost everyone had their children baptized. In his characteristically spirited manner, the head of the Soviet Government parried with: 'Russians are clever people, you know; they iust want to be reassured.'

But reassured about what? The possibility of divine wrath in the after life, or a possible change in the Government's attitude? Mr Khrushchev's quip[1] leaves us hanging in the air. The fact is that it is infinitely simpler to take a child wrapped in a shawl to a church than it is to get past one's neighbours while wearing one's Sunday best or a white dress and veil. 'What will people say?' is a question to be reckoned with even outside capitalist countries.

It was after I had considered this state of affairs that I decided not to include student circles in my investigation. It would have

[1] Russian humour has come up with another one, which is almost proverbial by now: 'Thank God, there is no God; but what if, God forbid, God really did exist?'

been as worth while as asking students at Saint-Cyr what they think of the Algerian war, or the officer-cadets at Sandhurst or West Point their opinions on the defence of the West. All these young people are too involved in their studies and sports, and too absorbed in their future, to be confidential with a passing stranger at the risk of jeopardizing their chances for promotion and advancement. Besides, youth is not the age for religious contemplation, though it is rather surprising to see boys and girls in the Soviet Union entering churches to pray and respectfully bowing their heads to members of the clergy.

One very astute observer, Miss Hélène Peltier-Zamoyska, has provided an extremely interesting approach to this point, basing her conclusions on many contacts with Russian young people.[1] She recognizes the almost complete ignorance of religious questions rampant in student circles, and the anticlerical prejudice circulating among them; she deplores the fact that nothing is being done to remedy this situation. According to her, the situation would be irremediable, if the society were not deeply influenced by another current—the hunger for culture:

'It is in that area that traditional Russian aspirations are most strikingly evident; the things that matter most, in their eyes, are spiritual values. . . . The most contradictory elements become all confused there and, in the midst of a Marxist train of thought and vocabulary, one often discovers decidedly Christian tendencies, secularized and stripped of the religious content. . . . The day when they discover that faith, far from stifling the intellect, helps it to expand, many of their preconceived notions will disappear. What they are instinctively looking for among Christians is the certitude of a moral judgment based on faith. . . .

One frequently finds among young people that the most sensitive and upright of them are suffering through a period of

[1] Hélène Peltier-Zamoyska, 'Quel témoignage peut toucher les esprits soviètiques?' *Informations catholiques internationales*, 1 April 1960.

genuine anguish because they do not know what to give their loyalty and devotion to. You are Christians, some of them said to me, you have had your chance; you know what is good and what is bad; you know how to act in life. . . . But we do not know. One day a thing is white, the next it is black. . . .

This nostalgia for transcendent principles according to which they can direct their personal lives leads some of them to turn towards Christianity, and even to convert. The starting point of almost every religious quest is a stirring of conscience in the face of injustice or deceit.'

It goes without saying that the nation's most dynamic atheists are perfectly aware that part of the country's youth are not able to shake off these religious tendencies. Without other means to combat them except education, they are content to hold them up to ridicule.

One newspaper recounts that in the small provincial city of Nesvij (in the district of Minsk), schoolchildren still believe in miracles and kneel before the altar praying, while explaining, 'Everybody does it, even our teachers.' Another newspaper, not without a touch of sardonic cynicism, describes all the *ex votos* covering the old walls of the wealthy industrial Erlanger family's mausoleum in a Moscow cemetery. Some of them invoke Divine goodness for success in examinations; in others, a young man asks the Lord to make a girl fall in love with him.[1] Once again, however, is it not a basically religious attitude which naively resorts to this sort of childishness?

Moving from young people to adults, we cannot but recognize (as we have just said) that the Church cannot expect much of the working classes. The situation is different among the country people, however, who still, despite the shift of about forty million of them from rural to urban centres, constitute most of the Soviet population. I myself saw men, women and children fill churches in rural areas; in a place where everybody goes to church no one

[1] *Literaturnaya Gazeta.*

need fear gossiping neighbours. This survival of religious observance has not failed to worry the civil authorities, and very sweeping investigations into its causes have been undertaken by scientific organizations. Their conclusions coincide *grosso modo* with mine.

A special commission set up by the Ethnographic Institute under the auspices of the Academy of Sciences travelled through four districts in central Russia (the provinces of Kalinin, Kostroma, Gorki and Yaroslav) in 1959 in order to form a clear and precise idea of the people's attitude towards religion. Though they declare with satisfaction that agricultural collectivization and educational advances have made certain old-fashioned customs such as prayers for rain or for a good harvest disappear, they nevertheless concede that a large part of village dwellers are still deeply attached to their Christian faith, despite all propaganda; even among young people, they say, a considerable number are still not sufficiently aware of the 'dangers inherent in religious ideas'. Since the war children are baptized more and more 'because the people are attracted by the beauty of the religious ceremony'. Parents and grandparents still have a strong hold on their offspring, grandmothers refuse to take care of unbaptized 'little pagans'; in the evenings the people sit about talking about God's omnipotence and discussing the lives of the saints. 'Our children are in our hands, and they do what we teach them to do,' one peasant said.[1]

If country people have had any change in attitude, it is not quite what the 'Godless' hoped it might be. 'Believers today are very different from believers before the Revolution,' the investigators admit.[2] 'We are no longer living in the days when religious ideas were intimately bound up with political notions of a reactionary character, and were put to use in the best interests of

---

[1] A Moscow taxi-driver—who was not a peasant, therefore, but belonged to the working class—said almost the same thing to me: 'I have two sons, one is still in school and the other is doing his military service; we taught them their prayers and we still encourage them to pray.'

[2] The results of the investigation were analysed in the magazine, *The Communist*, VIII (May 1960); this periodical is the official organ of the Party.

the exploiting classes. In our Socialist society the majority of believers are sincere patriots and play an active role in the construction of socialo-communism.' And what can one do to combat people like that? 'Activate our propaganda machinery,' the investigators reply, without labouring under any illusions, 'and improve its methods.' Are not they the first to admit that, in the regions they visited, religious marriage ceremonies are becoming popular again, a phenomenon which is easily explained by a civil ceremony's wan and absolutely colourless atmosphere?[1]

It would be extremely interesting if we had as detailed and official information about the attitude of intellectuals. Naturally, however, we shall never get them; more disciplined and closer to the sources of power, the Soviet's scholars, technicians, and bureaucrats are, because of their very position, constrained to the utmost reserve. It is hard to imagine, under present conditions, an academician, an ambassador, a high-ranking military man or an editor make open profession of his loyalty to the Church.[2] But this neutral attitude affected by intellectuals proves nothing; here, more than elsewhere, it is a question of knowing a man's innermost convictions. Knowing their secrets would be extremely important, because these men are the very brain of the nation; they already exercise influence today, and will continue to exercise it even more tomorrow, on the whole political life of the U.S.S.R. and the entire present and future spiritual evolution of the Russian people.

As an illustration, let me mention here a few of the interesting statements I heard from people in these highly educated circles, people who are profoundly aware of their responsibilities. Thus, a

[1] Civil authorities have tried to remedy this situatoin by opening special halls with buffets, gift-shops, etc., at Leningrad (and in Moscow and other cities as well) for civil weddings. It is still too soon to say how successful the operation has been.

[2] One day, during a celebration of the liturgy by the Patriarch in his cathedral, I saw an energetic and intelligent looking colonel, his chest covered with decorations, kneeling in prayer before the relics of St Alexei, Metropolitan of Moscow. It almost seemed that he wanted to make public manifestation of his attitude before a congregation of several thousand. That was a unique case, of course. I was told that generals who attend the services usually ask the celebrant to give them Communion behind the altar.

specialist in nervous diseases, member of the Faculty of Medicine, ingenuously admitted to me that he frequently visits churches, where the services and the faces of the people 'act as an excellent sedative on me'. Or I can recall what a leading biologist said to me, indignant that his contemporaries considered reading Dostoyevsky too difficult and citing a passage from *The Brothers Karamazov*: 'Take away man's faith in immortality—and everything will be allowed.'

Another university professor made a longer admission: 'I am only forty-five years old, so I received all of my education during the Stalin era. In those days Helvetius was my bible and I was naive enough to believe that we would be able to realize his doctrines.

'Afterwards, I had only one desire: gradually to free myself from deception; Romain Rolland says that men born in slavery do not even suspect that such a desire as that can exist. Like all of my generation, I did not read the Bible, but often read deeply in the works of Korolenko and Tolstoy, and I found a concept of life in them that was very close to my own.

'Am I for religion? I think I can answer that in the affirmative, because I recognize the existence of a transcendent principle. I know what I must do, and what I may not do. I strive always to be aware of man's position on earth. Perhaps that is only what we can call the "arithmetic" of religion, but I have no hope of reaching its "higher mathematics". I should have to have far more freedom to think at my disposal to penetrate those upper regions. But cannot the whole history of humanity be summed up as a struggle for spiritual independence?

'Whatever is forcibly imposed upon us does not penetrate our soul, nor can it send out new shoots; sooner or later, in ten years or in a hundred, it is destined to disappear without leaving a trace.

'And every attempt at stamping out faith will fail. I do not know if all my contemporaries think as I do, but there is every chance that they will arrive at the same conclusions before the end of their life, at the price of a long struggle with themselves.'

And then he rang the changes on a familiar theme: 'The tendency towards the spiritual can never be destroyed, especially in this country. With us, even atheism has become a religious faith, exactly as Dostoyevsky predicted it would be when he had Versilov, in *The Adolescent*, say: "The Russian atheist is not a simple atheist; his whole being is steeped in faith in atheism." People are trying to divert religious inclinations into a new direction, by divinizing the outstanding Revolutionary figures. You can judge for yourself what results that can give.'

And someone else declared: 'Do not have any preconceptions about the future. The time for spiritual regeneration is not near. But how could anyone doubt that the Church will be one of the elements in the evolution to come?'

More than all these, however, I especially recall the long conversation I had with a young schoolmistress in a provincial city. Everything about her reminded me of one of Turgenev's heroines: her white dress, her smooth, blonde hair, her pure expression and subdued impassioned enthusiasm. She was highly cultured, widely read and what she said came from the bottom of her heart. We were sitting on a high hill in the shade of a very old cathedral, and the broad countryside, stamped with melancholy and peaceful beauty stretched out before us. It was the countryside of the eternal Russia, with its fields following one another off into infinity, its forests of birches and firs, and its modest villages, from whose midst sprang gilded cupolas.

'The spiritual aspirations of our young people,' she said, 'cannot be satisfied with the sustenance they get from clubs and party lectures, which have a glacial atmosphere about them and where they never meet anything but indifference. Marxism in its present form is tending to become a dogma; take away one iota and the whole structure will collapse. Everyone knows that, and the ones who call themselves "orthodoxalists" are simply deceiving their comrades or are afraid of being denounced for telling the truth. Nor should we be surprised that young people are instinctively driven to personal reflection and, sometimes, even towards the Church: the beauty of the music and the impressive ritual could hardly help affect minds which are still not completely formed.

'It would be wrong to conclude from all this, however, that we are ready to renounce socialist doctrine. But even within the Party itself there are subtle currents which, sooner or later, will bring us to the stage where we shall have to revise our theory of knowledge, especially the points touching on reality's reflection in thought. There is one question which is constantly exercising our minds: if there is a link between matter and energy, should not the same link also exist between the mind and matter, which is a reflection of mind? Which of the two principles—mind or matter—precedes the other?

'Which road will we finally take? Certainly not the one laid out by the Slavophiles; it would lead us straight into an impasse. If, as you put it, they were "suppressed", it was probably because their doctrines were not so constructed as to endure through the evolution of national thinking. No police system could ever "suppress" Pushkin or Tolstoy.

'I never cease to be surprised that the Church's ritual is so archaic; I do not think it is adapted to the times we are living in. I must admit, however, that there is one idea constantly going through my mind: why is it that one so often sees such a luminous [*prosvetlionny*] expression on a priest's face? I still haven't found the answer.'

.   .   .   .   .

During the forty years of the Soviet regime the propaganda system of the 'Godless' has undoubtedly led a major part of the country to accept materialist doctrine. But it has failed to destroy the Church, or even to root out the masses' profound religious feelings. It is even the first to admit that failure.

A contributor to the influential *Philosophical Questions* (*Voprosy Filosofi*) very recently wrote: 'Preachers in every religious group have become more active; bishops are seen in their various parishes more often; a good number of believers are more interested in religion than they used to be.' An article which attracted attention when it was published in *Pravda* on 2 August 1959 quite frankly admitted that 'scientific atheist propaganda is not up to the task imposed upon it'. The writer condemned 'its unrestrained tone, which is bound to offend the sensibilities of believers and is irreconcilable with that freedom of conscience which is the keystone of Soviet democracy'. The article also made the surprising admission that: 'The clergy have demonstrated great resources of subtlety and finesse in their efforts at reviving the religious spirit of the masses, who have become more and more indifferent. They no longer stop at using faith in relics, intimidating children and putting pressure on parents, to gain their ends; what they are doing now is working to adapt religion to science and modern conditions, and to convince men that Communist ideas can be reconciled with religious notions.'

It is not difficult to find the reason for this stalemate facing militant materialism. Its propaganda has never hit the essential point: religious sentiment, the aspiration towards the infinite which is ineluctably rooted in men's hearts. The propaganda insists that this mentality was only generated slowly, at a very precise stage in social evolution. The most competent expert research into prehistoric attitudes have demonstrated that the contrary is true. In his *Naissances mystiques* (Paris, 1959) Mircea Eliade writes: 'Ecstatic experience under all its many aspects is very probably inherent in the nature of man, in the sense that it is an integral part of man's consciousness of himself.'

Atheist propaganda considers religion as a superstructure thrown up over some or other economic system, which it sees as the true basis of society. But though Christianity first appeared during an epoch of slavery, that did not prevent it from adapting itself to feudalism, then capitalism and finally, as we see it today, subsisting in a world preparing for the transition from Socialism to Communism. The propaganda hurls itself against superstitions inherited from paganism, and lashes out at the abuses of the clergy and their many ties with reactionary elements; but it forgets that genuine religion has nothing to do with politics, and that a truly religious man, devoted to a transcendent idea, is not likely to be immoderately swayed by the defects of ministers of religion who are, after all, only ordinary human beings.

This propaganda has very broad aims: it wants to destroy not only revealed religion, but even idealist philosophy. 'Such a philosophy,' one leading Soviet journal declared, 'is certainly linked with knowledge, while religion is not a form of knowledge, does not bother with investigating phenomena, and insists on a blind and unconditional faith in divine providence. On the whole, however, idealist philosophy seems an ally of religion; it has the same origin and the same goals.'

If we admit this position, however, can we overlook the fact that it is impossible to impose materialism integrally upon all humanity? To achieve that end, it would not be enough to burn down churches and houses of worship; we should also have to burn or, at least, refute once and for all all the works of every author who down, through the centuries, has proclaimed the principle of spirituality. And who could assure us that new thinkers of that ilk would not rise up, perhaps even on the very day after the *auto-da-fé*?

Attempts have been made to convince us that, with science making more and more important advances, tendencies like these would no longer have the slightest chance of developing. This, it seems to me, is precisely the fundamental point on which the enemies of religion and idealistic spiritualism have the weakest arguments to put forth. We are no longer living in Voltaire's optimistic times with its candid creed of unlimited progress. And we have outgrown the days when Ernest Renan could write: 'We reject the supernatural for the same reasons that we reject centaurs and hippogriffs: because no one has ever seen any of them.'

Modern scholars and scientists themselves admit that we are

surrounded by the supernatural, that our knowledge is limited, that determinism cannot explain every phenomenon of matter, to say nothing of the manifestations of the spirit. The most eminent of them today loudly proclaim that religious activity and scientific activity are carried on on two different levels, one as legitimate as the other.

I certainly have no intention of developing a philosophic thesis on this point here. Let me, rather, cite a few passages from books available to anyone and written by some of our most famous modern thinkers; I need only reach out my hand to find any of these books within reach on the shelves of my library

Listen, for instance, to Einstein, who certainly had nothing about him of the believer, and who even hesitated to admit the existence of a personal God. He knows, however, that the scientific method 'can only teach us how facts are connected with one another and how they are conditioned by one another, nothing more'. He also realizes that religion is 'humanity's old attempt to become fully and clearly aware of supra-personal values'. And he concludes:

'If we conceive of religion and science in terms of these definitions, any conflict between them then seems impossible. For science can only affirm what is, but not what ought to be; outside its own domain, all sorts of value judgments remain necessary. . . . And this is the domain of religion. . . . Science without religion is crippled, religion without science is blind.'[1]

The same point of view is more amply developed by Hans Reichenbach, the eminent professor of the University of California:

'It is useless to ask scientific philosophers to justify a hierarchy of values. These values are as important to them as they

[1] A. Einstein, *Scientific, Moral and Social Concepts*, Paris: 1952 (the chapter on 'Science and Religion'.

are to anyone else, but they believe that we cannot resolve them scientifically.

. . . The typical ancient philosopher gave his student maxims and counsels for living and promised him that, by studying works of philosophy diligently, he would come to know good from evil. The scientific philosopher tells him quite frankly that he must expect nothing from his teaching, if what he is interested in is leading the good life.[1]

Sri Aurobindo, the great Hindu teacher, agrees with this. According to him, the only contribution which reason and science can make towards harmonizing the chaos of the cosmos is to stabilize a thing in 'an artificially arranged and mechanized unity of material life'.

'At the same time,' he says, 'Science has put at man's disposal many potencies of the universal Force and has made the life of humanity materially one; but what uses this universal force is a little human individual or communal ego with nothing universal in its light of knowledge or its movements, no inner sense of power which would create in this physical drawing together of the human world a true life unity, a mental unity or a spiritual oneness.'[2]

At bottom there is nothing really new in these ideas. A contemporary of the Encyclopaedists, Lomonossov, the famous Russian thinker and poet, who is ordinarily cited by Soviet publicists as a convinced atheist, wrote long ago that 'science and faith are sisters, daughters of the same Father, who never contradict one another unless their admirers make them vain'. In another passage, he prophetically heralded the age of the Sputnik, 'the days when men will reach the planets', and reflected:

'Some people wonder if there are beings like us on other

---

[1] Hans Reichenbach, *Rise of Scientific Philosophy*, University of California Press, 1954.
[2] Sri Aurobindo, *The Life Divine*, Calcutta: 1940, II (2), p. 1160.

planets and if their religion is the same as ours. If they really want to know and convert them, let them go to Venus to baptize them. I fear, however, that their work will come to nought, for the ways of salvation are many.'

And, moving on to the problem we are discussing, he writes:

'Any mathematician who wanted to measure the Divine will with a compass would finish with a wrong solution; just as a theologian who thought he could learn astronomy and chemistry from the Psalms. Preachers of the Gospel show us the ways of virtue and salvation. . . . Astronomers discover the temple of divine beauty and grandeur, and strive to find the means of guaranteeing our temporal happiness.'[1]

There is, however, a difference between the situation those people were in and ours. 'One of modern theoretical physics' most interesting conclusions,' writes Johannes Hohlenburg,

'lies in recognizing that the objective experience of universal value is absolutely inconceivable, because its result will always depend upon the one experiencing and the structure of his experience. Contrary to what was formerly believed, it is now clear that it is impossible to eliminate errors resulting from the fact that experience is had by one man in one specific place, at a particular time, with particular material, and that, in principle, this impossibility cannot be suppressed.'[2]

Thus science herself has arrived at the point where she defines the limits of her own possibilities by using scientific methods; our authorities for that are Nils Bohr, Max Planck, Heysenberg and Prince Louis de Broglie.

This evolution in modern thought goes beyond mathematics and physics. With unsurpassed clarity, Bergson has shown us the

[1] M. Lomonossov, *Selected Philosophical Works* (in Russian) Moscow: 1950.
[2] Johannes Hohlenburg, *The Works of Søren Kierkegaard*, Routledge, London, 1954.

importance of intuition, an element which is opposed to reason and is its complement.

Freud and his disciples have thrown light into the depths of the human soul. Scientific psychology has benefited enormously by this new knowledge to completely revise its notions of matter and mind.

On this subject Julian Huxley writes:

'The expression "God", like the expressions "energy" or "justice" for example, has a basically scientific meaning. . . . Physical and biological science, in discovering the unity of matter and energy, and the operative direction of cosmic evolution, has provided a real basis for what, until now, has been nothing but theological speculation. Psychological science, by revealing part of the mind's mechanics, helps us appreciate the value of what is called mystical experience, establishes the fundaments for spiritual education and development appropriate to the human mind, and shows us how the notion of God can be effective as the predominating idea in the extremely important process of sublimation.[1]'

And one last passage which, at first sight, does not seem to relate directly to the connections between science and religion. It is an excerpt from the address delivered in December 1960 at Stockholm by Nobel-prize winner Saint-John Perse:

'When we take stock of the drama of modern science pursuing its rational limits in the mathematical absolute; when, in physics, we see two key doctrines proposing, one a general principle of relativity, and the other a quantum principle of uncertitude and indeterminism limiting forever even the exactitude of physical measurements; when we have heard the greatest scientific innovator of this century, the originator of

[1] Julian Huxley, *Essays of a Biologist*. See also his article in the *Neue Zürcher Zeitung*, 27 August 1960.

modern cosmology, reply in terms of the most vast intellectual synthesis of equations and invoke intuition to the aid of reason, and proclaim that "the imagination is the true soil of scientific germination", going as far as to appropriate to the thinker the benefit of a real "artistic vision"—are we not right to claim that the poetic instrument is as legitimate as the logical instrument?'

The speaker was only concerned with defending the rights of poetry; but is not his reasoning just as applicable, word for word, to the defence of the 'religious instrument'?

Another great French poet, Jules Supervielle, wrote the following a short time before his death: 'Each man has his own God, who serves his personal need, even if his faith in Him is not very strong. It is something like a poetic concentration, a quick way of attaining the Absolute with ease.'

Judging by the evidence we have, there will always be one area closed to science. Though scientists may succeed in establishing interplanetary communications, improving the structure of our society beyond all legitimate hope, and prolonging our life on earth, they will always remain baffled by the unfathomable mysteries of birth, suffering, death and eternity. 'The State won't be able to help us once we're dead,' say the Russian peasants. And Rosanov, whom we have already cited, declares: 'On this planet, death is the strongest of all forces. Is there a soul? Is there an after life? These notions are far more important than any Revolution.'

On this point, we could hardly fail to agree with the Patriarch of Moscow's declaration that: 'Side by side with the visible world, there is an invisible world whose reflections men can perceive. Faith opens up to us a spiritual world, an eternal world, and thus answers the greatest problems of human thought.'[1]

.   .   .   .   .

[1] *Annals of the Patriarchate of Moscow*, IX, 1957.

The outcome of the struggle between materialism and spiritualism does not depend entirely upon the Russians. The whole world has a share in it; supposing, contrary to all probability, that religious thinking should disappear from the world on a single day, it is certainly not under the unfavourable conditions extant in the Soviet Union that it could survive. Having said this, we are forced to admit, not without some regret, that the battle between believers and unbelievers going on in that country is being waged on a relatively low intellectual level, at least as far as we can see. (for, of course, we have no idea what goes on in the depths of men's souls).

Fortunately, things cannot remain as they are. Russians may not be very prone to metaphysical anguish, but they are more avid than other peoples for *pravda*, an untranslatable idea combining 'truth' and 'justice' at one and the same time.

The obstacles which today stand in the way of satisfying their desires will inevitably be overthrown. There is no thoughtful Russian (including members of the Party) who at this moment does not wish that cultural contacts with the world outside Russia could be strengthened. Any research specialist would not have the slightest difficulty, either in Moscow or in Leningrad, in getting any book he wanted through the great national libraries, even anti-materialist books published in Western countries. But the Soviet's 'ordinary citizen' who is eager to educate himself has no access to all the sources of modern knowledge. He has never read Bergson, perhaps has never even heard of him. Though he may know Jean Paul Sartre as a playwright, he knows nothing about his philosophical writings. New foreign literature is not advertised in newspapers nor is it displayed in bookshop windows, if it does not conform to present official doctrine.

The day when the curtain will be lifted is probably drawing near. Better equipped, the Church will be able to settle down to working out a national theology, and will then be capable of influencing all the many intellectual circles which have avoided her since the days of Peter the Great.

Agnostics, in their turn, will find themselves forced to admit with the great Catholic Thomist, Étienne Gilson, that 'the universe of science has never been closer to the universe of Scripture than it is today;'[1] and with Lord Russell, the most eminent of the West's atheist thinkers, that 'science can neither demonstrate nor refute Christianity's three fundamental doctrines: God, immortality and free will'.[2]

Standing as they do at the crossroads of East and West, they will find themselves obliged to pay more attention to the deeply spiritual teachings of Hinduism. They will also begin to understand the value of symbols, which now escapes them completely. They will strive to reconstitute man's interiority in their dialectical reasoning. And it will be in those days that the world will witness that 'great thaw of Russian thought' about which Khomiakov dreamed as long as a hundred years ago.

It would, naturally, be childish to imagine, as some old émigrés do, that this 'thaw' will bring us closer to a resurrection of 'Holy Russia' as she was in the past.[3] And it would be just as unrealistic to wait for one or the other of the two opposing camps to repudiate its beliefs. Thus, for example, expecting the Soviet Government to reintroduce religious education would be tantamount to asking Western universities to set up faculties of astrology or alchemy, disciplines as obsolete to Westerners as Christianity is to the Soviet Government.

But no one is asking for that. It is not even a question of establishing a foundation for collaboration between Christians and the Soviet authorities. In 1944 Paul B. Anderson was able to declare that 'millions of Christians are already involved in doing it'.[4] Though he is a highly tolerant and far-seeing representative of the Catholic world, Father A. Wenger does not seem to have appreciated this attitude when he wrote that: 'Supporting the Soviets may be considered one of the Russian Orthodox Church's

---

[1] Étienne Gilson, le Philosophe et la théologie, Paris: 1960.
[2] Bertrand Russell, Science and Religion, O.U.P., London: 1935.
[3] A. V. Kartashov, la Réconstitution de la Sainte Russia, Paris: 1956.
[4] Paul B. Anderson, op. cit.

obligations, and a condition for survival, but it is also an indirect
—and certainly involuntary—contribution to the great Marxist
idea.'[1]

For Christians in the Soviet Union, however, the question no
longer arises. Anderson writes:

> 'Millions of them work the soil, operate machines, take
> care of the sick, worship, sit on the soviets in factories and
> collective farms, and fight in the ranks of the Red Army.'

Patriarch Alexei supported this point of view when he
declared:

> 'It is in this way that the Russian Orthodox Church is
> accomplishing her mission of salvation under new conditions:
> she is preparing her members for eternity through the trials of
> their temporal existence, and, by the moral training she gives
> them, also helps her people. Blessing the work that these
> people are accomplishing for the social community, the
> Church contributes thereto by her peculiar activity within the
> framework of her own religious position; nor is she hindered
> in any way in this activity by the State, which by no means
> obtrudes into her internal affairs. . . .
> These conditions, which are so favourable to the life and
> activity of our Church, make it possible for us to look forward
> to her future with assurance, in the hope that she will be able
> to realize new progress and will be even more prosperous.'[2]

If this desire is to be realized, there will first have to be some
change in the Government's standpoint. We cannot possibly
accept the view recently put forth by Professor Pierre Pascal, in a
Paris periodical, that 'the Soviets cannot recognize any right of
religion to exist, and the persecution of religion will not stop'.

---

[1] A. Wenger, *La Russie de Khrouchtchev*, Paris: 1960.
[2] *The Russian Orthodox Church*, Moscow: the Patriarchate of Moscow, 1958.

The facts themselves prove the learned biographer of Avvakum wrong; churches in the Soviet Union have legal 'existence', and no representative of any of them complains of 'persecution' today. What believers have not got is complete equality of rights, the material and moral possibility of openly defending their doctrines.

Since 1917 governmental policy has not followed a uniform course; initially intransigent, it has shown marked goodwill towards the Church since the end of World War II, but has become somewhat more stiff-necked during the past two years. It will continue to change since permanent evolution cannot be stopped anyhow.

There is no possibility of a return to the methods used during the Civil War. Though a publicly professed atheist, the present head of the Soviet Government has always acted tolerantly and his frequent references to the Bible and Christian morality have probably not passed without surprising the more dogmatic members of the Party.

Speaking to an Indian delegate, Pandit Sunderlala, on 16 May 1959, he said: 'I am not a religious man, and you believe in religion. But no one would be right to conclude from that that there will be hostility between us. . . . Though we are atheists, we do not allow ourselves to indulge in antagonism towards people with religious affiliations. We have never stirred up animosity among people over religion, nor among states because of ideo-logical differences, and we do not intend to do so in the future. We are not only tolerant of religious people, we also respect them.'

The day Mr Krushchev's office passes on to another man his successor will find himself unshirkably obliged to pursue the same line, at the risk of alienating the sympathy of tens of millions of his fellow-citizens.

In the West not enough account is taken of the fact that the revolutionary period in the Soviet Union is over and done with; Beria's downfall was its last stage. Destructive passions have given place to constructive dynamism. The Government has finally been effectively stabilized and most of the people await nothing except an amplification of their well-being. On this score, it may be well to recall Mr Macmillan's words before the General Assembly of the United Nations on 29 September 1960: 'Materially, the masses [of the whole world] want peace, prosperity, advancement. But they perhaps want something more: the opportunity to think for themselves about the most profound problems facing us during our brief stay on earth—relations between human beings, and relations between men and God.'

The evolution of the Russian people, and perhaps also of the Party, will proceed along those lines. Looking back at the past, we are obliged to concede that 'Marxism has used the natural inclinations of the Russian soul—its religiosity, its dynamism, its stubbornness, its faith in Russia's special destiny, its love of sacrifice, its quest for social justice and the kingdom of God on earth.'[1]

And we must also agree with Brice Parain, an outstanding French author and a man intimately familiar with the Soviet soul, when he writes: 'There is no other way to explain the tremendous appeal of the Russian revolution than by a grafting of Bolshevism onto Christian messianism—the kingdom of God on earth preparing for the end of time.'

Today, after forty-two years of an agnostic regime, religion still penetrates every pore of Russian life. Be he believer or un-believer, a Soviet citizen need only go out into the streets to see rising before him the gilded domes of old churches. In the Moscow underground, he sees the station walls decorated with mosaics depicting the exploits of St Alexander Nevski; should he go to the ballet at the Bolshoi Theatre, he will see a pious Franciscan friar blessing the union of Romeo and Juliet; at the opera, he will hear Boris Godunov confessing his sins and begging for God's mercy: at the Art Theatre, he will watch the moving scene in *The Brothers Karamazov* where staretz Zossima appears.

Or in his own home perhaps he will leaf through the works of

[1] Berdayev, *Origins of Russian Communism*, G. Bles, London, 1937.

his favourite author, Leo Tolstoy, the man who wanted to consecrate his life to 'the creation of a new religion, conformed to humanity's evolution, a religion of Christ stripped of its mysteries'.[1] If he turns to more modern authors he will come across a great contemporary success, Sergei Borodin's *Dmitri Donskoy*, which sold hundreds of thousands of copies, was awarded the Stalin Prize and recalls the immense role played by the Orthodox Church in his country's destiny. He might even spend some time looking through one of the albums of superb reproductions of ikons which the state published in 1960 on the occasion of the sixth centenary of the painter-monk Andrei Rublev.

From time to time, even periodicals will remind him of the value of religious art. One daily printed a long eulogy of lovely provincial churches and added: 'These monuments of our past should be used, because our country has so many of them, for the education of our youth. Only the most ignorant can remain indifferent to the glorious heritage handed down to us by our ancestors.'[2] Another widely circulated periodical published a poem whose author apostrophized the famous church of Nerli, built near Vladimir on the picturesque banks of a river: 'On this spot, you seem indispensable, as though you had not been created by an architect, but by the Earth herself, and your magnificence shines eternally.'[3]

Who is the Russian who can resist all this evidence and not say to himself, with the novelist Dudintsev, 'Not by bread alone...'?

This peculiarly religious—and Russian—atmosphere is bound to contribute, in the more or less distant future to a *rapprochement* of the positions now so hostilely maintained in the Soviet Union by religion and Communism. Rising above strict observation of ritual, the Church should then be able to work out a more purified doctrine which agnostics will find more approachable and comprehensible. For their part, the agnostics may yet come to the

[1] Leo Tolstoy, *Journal*, entry for 4 March 1855.
[2] *Utchitelskaya Gazeta*, 16 July 1959.
[3] *Literaturnaya Gazeta*, 11 August 1959.

point where they will no longer look upon religion as 'a gardener looks at ivy, or a soldier at a machine-gun nest.'[1]

During a visit to Moscow, Giorgio La Pira, former mayor of Florence and a great Christian, told the guests, who included some of the leading figures in the Soviet Government, at a banquet: 'You put great stock in realism. Fine, but realism should be analysis and evaluation of all authentically popular realities, and religion is one of them.'[2]

Can we go farther, and imagine the possibility of an effort at synthesizing these two doctrines, which are so opposed? Berdayev wrote:

'The Russian intellectuals who committed themselves to Marxist theories are believing men. . . . The eschatological doctrines of former times have taken on the character of a Last Judgment, equivalent to a social revolution, paving the streets of the Communist society's Eternal City.'[3]

And elsewhere he declared:

'The idea of a classless society, founded on labour, in which the one works for the others and for all with a sublime goal in view, does not imply a denial of God: on the contrary, it would be in greater conformity with Christianity than the one upon which the Capitalist bourgeoisie is founded.'[4]

Taking a purely philosophic standpoint, he continues: 'Dialectical materialism presupposes reason; matter which would consist merely of colliding atoms could have no place in it. Dialectical materialism, therefore, presupposes Logos to be in matter, the reason within an irrational process.'

An attentive reading through Engels, Marx and Lenin will

[1] Anderson, op. cit.
[2] *Informations catholiques internationales*, 1 November 1959.
[3] Berdayev, op. cit.
[4] Berdayev, *le Psychologie religieuse russe et l'athéisme communiste russe*, Paris: 1931.

lead to many passages which are not so far from Berdayev's reasoning. For all three, matter is an objective reality. Engels and Lenin emphatically insist on the reality of Absolute Truth, which is identical with absolute energy, with absolute Being. Lenin wrote: 'The extent of our knowledge of objective absolute Truth is conditioned historically, but the existence of such a Truth is not conditioned.'[1]

'Materialism,' writes Tiran Nersoyan, 'was generated by an opposition to Hegelian idealism, and it so happens that Christian philosophy itself is radically opposed to philosophical idealism in any form; the Christian's ultimate reality is not an idea, but a substantial being. It is here, paradoxical though it be, that religion and Communism are tangent to one another.'[2]

In effect, of course, dialectical materialism and Christian philosophy are both monist. Both believe in a substantial being beyond phenomena; both admit that the soul is the essence of this being and that phenomena are produced by a perduring motion of this being. One could say that the divine essence is the final form of the dialectical process.[3]

This does not, however, by any means preclude the fundamental divergence there is between the two ideas. Because materialism rejects God, its disciples cannot consider man as the child of God; because human relations are dependent upon economic conditions, Christian teaching must seem based on an exaggerated individualism.

But there is even a reply to this objection: the Russian and Orthodox position formulated long before the advent of the Soviets has always been that man can certainly be lost, by himself, but cannot be saved except as part of the community of mankind.

---

[1] V. Lenin, *Anti-Dühring*, VII.

[2] Tiran Nersoyan, *A Christian Approach to Communism*, London: 1942.

[3] In connection with this idea, I should like to cite an astonishing text of the apocryphal 'Gospel of St Thomas', which was discovered in upper Egypt in 1955 (verse 555): 'If someone asks you whence you have come, reply: "We come from Light, from where Light was born." If someone asks you who you are, reply: "We are his sons and the elect of the Living Father." If someone asks you what was the sign given you by your Father, reply: "*It is motion, and rest.*" '

This is the great 'Sobornost' doctrine, in reference to which that great statesman and Hindu philosopher, Sri Radakrishnan, told me one day that 'it forms the natural link between Communism and religion.'[1]

What does an Orthodox believer mean when he says 'Sobornost'? 'It means "catholicity" in its literal sense, but has overtones of community, unity amidst liberty, the triumph of harmony over chaos and of love over hatred and fear.'[2]

The man I consider the most eminent of all contemporary thinkers, Pierre Teilhard de Chardin, palaeontologist, member of the Academie des Sciences of Paris and Jesuit priest, recognized openly that cosmic evolution is leading us towards human socialization:

'The collectivization, now accelerated, of the human species, is nothing else than a superior form assumed by the work of moleculization on the surface of our planet. . . . For a century, a transformation has been going on before us, irresistibly. In the "totalitarian" political systems, whose excesses the future will assuredly adjust, but whose tendencies or profound intuitions it will doubtless accentuate, the citizen sees his centre of gravity gradually being transferred, or at least referred, to that of the national or ethnic group of which he is a member; this will by no means be a return to primitive or undifferentiated forms of culture, but the apparition of a clearly defined social system wherein a wise organization geometrizes the masses and tends to impose upon each individual a specialized function.'[3]

Every Russian Communist could subscribe to those words, even if he considered it impossible to accept Teilhard de Chardin's final conclusion, according to which 'place for a God is discovered

[1] Cf., on this point, S. Radakrishnan, *Religion and Society*, London: 1947.

[2] N. Zernov, *The Church of the Eastern Christians*, London: 1942.

[3] Pierre Teilhard de Chardin, *L'Avenir de l'homme*, Paris: 1959; cf. also the same author's *The Phenomenon of Man*, London: 1960.

over and above the world ... and the Cross becomes the symbol, the way, and even the sign of progress'.

As it happens, the Russian Communists themselves, though they do not know it or admit it, are in the process of building a society which could be called 'Christian', a society in which habitual mutual assistance must reign, with no preoccupation about money, the communal spirit and a humanitarian and pacifist ideal.[1] History is the reflection of the class struggle, of the evolution of production. But the human soul remains true to its own impulses; has an evolution to pass through which is leading it towards collectivism but does not destroy its fundamental essence—the quest for the Infinite.

In 1880, a few months before he died, Dostoyevsky wrote: 'The Russian soul, the genius of the Russian people, is more capable than anything else of incorporating the idea of universal unity and fraternal love, pardoning its enemies, understanding those who have suffered, and resolving all contradictions.'

Will future events confirm this opinion? As long as the world turns, there will be men who believe in God and others who deny His existence. But the days of Crusades have passed; in our times, two divergent ideologies—religion and anti-religion—will have to be able to confront one another in an atmosphere of mutual understanding. On this Christmas Day of 1960, as I end my book, I cannot help but recall the words which the Bible tells us the heavenly hosts used to announce the Nativity: 'Peace on earth to all men of good will.'

[1] Cf., on this point, Heinz Robert Schlette, *Sowjethumanismus—Prämissen und Maxim Kommunistischer Pädagogik*, Munich: 1960.

Index